The Use of
Traditional Materials
in Colossians

The Use of Traditional Materials in Colossians

BY GEORGE E. CANNON

MERCER UNIVERSITY PRESS
MACON, GEORGIA 31207

ISBN 0-86554-074-8

All books published by Mercer University Press are produced
on acid-free paper that exceeds the minimum standards set by the
National Historical Publications and Records Commission

Library of Congress Cataloging in Publication Data

Cannon, George E., 1923-
    The use of traditional materials in Colossians.
    Bibliography: p. 231
    Includes index.
    1. Bible. N.T. Colossians—Criticism, interpreta-
tion, etc. I. Title.
BS2715.2.C36   1983   227'.706   83-8181
ISBN 0-86554-074-8

Table of Contents

Preface

Several years ago, while teaching a foundation course in the General Epistles, I became fascinated with the research of R. Perdelwitz, P. Carrington, F. Cross, and especially E. Selwyn on the backgrounds of 1 Peter. It struck me at the time, as it no doubt has others, that there were numerous similarities in content and approach between 1 Peter and Colossians and Ephesians. Perhaps the presence of common materials in these three epistles could throw some light on the vexing problem of the authorship of Colossians and Ephesians. Since I was persuaded that Ephesians was dependent upon Colossians, I began to investigate the latter and discovered that most of the literary and theological problems which cast doubt on the Pauline authorship of Colossians were related to passages that either consisted of or alluded to traditional material.

My interests in this subject were interrupted by an invitation to teach at Bethel Theological Seminary in St. Paul, Minnesota. The adjustment from college to seminary teaching and the need to prepare new courses made it necessary for me to put aside my interest in the use of traditional materials in Colossians until my sabbatical. That sabbatical not only provided me with the opportunity of continuing research in Colossians but of fulfilling a hope that I had abandoned: continuing work in a doctoral program.

I was an older student in my forties when doing graduate work at Union Theological Seminary in New York City. I wish to thank my mentor, W. D. Davies, for his encouragement in those days and for the profound way he has influenced not only my understanding of the New Testament but also of the ministry and profession of teaching.

Special thanks are due my friend and colleague, Dean Gordon Johnson, whose confidence and trust I deeply value; and to the Board of Regents of Bethel Seminary who supported my endeavors with a full salary during my year of sabbatical.

Needless to say I am most grateful to Fuller Theological Seminary for giving me the opportunity to continue doctoral studies; and to Professor Ralph P. Martin whose help, counsel, and expertise have been invaluable to me.

In prefaces to books and dissertations it has become as traditional for authors to give thanks for the support of wives as it was for the writers of letters in the New Testament period to give thanks for their readers. Who, aside from the author himself, knows of the agonies and joys of writing more than the wife of the author? In my case very special thanks are due to my wife, Florence, without whose love and support this work would never have been completed.

1

An Additional Approach to the Problem of the Authenticity of Colossians

Ever since 1838 when Ernst Theodore Mayerhoff disputed the Pauline authorship of Colossians, the authorship of the letter has been questioned.[1] The issue is still far from being settled. Though there are many recognized New Testament scholars who accept the genuineness of the Colossian letter, there are perhaps even more who cannot accept it as a direct product of the Apostle Paul and who, therefore, carefully and deliberately omit it from any discussion of Paul's own historical situation or explanation of his own immediate theology. Nearly always the case against the Pauline authorship of Colossians has been based on linguistic, stylistic, and theological reasons. Those who argue for the genuineness of the letter usually try to show the inadequacy of those criteria.[2] Such an approach has left the issue at an impasse. This

---

[1]Since Colossians begins and ends with the claim that Paul the Apostle wrote it (1:1 and 4:18), the words "genuineness" and "authenticity" will be used to indicate the veracity of that claim.

[2]Ernst Percy's work, *Die Probleme der Kolosser-und Epheserbriefe*, Acta reg. Societatis Humaniorum Litterarum Lundensis 39 (Lund, 1946) is a well-known example of this approach. The strength of Percy's work is also its weakness. Its strength lies in the thorough investigation of nearly every problem about authorship related to

study will attempt to add an additional approach to the problem by examining it in the light of the use of traditional materials in the letter. The purpose will be to examine Colossians in the light of the presence and use of traditional materials and to observe the use of those materials from the perspective of the special aspects of the gospel which Paul emphasized from his view of himself as the uniquely appointed apostle to the Gentiles. If the use of the traditional materials in Colossians can shed no direct light on these central issues, then the letter probably should be regarded as the product of a later "deutero-Pauline" school. On the other hand, if Colossians deals directly with those issues and the use of traditional materials is related to specific concerns of Paul about them, the letter should be regarded with more confidence as a reliable source for Paul's historical circumstances and his theology.

As I have noted above, an increasing number of New Testament scholars are firmly persuaded that Paul did not write the letter to the Colossians.[3] The two major reasons for this conviction are the literary composition of the letter (style and vocabulary) and its theology (especially its Christology, ecclesiology, eschatology, ethics, and doctrine of baptism).[4] If it could be demonstrated that these problems are primarily related to the author's use of traditional materials and that the way in which he uses them is in full accord with the theological perspectives of the undisputed Pauline letters[5] and with Paul's special understanding of his own apostolic mission and gospel, a very strong case for the authenticity of the letter to the Colossians would have been made.

---

language, style, and theology. Its weakness lies in the failure to deal adequately with the reason why so many problems exist.

[3]A typical overstatement of this persuasion is made by Jack T. Sanders: "That Colossians, Ephesians, 2 Thessalonians, 1 and 2 Timothy, Titus, and 1 Peter are pseudonymous and imitate Paul's style and thought is not to be debated here but rather accepted as an assured result of critical historical scholarship." *Ethics in the New Testament* (Philadelphia: Fortress Press, 1975), p. 67, footnote.

[4]Two helpful excursuses on both of these issues are to be found in Eduard Lohse, *A Commentary on the Epistles to the Colossians and to Philemon*, trans. William R. Poehlmann and Robert J. Karris (Philadelphia: Fortress Press, 1971), pp. 84-91 and 177-83.

[5]By "undisputed letters" I mean Romans, 1 Corinthians, 2 Corinthians, Galatians, Philippians, 1 Thessalonians, 2 Thessalonians (though some dispute this), and Philemon.

It is clear that the author regarded tradition as of utmost importance for his readers. This is evident by his admonition in 2:6, 7: Ὡς οὖν παρελάβετε τὸν Χριστὸν Ἰησοῦν τὸν κύριον, ἐν αὐτῷ περιπατεῖτε, ἐρριζωμένοι καὶ ἐποικοδομούμενοι ἐν αὐτῷ καὶ βεβαιούμενοι τῇ πίστει καθὼς ἐδιδάχθητε, περισσεύοντες ἐν εὐχαριστίᾳ. The use of the quasi-technical term παραλαμβάνειν[6] and the verb διδάσκειν indicates that the author was concerned that his readers remember and hold fast to the traditions which they had received from their earliest teaching.[7] This would mean that whatever the original sources of those traditions may have been, the writer was either in basic agreement with their teaching as set forth in the forms received by the Christian community or that they were so well-known to the readers that they would immediately recognize any alteration or "correction" made by the author. It is to be expected, then, that he would refer to those traditions in his letter. His readers are admonished to keep on ordering their behavior (περιπατεῖτε) on the basis of the traditions which they had received about Christ (παρελάβετε τὸν Χριστὸν Ἰησοῦν τὸν κύριον). They were to be established and built up in Christ as he was set forth in the traditions and to be confirmed in the faith (with the article) just as they had been instructed (καθὼς ἐδιδάχθητε). Their ethical conduct was to be based upon the received Christology. For this reason the readers were warned against being victimized by a philosophy that was not κατὰ Χριστόν but was based on the παράδοσιν τῶν ἀνθρώπων which was κατὰ τὰ στοιχεῖα τοῦ κόσμου (2:8).

Do these statements of the author which indicate the importance of the Christological and paraenetic traditions point to a period subsequent to Paul's day when an emphasis upon an approved theology and an approved manner of conduct was necessary? The Pastoral Epistles, which most would regard as post-Pauline, surely stress both of these features. The excessive enthusiasm and pneumatic zeal already in evidence (especially in the Pauline churches) would practically demand

---

[6]See Oscar Cullmann, *The Early Church*, trans. A. B. J. Higgins and S. Godman (London: 1956), pp. 55-99 and W. D. Davies, "Reflexions on Traditions: The Aboth Revisited," *Christian History and Interpretation*: studies presented to John Knox, pp. 127-59. The use of παραλαμβάνειν, παραδιδόναι, and παράδοσις in Gal. 1:9-12; 1 Cor. 11:2, 23; 15:1-3; Rom. 6:17; 1 Thess. 2:13, 4:1; and 2 Thess. 2:15, 3:6 indicates an authoritative transmission of the traditions.

[7]See also Col. 1:5-7.

an emphasis upon correct doctrine authenticated by approved men and upon orderly and ethical conduct in the later churches. Acts and the Pastoral Epistles became the seed beds for the later doctrine of apostolic succession which grew out of this need. A post-Pauline provenance for these kinds of problems is most reasonable, but they were not limited to the post-Pauline period.

There is ample evidence within the undisputed letters of Paul that the Apostle was very much concerned about libertinism, disorder, and self-centered enthusiasm within his churches. This is evident not only in the Corinthian correspondence and Philippians, but also in those famous letters which deal primarily with the Jew-Gentile problem: Romans and Galatians.[8] One gets the impression that Paul's primary concern for his churches was not so much the Jew-Gentile problem as it was the pneumatic enthusiasm (which Paul regarded as a kind of "over-realized" eschatology) that was probably enhanced by a kind of triumphalism influenced by the religious ecstasy practices of the day and by traveling emissaries who regarded themselves as "divine men."[9] Paul's way of addressing this problem was similar to the approach used in Colossians in that he handled it Christologically and paraenetically. He stressed that the exalted Lord was also the crucified Messiah. The Messiah's mission was to wage a warfare of liberation from the evil powers. His ministry was therefore marked by conflict, suffering, rejection, and total obedience to the will of His Father.[10] The Messiah's followers, namely, the church, were to be those who continued the messianic mission until the Parousia. Hence, until that great event, the life of the church would be characterized by suffering, obedience, and

---

[8]The Judaizers in Galatia may have had some success in getting Galatian Christians to "live Jewishly" with respect to circumcision, food laws, etc., but they had little effect on and showed little concern for the ethical behavior of the Galatians. The closing paraenesis of the letter (5:13-6:10) is totally given over to dealing with the problems of libertinism, brotherly love, and responsible living. The same is true in the paraenetic section of Romans. Though the historical situation of the Roman church and the purpose of the Roman letter are much debated issues, the paraenetic section of the letter shows a clear concern for ordered behavior.

[9]See R. Jewett, "Conflicting Movements in the Early Church as Reflected in Philippians," *NovT* 12 (1970): 362-90.

[10]It is true that the Christological emphasis in Colossians is sometimes quite different, but that was made necessary by the special situation faced by the Colossians. This will be treated in greater length in chapter 6.

responsible living. The Apostle's other approach was paraenetic. He calls his churches to brotherly love, order, and engagement in the messianic conflict. Many of his admonitions are in somewhat standard forms which also appear in his other letters and in other New Testament and early Christian documents. It is clear, then, that the Apostle Paul faced problems of doctrinal error and disorder in his churches and that the use of commonly accepted teachings about Christ and about proper conduct would have been most useful to him.

A further question needs to be asked. It is commonly accepted that traditional materials are used in 1 Peter, Colossians, and Ephesians. Is there any evidence of the regular use of such materials in the undisputed Pauline letters? The question can be answered in the affirmative. Besides Paul's direct references to the importance of traditions in Galatians, Romans, 1 Corinthians, and 1 and 2 Thessalonians (as we have noted above, in footnote 6), research during the past half century has demonstrated that Paul's letters not only contain firmly formulated materials of a hymnic and confessional nature, but they also contain a plethora of less formalized materials which can be recognized as traditional on the grounds of style, language, context, and theological peculiarities. A. M. Hunter's record of research in this connection is interesting. In 1940 he regarded himself as a sort of pioneer in the investigation of pre-Pauline influences on Paul. Twenty years later he was more firmly persuaded of his basic conclusion that Paul was dependent on pre-Pauline Christianity than ever. He felt that his earlier work was "dated" because so much additional research had been done in the area. He, therefore, added an appendix to his earlier work to strengthen his original thesis.[11]

In a more recent work, Klaus Wegenast made a thorough investigation of the use of tradition in Paul and the deutero-Pauline letters. He clearly established the widespread use of traditional materials in both of these categories. He is persuaded that Paul's use of such material was quite unlike late Judaism's practice of carefully passing on such traditions in basically unaltered forms. Paul rather used the old forms to present his revealed gospel.[12] Although Wegenast regards Colos-

---

[11]Archibald M. Hunter, *Paul and His Predecessors* (Philadelphia: The Westminster Press, 1961), pp. 116-50.

[12]Klaus Wegenast, *Der Verständnis der Traditionen bei Paulus und den Deutero-paulinem*, Wissenschaftliche Monographien zum Alten und Neuen Testament 8 (Neu-

sians as a deutero-Pauline letter, he concludes that the traditions are used in the same way they are in the undisputed letters.[13]

Still more recently, Wiard Popkes made a study of the widespread use of the verb παραδιδόναι in the New Testament. He limited his investigation to the use of the term as it relates "to the way of Jesus in his humiliation" in order to discover the theological purpose of the early church's use of the "Christus traditus" in this connection.[14] He first made a study of the prehistorical use of the term *Dahingabe*[15] and then investigated the use of (παρα) διδόναι in the New Testament.[16] Since he was primarily concerned with the use of traditional materials pertaining to the significance of the death of Christ, he limited his investigation accordingly. With regard to the Pauline letters, he dealt primarily with Romans 4:25 and 8:32 and Galatians 1:4 and 2:20, but he also demonstrated the influence of this tradition in a variety of other places in the letters of Paul where the verb is not used. With reference to the deutero-Pauline letters, he discussed the use of the verb in Ephesians, 1 Timothy, and Titus. Since the (παρα)διδόναι form is not used in connection with the death of Christ in Colossians, Popkes omitted Colossians from his discussion. This is unfortunate because there is a very distinct stress on the death of Christ in Colossians (1:20, 21; 2:11-14, 20ff.) and, as we shall show later, this emphasis is explicitly connected with traditional materials related to the Christ-hymn in 1:15-20 and in the traditional baptismal concepts.

From the late fifties to the seventies, research in the confessional and hymnic materials of the New Testament flourished. Nearly all of these studies include special sections on the Pauline and deutero-Pauline writings, and nearly all of them place Colossians in the latter category.[17] At the same time interest in ethical paraenesis or commun-

---

kirchen, 1962), pp. 34-120. See his survey of early literature on the subject of tradition in the N.T. in his footnotes on pp. 9-10.

[13]Ibid., pp. 121-30.

[14]Wie kommt die Gemeinde dazu, vom "Christus Traditus" zu sprechen, welche Gedanken greift sie auf, was ist die Absicht dieser Verkündigungsform, und welche Theologie kommt darin zum Ausdruch? *Christus Traditus. Eine Untersuchung zum Begriff der Dahingabe im Neuen Testament* Stuttgart/Zürich: Zwingli, 1967), p. 9.

[15]Ibid., pp. 11-130.

[16]Ibid., pp. 131-296.

[17]Literature in this field is voluminous. A selective chronological list includes: O.

ity regulations was also quite evident. Although research in the latter field has been less prolific than in the former, it is nevertheless significant.[18] In addition to the doctrinal and ethical traditions, there are also traditional forms and styles associated with the epistolary genre of the

Cullmann, *Die Christologie des Neuen Testaments* (Tübingen, 1957; E. T.: Philadelphia: Westminster Press, 1963); J. M. Robinson, "A Formal Analysis of Col. 1:15-20," *Journal of Biblical Literature* 76 (1957): 270-87; G. Bornkamm, "Zum Verständnis des Christus-Hymnus Phil. 2:6-11" *Studien zu Antike und Urchristentum, Gesammelte Aufsätze*, vol. 2. Beitrage zur Evangelischen Theologie, 28 (Munich, 1959); E. Käsemann, "Eine urchristliche Taufliturgie" and "Kritische Analyse von Phil. 2:5-11," *Exegetische Versuche und Besinnungen, Gesammelte Aufsätze*, vol. 1 (Göttingen, 1960); R. P. Martin, *An Early Christian Confession; Philippians 2:5-11 in Recent Interpretation* (London, 1960); E. Schweizer, "Die Kirche als Leib Christi in den paulinischen Antilegomena," *Theologische Literaturzeitung* 86 (1961); H. Hegermann, *Die Vorstellung vom Schöpfungsmittler im hellenistischen Judentum und Urchristentum*. Text und Untersuchungen zur Geschichte der altchristlichen Literatur 82 (Berlin: Akademie—Verlag, 1961); E. Bammel, "Versuch zu Colossians 1:15-20," *Zeitschrift für die neutestamentliche Wissenschaft und die Kunde der älteren Kirche* 52 (1961): 88-95; V. Neufeld, *The Earliest Christian Confessions* (Grand Rapids: Wm. B. Eerdmans, 1963); D. Georgi, "Der vorpaulinsche Hymnus Philippians 2:6-11," *Zeit und Geschichte, Dankesgabe an Rudolph Bultmann zum 80 Geburtstag*, ed. E. Dinkler (Tübingen: J. C. B. Mohr, 1964); G. Strecker, "Redaktion und Tradition im Christushymnus Philippians 2:6-11," *Zeitschrift für die neutestamentliche Wissenschaft* 55 (1964); A. Feuillet, "L'hymne christologique de l'Epitre aux Philippiens (2:6-11)," *Revue Biblique* 62 (1965); H. J. Gabathuler, *Jesus Christus, Haupt der Kirche—Haupt der Welt: Der Christhymnus Colosser 1:15-20 in der theologischen Forschung der letzen 130 Jahre*, Abhandlungen zur Theologie des Alten und Neuen Testaments 45 (Zürich: 1965); R. Deichgraber, *Gotteshymnus und Christushymnus in der frühen Christenheit: Untersuchungen zu Form, Sprache und Stil der früchristlichen Hymnen*, Studien zur Umwelt des Neuen Testaments 5 (Göttingen, 1967); N. Kehl, *Der Christhymnus im Kolosserbrief: Eine motivgeschichtliche Untersuchung zu Kol 1:12-20* (Stuttgart, 1967); K. Wengst, *Christologische Formeln und Lieder des Urchristentums*. Studien zum Neuen Testament 8d. 7 (Gütersloh: Gütersloher Verlaghaus [Gerd Mohr] 1972); J. Biggs, *Creation and Redemption. A Study in Pauline Theology* (Leiden, E. J. Brill, 1971); J. Sanders, *The New Testament Christological Hymns. Their Historical Religious Background* (Cambridge: University Press, 1971).

[18]Some of the more notable works on this subject are: K. Weidinger, *Die Haustafeln: Ein Stück urchristlicher Paränese*, Untersuchungen zum Neuen Testament 14 (Leipzig, 1928); B. Easton, "New Testament Ethical Lists," *Journal of Biblical Literature* 51 (1932): 1-12; A. Vögtle, *Tugend-und Lasterkataloge im Neuen Testament: Exegetisch, religions-und formgeschichtlich untersucht*, Neutestamentliche Abhandlungen 16, 4.5 (Munster i.W., 1936); K. Rengsdorf, "Die neutestamentlichen Mahnungen an die Frau, sich dem Manne unterzuordnen" in *Verbum Dei manet in aeternum, Festschrift für Otto Schmitz*, ed. Werner Poerster (Witten, 1953), pp. 131-45; D. Daube, "Haustafeln" and "A Baptismal Confession" in *The New Testament and Rabbinic Judaism*) University of London: The Athlone Press, 1956), pp. 90-140; H. Wendland, "Zur sozial-ethischen Bedeutung der neutestamentlischen Haustafeln" in

New Testament letters.[19] When one considers all of these elements, it can be seen that Paul was very much influenced by the traditional teachings and forms of his day. The power of tradition affected him more than was once realized. Research dealing with the presence of those traditions will continue to have a marked impact upon our understanding of the historical situation and theological concerns of the Apostle Paul.

The fact that Colossians contains a significant amount of traditional material, therefore, does not in itself indicate a post-Pauline provenance. The very presence of those materials may rather point to the genuineness of the letter as the product of Paul himself. If it can be shown that the problems of authenticity which are related to the literary composition and theology of the letter are specifically linked with the use of traditions, the case for the genuineness of the letter will be greatly enhanced, though certainly not proved.

Another matter must be investigated before the argument for or against the Pauline authorship of Colossians can be considered. Is the use of the traditional materials in Colossians compatible with the theology set forth in the undisputed letters of Paul? If so, how strong is

---

Die Leibhaftigkeit des Wortes, Festschrift für Adolph Köberle (Hamburg, 1958), pp. 34-46; S. Wibbing, *Tugend-und Lasterkataloge im Neuen Testament und ihre Traditionsgeschichte unter besonderer Berücksichigung der Qumran-Texte*, Beihefte zur Zeitschrift für die neutestamentliche Wissenschaft und die Kunde der älteren Kirche 25 (Berlin, 1969); D. Schroeder, *Die Haustafeln des Neuen Testaments: Ihre Herkunft und ihr theologischer Sinn*, unpublished dissertation, (Hamburg, 1959); E. Kamlah, *Die form der katalogischen Paränese im Neuen Testament*, Wissenschaftliche Untersuchungen zum Neuen Testament 7 (Tübingen, 1964); J. Sampley, *"And the Two Shall Become One Flesh." A study of the Traditions in Ephesians 5:21-23* (Cambridge: University Press, 1971); J. Crouch, *The Origin and Intention of the Colossian Haustafel*, Forschungen zur Religion und Literatur des Alten und Neuen Testaments (Göttingen, Vandenhoek und Ruprecht, 1972); D. Schroeder, "Haustafeln," *The Interpreters' Dictionary of the Bible*, Supplementary Volume, ed. George Arthur Butrick (New York and Nashville: Abingdon, 1962), pp. 546-47.

[19]Research in this area was largely stimulated by the work of P. Schubert, *Form and Function of the Pauline Thanksgivings*, Beihefte zur Zeitschrift für die neutestamentliche Wissenschaft 20 (Berlin: Topelmann, 1939), and has been carried on by American scholars for the most part. Good overviews of this research are provided by J. L. White, *The Form and Function of the Body of the Greek Letter: A Study of the Letter-Body in the Non-Literary Papyri and in Paul the Apostle*, second edition, corrected, Society of Biblical Literature Dissertation Series (Missoula: Scholars Press, 1972), and by W. Doty, *Letters in Primitive Christianity*, New Testament Series (Philadelphia: Fortress Press, 1973).

that compatibility? To show that the theological perspectives of Colossians do not conflict with the theologies set forth in the *Hauptbriefe* may be significant, but it would be inadequate. If it could be shown that the way in which the traditions are used indicates a close correspondence to the theological perspectives of the undisputed letters, that would make a stronger case. To go one step further, if it could be demonstrated that the use of those traditions are explicitly related to the special emphases which Paul makes with respect to his own proclamation of the gospel and to his view of himself as the unique apostle to the Gentiles, then, it seems to me, the argument for the authenticity of Colossians becomes very strong indeed. Recent Pauline studies have given a great deal of attention to these two matters and they play a more central role in Colossians than may be realized.[20]

To summarize: The authenticity of Colossians is usually judged on the basis of its theological, lexical, and stylistic features. An examination of the use of traditional materials in Colossians will throw additional and important light on those features. Furthermore, such an examination will help in arriving at a clearer understanding of the theology of Colossians and will enable us to make a more adequate comparison of its theology with that of the undisputed letters of Paul. It will also cause us to think more specifically about the Apostle's understanding of the gospel and his own special ministry to Gentiles. It is my thesis that this procedure will point to the strong probability of the Pauline authorship of Colossians and lead to the conclusion that the letter may be used with more confidence as a source for his theology and historical situation.

My procedure will be to examine the probable presence of confessional and hymnic materials in chapter two, of paraenetic materials in chapters three and four, and of traditional forms and styles in chapter five. Chapter six will consider the use of the traditional materials in the letter, compare the theological perspective of Colossians with the undisputed letters of Paul, and relate this to the problems of authorship and purpose.

---

[20]Documentation for this remark will be found below, in the final chapter. The recent controversial work of E. P. Sanders, *Paul and Palestinian Judaism: A Comparison of Patterns of Religions* (Philadelphia: Fortress Press, 1977), is an especially provocative source of ideas.

2

Confessional and Hymnic Materials in Colossians

In this chapter we shall attempt to establish the traditional character of three passages which serve as the basis for the very important Christological teaching of the letter to the Colossians. In Colossians 2:6 the readers are admonished to walk in the light of the teachings which they had received about Christ. Colossians 1:12-14; 1:15-20; and 2:9-15 are reminders of those Christological teachings. On the grounds of their style, language, and contents they appear to be liturgical materials of a confessional and hymnic nature. Even though the second passage (Colossians 1:15-20) has been the object of much investigation,[1] we shall include it because of its importance to this study and for the sake of completeness.

---

[1]See James M. Robinson, "A Formal Analysis of Colossians 1:15-20," *JBL* 76 (1975): 271-75, and Ralph P. Martin, *Colossians and Philemon*, pp. 61-66, for a survey of these studies. For a complete history of the interpretation of Colossians 1:15-20 from Schleiermacher to Conzlemann, see Hans J. Gabathuler, *Jesus Christus, Haupt der Kirche-Haupt der Welt: Der Christhymnus Kolosser 1, 15-20 in der theologischen Forschung der letzen 130 Jahre*, Abhandlungen zur Theologie des Alten und Neuen Testaments 45 (Stuttgart: Zwingli, 1965), pp. 11-124.

THE TRADITIONAL CHARACTER OF
COLOSSIANS 1:12-14

Although a great deal of attention has been given to the hymnic style of Colossians 1:15-20, less has been written about the traditional character of 1:12-14. One of the reasons for this is obvious. It is usually treated as a part of the prayer in 1:9-11 because the participle εὐχαρισ-τοῦντες which begins verse 12 is found in a cluster of three other participles in verses 10 and 11 (καρποφοροῦντες, αὐξανόμενοι, and δυναμούμενοι) which all seem to modify περιπατῆσαι in verse 10.[2]

However, it seems to me that the writer introduces a new thought in verse 12 which is separate from the prayer in verses 9-11 and that he introduces the new section by using traditional confessional materials which make up verses 12-14. There are four reasons for this opinion.

The Significance of Εὐχαριστεῖν

Lohse (following Lohmeyer and recently endorsed by Martin) asserts that "Paul never closes the intercessions in his letter with thanksgiving or with a summons to it" and that, therefore, the words μετὰ χαρᾶς εὐχαριστοῦντες "are directed to the whole community and, therefore, cannot be viewed as a connecting link to the prayer and thanksgiving, which opens the letter with the apostle's thanks to God for the good condition of the community."[3] This observation, while correct, must not be given too much weight because we have only a few letters by Paul and he does not mention his intercession for his readers in all of them.[4]

---

[2]Typical of this position is C. F. D. Moule who says, "εὐχαριστοῦντες is more naturally construed with the preceding participle." *The Epistles to Colossians and Ephesians*, p. 55. In a more recent commentary (1970), J. L. Houlden, basing his reason on Schubert's *Form and Function of the Pauline Thanksgivings* places verses 12-14 in the larger context of 3-14 which he regards as a liturgical utterance such as Paul was "accustomed to make in solemn liturgical gatherings of his churches," *Paul's Letters from Prison*, pp. 52, 149.

[3]Eduard Lohse, *A Commentary on the Epistles to the Colossians and to Philemon,* trans. William R. Poehlmann and Robert J. Karris, Hermencia Series (Philadelphia: Fortress Press, 1971), p. 33.

[4]There are but nine instances of prayer for the readers in all thirteen letters attributed to Paul. (Rom. 1:10ff.; 2 Cor. 13:10; Eph. 1:15ff.; Phil. 1:9ff.; Col. 1:9ff.; 1 Thess. 1:2ff.; 2 Thess. 1:11ff.; 2 Tim. 1:3ff.; and Philemon 4ff.

The main reason for the significance of εὐχαριστεῖν in our discussion is its probable relationship to confession in the Septuagint, Hellenistic Judaism, and the early church. In 1942 Günther Bornkamm advanced the proposition that εὐχαριστεῖν is a technical term introducing a confession.[5] In recent times this observation has been developed further by Lohse. Because he packs so much information in a single paragraph, I shall quote him in full:

> The verb εὐχαριστεῖν (to give thanks) does not appear often in the *LXX*, and does so only in books which lack a Hebrew original (for example, Judith 8:25; Wisd. Sol. 18:2; II Macc. 1:11; 10:7a; 12:31; III Macc. 7:16). In the Psalms the summons to thanksgiving is given by the hiphil form of *yadah* (to know), and this form is usually translated in the *LXX* as ἐξομολογεῖσθαι (to confess, to praise) as in *LXX* Ps. 135:1, 2, 3, 26; 137:1, 2, 4; et cetera. The noun form *todah* becomes ἐξομολόγησις (confession, praise) as in *LXX* Josh. 7:19; Ps. 41:4; 92:4; 95:6; et cetera. Later, in the linguistic usage of Hellenistic Judaism, ἐξομολόγεῖσθαι (to confess, praise) was replaced by εὐχαριστεῖν (to give thanks). Thus Philo almost always uses the latter verb as the expression for thanks offered to God. In view of this transition from ἐξομολογῆσθαι to εὐχαριστεῖν Origen can state that "to say 'I confess' is the same as saying 'I give thanks'" (Orat. 6 τὸ ἐξομολογοῦμαι ἴσον ἐστι τῷ εὐχαριστῶ) [Trans.] The Greek εὐχαριστεῖν thus corresponds to the Hebrew *yadah* in the hiphil, which served to introduce the song of thanks and praise.[6]

Lohse then proceeds to show that the same phenomenon occurs in the *Hodayoth*, the hymns of praise of the Qumran community.

To summarize: εὐχαριστοῦντες does not belong with the other participles that are a part of the prayer for the Colossians but it rather begins a new section in the chapter. It functions as a participial imperative by which the readers are called upon to give thanks to the Father.[7] In Hellenistic Judaism this was the same as gratefully confess-

---

[5]G. Bornkamm, "Das Bekenntnis im Hebräerbrief," *Studien zu Antike und Urchristentum*, pp. 188-203. This article first appeared in *Theologische Blätter* 21 (1942). It made such an impression on Käsemann that he asserted that if Bornkamm's thesis is correct then the "connexion between verse 12 and what follows becomes nothing less than mandatory" ("Primitive Christian Baptismal Liturgy," p. 153). However, Käsemann did not follow Bornkamm's hypothesis that the liturgical gathering of the Christological hymns came out of a Eucharistic setting (Bornkamm, "Das Bekenntnis," pp. 196-200).

[6]Lohse, *Colossians*, p. 34. He depends heavily on J. M. Robinson's article "Die Hodajot-Formel in Gebet und Hymnus des Frühchristentums" in *Apophoreta: Festschrift für Ernst Haenchen*, pp. 194-235.

[7]See Blass and Debrunner, *A Greek Grammar of the New Testament and Other Early Christian Literature*, p. 175. R. P. Martin also accepts this grammatical function, *Colossians and Philemon*, p. 53.

ing what the community knew about the Father. If this analysis should be true, then we could readily conclude that everything after the participle εὐχαριστοῦντες in verses 12-14 is traditional confessional material.[8]

The Change of Pronouns

One of the most obvious indicators that the writer was drawing upon an outside source (or sources) in 1:12-20 is the change from the second person plural pronoun in verse 9 to the first person plural in verses 12ff. There is a dispute over the text in verse 12. Should the form be ὑμᾶς or ἡμᾶς? B. Metzger, writing on behalf of the Editorial Committee of the United Bible Societies' Greek New Testament, states that "a majority of the Committee preferred ὑμᾶς, regarding ἡμᾶς as an assimilation to verse 13."[9] But there is as much manuscript evidence for saying that ὑμᾶς is an assimilation to verse 9.[10] Indeed, in the light of the probable confessional character of verse 12, I am inclined to think that the reading should be ἡμᾶς.

Stylistic and Linguistic Features

Even though style and vocabulary are not in themselves adequate criteria for establishing the presence of traditional material, they are helpful pointers when used in conjunction with other tests. There are present in verses 12-14 not only stylistic features which bear the stamp of the liturgical genre, but also words and phrases which are either not used at all in the other letters attributed to Paul or are used in a different way.

---

[8] As Käsemann puts it: "we should merely have to insert a semicolon and quotation marks after εὐχαριστοῦντες and all would be clear." "Primitive Christian Baptismal Liturgy," p. 154.

It is interesting to observe that the noun εὐχαριστια occurs in 2:7 in a context which (as we previously noted) is one in which the writer called upon his readers to walk in the light of the received Christological tradition, "rooted and built up in him and established in the faith just as you were taught, abounding in εὐχαριστια." If Lohse is right about the confessional character of εὐχαριστια, this participial phrase would be another reminder to the Colossians of their need to immerse themselves in the received traditions (2:8).

[9] B. M. Metzger, *A Textual Commentary on the Greek New Testament*, Companion Volume to the United Bible Societies' Greek New Testament, 3rd ed. (London and New York, 1971), p. 620.

[10] ἡμᾶς A C D G K P 33 81 88 181 326 330 436 45! 614 630 1241 1877 1962 2492 2495, *United Bible Societies' Greek New Testament*, p. 694.

Norden has shown that the presence of participial constructions and relative clauses is a characteristic of the formulary style.[11] Those features are present in τῷ ἱκανώσαντι, ὅς ἐρρύσατο ἡμᾶς, and ἐν ᾧ ἔχομεν. Vawter notes that "the same criteria which clearly mark the *Wortschatz* of verses 15-20 as non-Pauline hold equally well for verses 12-14."[12] Ἱκανόω is found only in Colossians 1:12 and 2 Corinthians 3:6 where it refers to the apostolic ministry, not to eschatological redemption. Μερίς recurs only in 2 Corinthians 6:15 in a passage many believe to be an insertion in the text of non-Pauline origin (2 Corinthians 6:14-7:1). Ἅγιοι is used many times by Paul to refer to Christians but only in Colossians 1:12 and in an apocalyptic statement in 2 Thessalonians 3:13 does it refer to angelic beings. Ῥύομαι always connotes a present or futuristic meaning when used by Paul to denote salvific deliverance. In verse 13 it is in the aorist.[13] The phrase βασιλεία τοῦ υἱοῦ τῆς ἀγάπης αὐτοῦ is without parallel in the New Testament.[14] Τὴν ἄφεσιν τῶν παραπτωμάτων is used in Ephesians 1:7 (probably because of the influence of Colossians) and nowhere else in the Pauline corpus. As Lohse notes,

---

[11]Eduard Norden, *Agnostos Theos, Untersuchungen zur Formengeschichte religiöser Rede*, 4th ed. (Darmstadt, 1956), pp. 168, 201-207, 383ff. Vernon Neufeld came to a similar conclusion about the criteria for detecting formulary material. His study placed primary stress on the ὁμολογεῖν-ὁμολογία word group as the pointer towards the presence of a confession or creed. He does not discuss the εὐχαριστεῖν-εὐχαριστία word group, but he does assert that "other verbs of a kerygmatic, didactic, or confessional nature also provide certain clues pointing to the *homologia*." Among the syntactical indicators of formulary material are participial constructions and relative clauses. Neufeld does not discuss Colossians 1:12-20 but his linguistic and stylistic methodology surely suggest the "creedal" nature of our passage. *The Earliest Christian Confessions*, ed. Bruce M. Metzger, New Testament Tools and Studies 5 (Grand Rapids: Eerdmans, 1963), pp. 13-20, 42-43, 140-41.

[12]B. Vawter, "The Colossian Hymn and the Principle of Redaction," *CBQ* 33 (1971): 68.

[13]Romans 7:24; 11:26; 1 Thess. 1:10. It should be noted, however, that the aorist ἐρρύσατο is not out of harmony with the "realized" aspect of Pauline eschatology.

[14]The concept of the reigning Son is also found in Hebrews and in Matt. 25:31. In 1 Cor. 15:20-28 Paul teaches that Christ will reign until he has overthrown all his enemies and then he will deliver up the Kingdom to God. So, though Paul does not use the phrases "Kingdom of the Son" or "Kingdom of Christ," he does refer to such a kingdom. The important matter for our study is the phrase "τοῦ υἱοῦ τῆς ἀγάπης αὐτοῦ."

Paul seldom speaks of the forgiveness of sins. He understands ἁμαρτία (sin) as a power which found entrance into the world through Adam's deed (Romans 5:12) and since then has exercised its tyranny over men.[15]

The Baptismal Motif in 1:12-14

A fourth possible evidence of the use of traditional materials in 1:12-14 is the presence of motifs related to baptism. Bornkamm, who argued that the "Son" designation for Christ had its roots in the primitive Christian *Taufbekenntnis*, nevertheless attempted to show that the early Christological homologies (including Colossians 1:12-20 came from an Eucharistic setting.[16] But Käsemann has shown to the satisfaction of many that the traditional unit in 1:12-20 has its real roots in the primitive Christian baptismal profession of faith.[17]

The Baptismal Character of the Colossians Letter. There is little doubt that the writer makes a strong appeal to the significance of baptism in this letter. The relationship of the readers to the sovereign Lord is based upon their experience of baptism (2:11-15). The basis of a style of life befitting the Christian community is based upon its identity with the death and resurrection of Christ in baptism (2:20-3:44). It is for this reason that the readers are to "put off" those traits and characteristics which were marks of existence in the kingdom of darkness and to "put on" those dispositions and manners which indicated that they were the chosen members of the kingdom of the Son (3:12-14).

The "Beloved Son" and "Forgiveness of Sins" Phrases. The unusual references to the kingdom of the beloved Son and the forgiveness of sins noted above have a clear conceptual association with baptism. The phrase τοῦ υἱοῦ τῆς ἀγάπης αὐτοῦ is probably a Semiticism and hence another way of saying "his beloved Son" (as it is translated in the

---

[15]Lohse, *Colossians*, p. 39.

[16]Bornkamm, "Das Bekenntnis," pp. 188-200.

[17]Käsemann gives five reasons for this conclusion: (1) The unparalleled phrase "βασιλείαν τοῦ υἱοῦ τῆς ἀγάπης" is a "paraphrase of the proclamation of Jesus as υἱος ἀγαπητός at his baptism." Pp. 43, 44. (2) "Deliverance from darkness and translation into the kingdom of God's Son "are unquestionably thought of as following from baptism." P. 44. (3) Forgiveness of sins was associated with baptism in the early church. P. 45. (4) The sense of Romans 6 indicates that baptism is the calling forth of a new creation, an eschatological concept which can be understood as a resurrection from the dead. Pp. 45, 46. (5) The total context of Colossians develops themes all of which point back to baptism. "Primitive Christian Baptismal Liturgy." Pp. 43-48.

Revised Standard Version). Such an expression calls to mind the pronouncement of the heavenly voice at the baptism of Jesus: "This is my beloved Son."[18] Similarly the expression "forgiveness of sins," so unusual in the Pauline letters but common in the Lukan writings, is associated with the central thrust of the gospel (Luke 24:47; Acts 5:31; 10:43; 13:38; 26:28) and hence with baptism. It is associated with the baptizing ministry of John the Baptist (Mark 1:4; Luke 3:3) and associated with baptism in the preaching and practice of the primitive church (Acts 2:38).

The Exodus Motif in 1:12-14. It has been pointed out by some that the verses under consideration contain terms that are associated with the story of the exodus of Israel from Egypt. In Exodus 6:8 (*LXX*) κλῆρος refers to the land which God promised to His people. Lohse observed that in Deuteronomy 32:9 and Joshua 19:9 both μέρις and κλῆρος are used to denote the apportionment of the land of Canaan at the conclusion of the Exodus.[19] The verbs ῥύεσθαι, μεθιστάναι, and the noun ἀπολύτρωσις all connote deliverance from a state of slavery and transference to a new condition.

As is well known, the exodus motif underlies much of the theology of the New Testament and can be detected in many of the New Testament documents. This is to be expected because the Exodus was a powerful expression of the saving activity of God. For this reason Judaism remembered and celebrated the Exodus from Egypt in all of its pilgrim festivals (Passover, Pentecost, and Tabernacles). For this reason the early Christians celebrated the new Exodus of the new Israel in the sacraments of baptism and the Lord's Supper. It is the eschatological significance of both of these rites that ties them to the Exodus motif.[20]

---

[18]This association is made by Houlden, *Paul's Letters from Prison*, p. 154; Lohse, *Colossians*, p. 38; Moule, *Colossians*, p. 58; and Martin, *Colossians*, p. 55.

[19]Lohse, *Colossians*, p. 35. See also Ralph P. Martin, "Reconciliation and Forgiveness in the Letter to the Colossians," in *Reconciliation and Hope, New Testament Essays on Atonement and Eschatology*, ed. Robert Banks (Grand Rapids: William B. Eerdmans Pub. Co., 1974), p. 106.

[20]It seems to me that Albert Schweitzer is right when he says that the Johannine baptism is "by no means as enigmatic as it is usually supposed." *The Mysticism of Paul the Apostle* (London: Adam and Charles Black, 1956; first printed, 1931), p. 231.

Although the relationship between the Exodus and the Lord's Supper is more apparent in the New Testament, the connection of baptism with the Exodus should not be overlooked. It is true that in Romans 6 being "in Christ" is contrasted with being "in Adam" and hence a Genesis or a new creation motif is present.[21] However, Paul associates baptism with Moses and the crossing of the Red Sea (1 Corinthians 10:1, 2) as well as with the Lord's Supper (1 Corinthians 10:3,4).[22] Wilfred Knox makes the following observation about the baptism passage in Romans 6:

> In Romans 6 it is stated in terms of the Christian revision of the *kerygma* of Judaism, in which the death and resurrection of Jesus replace the Exodus from Egypt. The proselyte through circumcision and the proselyte's bath was enabled to come out of Egypt and pass through the Red Sea into the promised land of Israel. The original salvation of the people was re-enacted in every Gentile who was prepared to come out of Egypt, the natural type of evil in a religion whose literature was dominated by the utterances of the prophets who had counselled submission to Babylon. Paul transfers the argument to the death and resurrection of Jesus. Those who share in it through faith and pass through the waters of baptism are delivered from the old Egyptian bondage to sin.[23]

Furthermore, it seems to me significant that the Lord's Supper, by virtue of its repetition as well as the futuristic "until he comes" statement in the tradition passed on by Paul, points to the "not yet" element in God's eschatological purpose.[24] But baptism points to the indicative fact of Christ's death and resurrection and the indicative reality of the forgiveness of sins. It, therefore, calls the Christian to live in the light of these accomplished realities and in anticipation of future resurrection.

(Though his own view is as enigmatic as any!). We may seek to understand it in terms of the Qumran cleansing rites or Jewish proselyte baptism, but we understand it best when we remember that John was regarded as the expected eschatological prophet who was to announce the coming of the Messiah and the inauguration of the New Age.

[21]Käsemann states that "In Judaism the deliverance from Egypt was understood as a new creation." *Essays in New Testament Themes*, trans. W. S. Montague (Naperville: Alec R. Allenson, 1964), p. 161.

[22]Paul's most often quoted statement about the new creation (2 Cor. 5:17) comes in a context sparked by Paul's comparison of himself with Moses.

[23]W. L. Knox, *St. Paul and the Church of the Gentiles* (Cambridge: University Press, 1939), p. 97.

[24]Indeed it was this very emphasis that the Corinthians with their "over realized" eschatology needed.

The language of Colossians 1:12-14 with its aorist indicatives (ἱκανώ-σαντι, ἐρρύσατο, μετέστησεν) and the affirmation of the present possession of redemption (ἐν ᾧ ἔχομεν τὴν ἀπολύτρωσιν) points more to baptism than the Lord's Supper.[25]

Summary

While the traditional character of Colossians 1:12-14 cannot be proved with certainty, the evidence points to the probability of such a conclusion. The opening participle εὐχαριστοῦντες points to the confessional character of these verses. The change of pronouns and the style and language strongly suggest that the writer drew on an outside source. And finally, the manner in which the concepts related to the Exodus motif are presented intimates that the sacrament of baptism was the source of the homology.

THE TRADITIONAL CHARACTER OF COLOSSIANS 1:15-20

We turn now to a passage that is generally recognized to be a composition with hymnic structure. Because of the vast amount of research that has already been done on the structure, source, and authorship of Colossians 1:15-20, the treatment of these items will take on the nature of a survey. We shall then give attention to the probable redactional statements in the passage and the theological implications of those editorial revisions. Lastly, we shall consider the relationship of the passage with 1:12-14.

Structure

A thorough review of the history of the interpretation of Colossians 1:15-20 can be found in Hans-Jakob Gabathuler's work.[26] These inter-

---

[25]Martin notes the important fact that "Paul's use of the word redemption usually contains an eschatological dimension, but this is not present here. Rather, the promise is a present experience within the church's fellowship and under the regime of Christ. Its content is crisply defined as consisting in the forgiveness of sins." "Reconciliation and Forgiveness," p. 108. The point of his essay is to give a reason for this change of emphasis. I shall later suggest that the emphasis on the "already" of eschatology was demanded by the Colossian situation.

[26]See above, fn. 17 to chapter 1. In addition Lohse lists twenty-three investigations of the hymn which he considers noteworthy, *Colossians*, p. 41. For an up-to-date

pretations contain a variety of approaches and no consensus on the original form of the passage has been reached. However, they all point to a basic literary structure that is hymnic in character. The following three influential reconstructions will help demonstrate this.

Eduard Norden (1913).[27] The earliest reconstruction which laid a foundation for other reconstructions was made by Eduard Norden. It is interesting to observe that he begins the analysis with verse 12 and divides the passage into three strophes.

1. . . . εὐχαριστοῦντες τῷ πατρὶ
   τῷ ἱκανώσαντι ὑμᾶς εἰς τὴν μερίδα τοῦ κλήρου τῶν
   ἁγίων ἐν τῷ φωτί

   ὅς ἐρρύσατο ἡμᾶς ἐκ τῆς ἐξουσίας τοῦ σκότους
   καὶ μετέστησεν εἰς τὴν βασιλείαν τοῦ υἱοῦ τῆς ἀγάπης αὐτοῦ
   ἐν ᾧ ἔχομεν τὴν ἀπολύτρωσιν, τὴν ἄφεσιν τῶν ἁμαρτιῶν

2. ὅς ἐστιν εἰκὼν τοῦ θεοῦ τοῦ ἀοράτου, *πρωτότοκος πάσης κτίσεως*
   ὅτι ἐν αὐτῷ ἐκτίσθη τὰ πάντα ἐν τοῖς οὐρανοῖς καὶ ἐπὶ τῆς γῆς
   τὰ ὁρατὰ καὶ τὰ ἀόρατα
   εἴτε θρόνοι εἴτε κυριότητες
   εἴτε ἀρχαὶ εἴτε ἐξουσίαι
   τὰ πάντα δι' αὐτοῦ καὶ εἰς αὐτὸν ἔκτισται
   καὶ αὐτός ἐστιν πρὸ πάντων
   καὶ τὰ πάντα ἐν αὐτῷ συνέστηκεν
   καὶ αὐτός ἐστιν ἡ κεφαλὴ τοῦ σώματος τῆς ἐκκλησίας

3. ὅς ἐστιν ἀρχή, *πρωτότοκος ἐκ τῶν νεκρῶν*
   ἵνα γένηται ἐν πᾶσιν αὐτὸς πρωτεύων
   ὅτι ἐν αὐτῷ εὐδόκησεν πᾶν τὸ πλήρωμα κατοικῆσαι
   καὶ δι' αὐτοῦ ἀποκαταλλάξαι τὰ πάντα εἰς αὐτόν
   εἰρηνοποιήσας διὰ τοῦ αἵματος τοῦ σταυροῦ αὐτοῦ
   δι' αὐτοῦ εἴτε τὰ ἐπὶ τῆς γῆς
   εἴτε τὰ ἐν τοῖς οὐρανοῖς

---

survey of the history of interpretation of Col. 1:15-20 see Martin, "Excursus: The Literary Form and Background of Colossians 1:15-20," *Colossians*, pp. 61-64.

[27]Eduard Norden, *Agnostos Theos*, p. 250.

James M. Robinson (1957).[28] Robinson's analysis springs from Norden. He omits verses 12-14. Notice that it differs widely from Norden's reconstruction and from the text of Colossians. It has remarkable symmetry. Fearing criticism similar to Käsemann's cynical comment about Lohmeyer's reconstruction ("a model of hymnic formation, without parallel in the New Testament"), he justifies the rearrangement by noting the striking parallels in the first three lines, which quite closely follow the text of Colossians. These lines, he believes, were written by an exacting composer. The other lines which are marked by disorder are attributed to another writer who was not concerned with parallelism and correspondence. The latter writer thus felt free to manipulate the material in order to bring about an orderly hymnic structure.[29] Few have been satisfied with Robinson's attempt to make order out of material which he himself says was composed by a redactor who was not really concerned about liturgical order.

Strophe A

ὅς ἐστιν εἰκὼν τοῦ θεοῦ τοῦ ἀοράτου
πρωτότοκος πάσης κτίσεως

ὅτι ἐν αὐτῷ ἐκτίσθη τὰ πάντα ἐν
τοῖς οὐρανοῖς καὶ ἐπὶ τῆσ γῆς

[καὶ] τὰ πάντα δι' αὐτοῦ καὶ εἰς
αὐτὸν (ἔκτισται)

καὶ αὐτός ἐστιν πρὸ πάντων

καὶ τὰ πάντα ἐν αὐτῷ συνέστηκεν

Strophe B

ὅς ἐστιν ἀρχή
πρωτότοκος ἐκ τῶν νεκρῶν

ὅτι ἐν αὐτῷ [κατοικεῖ] πᾶν τὸ
πλήρωμα [τῆς θεότητος] (σωματικῶς)

καὶ δι' αὐτοῦ [ἀποκαταλλάξαι] τὰ
πάντα εἰς αὐτόν

---

[28]James M. Robinson, "A Formal Analysis of Col. 1:15-20," *JBL* 76 (1957): 286.

[29]Ibid., pp. 286-87.

καὶ αὐτός ἐστιν ἡ κεφαλὴ τοῦ
σώματος
ἵνα γένηται ἐν πᾶσιν αὐτὸς
πρωτεύων

Eduard Schweizer (1961).[30] Schweizer, like Robinson, begins with verse 15. His arrangement consists of three strophes and follows the order of the text of Colossians exactly. He omits the following four phrases and regards them as redactions made by the author of Colossians: (1) "things visible and invisible whether thrones or dominions or principalities or authorities" in 16b; (2) "the church" in 18a; (3) "in order that he might be preeminent in everything" in 18c; and (4) "making peace by the blood of his cross (διὰ αὐτοῦ is omitted in some manuscripts) whether things upon the earth or things in the heavens" in 20b. Notice that strophes 1 and 3 consist of three statements of exactly parallel lines and that the middle strophe (2) is made up of three lines beginning with καί, each of which asserts a relationship of Christ to all things.

1. ὅς ἐστιν εἰκὼν τοῦ θεοῦ τοῦ ἀοράτου
    πρωτότοκος πάσης κτίσεως
    ὅτι ἐν αὐτῷ ἐκτίσθη τὰ πάντα
    ἐν τοῖς οὐρανοῖς καὶ ἐπὶ τῆς γῆς
    τὰ πάντα δι' αὐτοῦ καὶ εἰς αὐτὸν ἔκτισται

2. [καὶ] αὐτός ἐστιν πρὸ πάντων
    [καὶ] τὰ πάντα ἐν αὐτῷ συνέστηκεν
    [καὶ] αὐτός ἐστιν ἡ κεφαλὴ τοῦ σώματος

3. ὅς ἐστιν ἀρχή
    πρωτότοκος ἐκ τῶν νεκρῶν
    ὅτι ἐν αὐτῷ εὐδόκησεν
    πᾶν τὸ πλήρωμα κατοικῆσαι
    καὶ δι' αὐτοῦ ἀποκαταλλάξαι
    τὰ πάντα εἰς αὐτόν

---

[30]E. Schweizer, "The Church as the Missionary Body of Christ," *NTS* 8 (1961, 1962): 6, 7.

All three of the above representative arrangements, though varied in detail, point toward a basic literary form that is hymnic in character. Martin's carefully worded statement is appropriate:

> The combined evidence of stylistic peculiarities (such as the repetition of words and phrases in verses 16, 20); the presence of identical words, (for example, 'first-born' in verses 15 and 18, coming in the same place in each hypothetical stanza); the use of constructions such as the ὅτι-clause in verses 16 and 19; and the incorporation of the formula 'from . . . through . . . to' (as in Romans 11:33-35) all these data show that we are reading a piece of carefully composed writing, set in a poetic mould and designed to be read as a self-contained whole and not a series of unrelated statements.[31]

The Authorship of the Hymn

An important consideration with regards to the traditional character of Colossians 1:15-20 is the authorship of the passage. Was it written by the author of the letter (whether it be Paul or a member of his circle)? If so, did he write it at the time of the composition of the letter or did he write it previously and include it in his letter? Let us examine the types of evidence and seek to draw a conclusion.

Linguistic Evidence. As is the case in verses 12-14, there are a number of terms in verses 15-20 which do not appear elsewhere in the Pauline corpus or else are used with a different meaning. The following statement by Lohse will verify this statement:

> Verse 15 has "image of God" (εἰκὼν τοῦ θεοῦ) which is used again only in 2 Corinthians 4:4 as a Christological predicate in the formula-sentence: "who is the image of God" (ὅς ἐστιν εἰκὼν τοῦ θεοῦ). In the whole New Testament, ὁρατός (1:16 "visible") appears only here; and while ἀόρατος (1:15 "invisible") appears a few times (Romans 1:20; 1 Timothy 1:17; Hebrews 11:27) it is never used elsewhere as a contrast to ὁρατός ("visible"). The Pauline letters do not mention θρόνοι ("thrones") elsewhere, and only Ephesians 1:21 uses κυριότης (1:16 "dominion"). The intransitive form συνεστηκέναι (1:17 "to be established") is otherwise not used by Paul. In a Christological context Paul speaks of Christ as ἀπαρχή (1 Corinthians 15:20 "firstfruits"), but never as ἀρχή (1:18 "beginning"). The words πρωτεύειν ("to be the first") and εἰρηνοποιεῖν ("to make peace") are hapaxlegomena in the New Testament. The word κατοικεῖν (1:19 "to dwell") reoccurs in Colossians 2:9, but this verse refers back to the hymn, and again in Ephesians 3:17. Ephesians 2:16 contains the other use of ἀποκαταλλάσσειν ("to reconcile"). The blood of Christ is mentioned by Paul only in connection with the traditional primitive Christian phrases which have to do with the vicarious death of Christ, and

---

[31]Martin, *Colossians*, p. 63.

the combination αἷμα τοῦ σταυροῦ αὐτοῦ (1:20 "blood of his cross") is without parallel.[32]

Although Lohse's conclusion that "these observations *exclude* the possibility that the author of this letter could have composed these verses by himself by using traditional phrases (italics mine)" is an extreme statement, the evidence at least suggests a non-Pauline provenance for the hymn.[33]

Theological Evidence. A study of the theology of this passage is a complicated task involving a consideration of the source of the hymn and redactions made by the author of Colossians. These matters will be considered later. For the moment we shall look only at the passage as it stands in the letter and seek to discover in a general way whether or not its theology is compatible with the theology of the undisputed letters of the Pauline corpus.

The obvious place to begin is with Christology. Two features immediately strike our attention: the affirmation of the preexistence of Christ as the Creator of all things and His position as the end or goal of creation. Although Christ is clearly set forth as the preexistent Creator in Hebrews and the Fourth Gospel, such a teaching is at best only hinted at in the undisputed letters of Paul. The classic hymnic unit used

---

[32]Lohse, *Colossians*, p. 42.

[33]Ibid. Lohse seems to be reacting to Kümmel's statement: "it is completely possible that the author of Colossians himself formed this hymn on the basis of traditional materials." (W. G. Kümmel, *Introduction to the New Testament*, p. 242). It should be observed that Kümmel recognizes the hymnic character of Col. 1:15-20 and the existence of traditional material. His real objective for making the above statement was to refute the post-apostolic dating of the letter. Vawter and Lohse both refer to the statement of Andre Feuillet who not only regards the hymn as Paul's, but as the "apex of Pauline Christology" (*Le Christ sagesse de Dieu d'après les épîtres pauliniennes*, Etudes Biblique [Paris, 1966]). Nicholas Kehl (*Der Christushymnus im Kolosserbrief*, 1967) is of the same opinion, "The basic form of the hymn stands firm in the Pauline theology, and it is rather unimportant whether the literary form is derived from Paul himself or from his circle. In its basic form it existed before the writing of the Colossian letter and sang of the realization of God's plan of salvation in the Christ-event which had begun" (trans. mine, p. 163). For other discussions which prefer the Pauline authorship of the hymn see W. D. Davies, *Paul and Rabbinic Judaism*, pp. 150-54; G. Maurer, "Die Begründung der Herrschaft Christi über die Mächte nach Kolosser 1:15-20," *Wort und Dienst*, Neue Folge 4 (1955): 79-93; C. F. D. Moule, *The Epistles of Paul the Apostle to the Colossians and to Philemon*, pp. 58-62.

by Paul in Philippians 2:6-11 may affirm Christ's preexistence,[34] but it does not ascribe to Him the work of creation. The same is true of other statements of Paul which obviously presuppose the Son's preexistence with the Father but relate that preexistence with the Son's redemptive work, not with creation (Galatians 4:4; Romans 8:3; 2 Corinthians 8:9).

Not only is Christ's preexistence as Creator an advance over the usual way in which Paul expresses his teaching about Christ, but also Christ's position as the goal or end of creation goes beyond the Christology set forth in the undisputed letters of Paul. Verse 16 declares that all things were created "through him" (δι᾽ αὐτοῦ) and "for him" (εἰς αὐτόν). However, in Romans 11:36 and in 1 Corinthians 8:6 it is the Father, not the Son, who is the goal of all things.[35]

Another area of theological concern is the doctrine of the church. It is generally acknowledged that the words τῆς ἐκκλησίας in verse 18

---

[34]Although most assume a "three stage" Christology (preexistence, incarnation, and exaltation) in Phil. 2:6-11, such an assumption is not *necessarily* required. If the passage is interpreted from the perspective of paralleling Christ with Adam and the Suffering Servant, only a "two stage" Christology is required. Such an approach not only makes it unnecessary to relate the passage to the almost impossible questions raised by a kenotic Christology (see G. E. Ladd, *A Theology of the New Testament* [Grand Rapids: Eerdmans Pub. Co., 1974], pp. 419-21; and James D. G. Dunn, *Christology in the Making* [Philadelphia: The Westminster Press, 1980], pp. 114-21), but it admirably corresponds with the central total obedience motif in the hymn itself and in the Philippian letter. The point being stressed, however, is that even if preexistence is implied in the hymn, it is not related to creation.

A. M. Hunter, who connects preexistence with the Son of Man title, says that although Paul never applies the "barbarous Greek phrase" ὁ υἱὸς τοῦ ἀνθρώπου to Jesus, it "trembles on Paul's lips" in his use of Psa. 8:6 in 1 Cor. 15:27 *(Paul and His Predecessors*, pp. 86-87). But 1 Cor. 15:27 does not discuss Christ as Creator and in the very next verse Paul states the very difficult teaching about the final subjection of the Son to the Father.

[35]E. Schweizer draws attention to the difference between the teaching of Col. 1:15-20 and the speech attributed to Paul in Acts 17:23-31. The hymn implies that we cannot understand the origin and goal of nature without believing in Christ. But the speech in Acts starts from the premise that Jews, Greeks, and Christians agree about God the Creator of all things. This is not only what the Old Testament teaches (Isa. 42:5 is quoted in Acts 17:24, 25), but is also taught in the Greek poem (quoted in verse 28). ("Christ in the Letter to the Colossians," *Review and Expositor* 70 [1973]: 456). Schweizer's point is not very clear. It was made against the backdrop of the New Delhi Conference and was made more for homiletical than exegetical reasons. Furthermore, it is perilous to use Acts as a source of Pauline teaching.

are a redactional addition to the original hymn.[36] This would indicate that the cosmological statement in the passage is brought into line with the ecclesiology of the redactor. How does the church as the body over which Christ is the head compare to the "body of Christ" statements in Romans 12 and 1 Corinthians 12? One clear difference is that in Romans and 1 Corinthians "head" is not contrasted with "body" but is regarded as one member among the others. Indeed, in 1 Corinthians 12:14-26 the ear, eye, nose, hand, foot, and head are all mutually dependent on one another. Moreover, the weaker, less honorable and presentable parts are given the greater honor.[37] Another, and probably more significant difference, is that in Colossians the church is given cosmic significance, whereas in the Roman and Corinthian correspondence the local situation was in mind.[38]

What inferences can be drawn from the statements about Christ and the church in Colossians 1:15-20? Even if one takes the passage as it stands and does not consider the probable redactions, the Christological and ecclesiological conceptions are markedly different from the undisputed Pauline letters. It should be pointed out that these theological expressions are not *necessarily* incompatible with the genuine letters of Paul. First Corinthians 8:6, which is almost certainly a traditional article of faith from the earliest church,[39] relates the preexistence of Christ and creation in a way very similar to the hymn in Colossians. W. D. Davies believes that Paul's description of Christ as the wisdom of God (1 Corinthians 1:24,30) coupled with his rabbinic background would not make the creating activity of Christ a strange

---

[36]Kehl cogently argues to the contrary that τῆς ἐκκλησίας belongs to the original hymn (*Der Christhymnus im Kolosserbrief*, pp. 93, 97). Gibbs thinks that Kehl's argument is convincing (*Creation and Redemption*, p. 105).

[37]The reference to the "less honorable" parts may be due to the fact that the Corinthians were exalting those members of the community with the more ecstatic and spectacular gifts at the expense of those with the more "ordinary" ones.

[38]Lohse concludes from these differences that a Pauline provenance is ruled out. "Thus it is not sufficient to state that in its statements about the church Colossians goes beyond the chief Pauline letters; the understanding of the church in Colossians cannot be explained as a simple evolution from earlier beginnings with Pauline theology." (*Colossians*, p. 55).

[39]Hurd, *The Origin of 1 Corinthians*, pp. 68, 278ff., 290-91; Gibbs, *Creation and Redemption*, pp. 59-73.

doctrine to him.[40] As for the headship of Christ over the church, such a concept could be understood in connection with the well-known tension between the "already" and the "not yet" in Paul.[41] If τῆς ἐκκλησίας was added by the author of Colossians, the cosmological statement about the headship of Christ becomes an ecclesiological one. If the phrase was not added, the statement was in a sense already an ecclesiological one from an eschatological perspective. It could imply that the eschatological reconciliation which does not yet include all things was already present in the church. The church is the unique sphere of Christ's redemptive grace. It has been translated into the kingdom of the Beloved Son. It must, therefore, demonstrate the indicative reality of the "already" by its manner of life.

Whether or not the Christology and ecclesiology of the hymn are compatible with Paul's own theological views is not the issue at this stage of our investigation. The primary matter is that they clearly differ from Paul's perspective. I am aware that this line of argument for the traditional character of the passage is only germane on the assumption that Paul is the author of Colossians. However, it seems useful to include it since the writer wrote in the name of Paul and since I will later argue for the probability of the Pauline authorship of the letter.

Stylistic and Contextual Evidence. Probably the clearest clue that the author of the hymn was using material that was already at hand is the presence of the stylistic features which can be seen from our previous treatment of the structure of the passage (pp.19-23). The precise parallelisms of the opening three lines in strophes 1 and 3 in Schweizer's arrangement show that the unit was very carefully composed. The

---

[40]W. D. Davies, *Paul and Rabbinic Judaism*, pp. 147-76. Davies seeks to demonstrate that Christ as the Wisdom of God is related to the understanding of Christ as the New Torah. After showing that sixth century B.C. Judaism used the figure of wisdom as a way of reconciling transcendence with immanence, he describes how wisdom became identified with Torah. He concludes with two theological implications which are not only germane to modern theology, but to the Colossian situation: (1) To claim that Torah was the instrument of creation was to declare that Nature and Revelation belong together (against Barth—and the Colossian heterodoxy). (2) Since Christ is the New Torah, the Wisdom of God, to live after Christ is the natural life. The Creator is the Redeemer. Nature and Grace are not antithetical (against Brunner—and the Colossian heterodoxy).

[41]See L. Goppelt, "Die Herrschaft Christi und die Welt nach dem Neuen Testament," *LuthRund* 17:1 (1967): 21-50.

relative clauses which introduce each of these strophes indicate their traditional character. The repetitious καί and the rhythmic pattern of strophe 2 which confesses the total Lordship of Christ over all creation betray the hand of a composer who artistically created a hymn of praise to the Creator-Redeemer.[42] Of course, the careful composer could have been the writer of the letter himself,[43] but the linguistic data which we previously considered probably rule that out.

The most forceful evidence for the existence of the hymn before the composition of the Colossian letter is the matter regarding the confessional nature of verses 12-14 (see pp. 12-14). Colossians 1:15-20 is connected with verses 12-14 by a relative clause. These verses serve as a "sort of introit"[44] which introduce the hymn. Therefore, the change of pronouns from the second person plural to the first person plural applies also to verses 15-20. It is not until verse 21 that the pronoun returns to the second person plural.

All of these considerations about the authorship of the hymn seem to point rather clearly to the conclusion that the author was not Paul the Apostle but someone whose ideas were either congenial to the Pauline school or whose words were so well known that the writer of the letter could revise them and the readers would immediately recognize the significance of the revisions. The larger issue concerning whether or not the writer of the letter was actually Paul the Apostle who included the liturgical materials in his letter will be taken up later.

The Source of the Hymn

Where did the hymn come from? Eduard Norden, who was one of the first to notice the doxological character of the passage, thought that it came from Stoic motifs mediated through Hellenistic Judaism.[45] C. F. Burney and E. Lohmeyer trace the source of the hymn to the Old Testament. Burney regarded it as Paul's own elaborate midrash on the first word in Genesis 1:1 (berê'shīth) in the light of the same word in

---

[42]Robinson argues for the existence of a pre-Pauline liturgical unit in Colossians on the ground of disorder as well as order ("Formal Analysis of Col. 1:15-20," p. 287).

[43]It is possible that 1 Cor. 13 was composed by Paul at a time previous to his writing of 1 Corinthians and was used by him because of the appropriate subject matter.

[44]Lohse's description of 1:12-14. *Colossians*, p. 33.

[45]E. Norden, *Agnostos Theos*, pp. 250-54.

Proverbs 8:22.[46] He regarded "firstborn of all creation" in Colossians 1:18 to be a direct allusion to "The Lord begat me as the beginning of His way" in Proverbs 8:22. In a similar Old Testament vein, E. Lohmeyer sought to find the provenance of Colossians 1:15-20 in the Jewish Day of Atonement.[47] He based his argument on ἀποκαταλλά- ξαι ("to reconcile") in verse 20. On the Day of Atonement the Creator and Lord of the whole world turns to His people. Thus, creation and reconciliation are linked together as they are in the Colossian hymn.

A number of New Testament scholars have traced the origin of the hymn to Stoic, gnostic, and Hellenistic sources. E. Käsemann noted that by removing eight words from the 112 word text every Christian motif would be eliminated. Furthermore, when verses 15-20 are contrasted to the liturgical, joyful, eschatological emphasis in 12-14, the "suprahistorical and metaphysical dramas of the gnostic Redeemer" stands forth. Therefore, he traces the source of the passage to a pre-Christian hymn based on the "gnostic myth of the Archetypal Man who is also the Redeemer," which myth is in a form characteristic of Hellenistic Judaism.[48] James Robinson, by analyzing each line of Norden's reconstruction, concludes that the hymn was associated with the logos, sophia, and anthropos speculations in Hellenistic Judaism. These concepts were crystallized in Judaism "and could be applied *en bloc* to Jesus."[49] Harald Hegermann also finds the Logos-Sophia speculations of the Hellenistic synagogues to be the most likely source of the hymn and directly relates the Colossian hymn to Philo's Logos

---

[46]C. Burney, "Christ as the APXH of Creation (Prov. 8:22; Col. 1:15-18; Rev. 3:14)," *Journal of Theological Studies* 27 (1926): 160-77. W. D. Davies was so impressed with Burney's argument that he said that Paul's picturing Christ as the image of Wisdom "has been convincingly proved by the work of Dr. C. F. Burney *(Paul and Rabbinic Judaism*, p. 151). Burney's hypothesis is overly ingenious. Although it points to the probable O. T. Wisdom source of the Christology, it is rather difficult to believe that Paul or anyone else would suddenly exegete a Hebrew text (in hymnic form!). See also Gabathuler's criticism in *Jesus Christus, Haupt der Kirche— Haupt der Welt*, pp. 28ff.

[47]Lohmeyer, *Die Briefe an die Philippen, an die Kolossen und an Philemon*, pp. 43-47. Lohse's devastating critique is appropriate: "Yet the term 'to reconcile'(ἀποκα- ταλλάξαι, verse 20) does not allude, even remotely, to a connection with Jewish conceptions of sacrifices and of the great Day of Atonement; moreover, the synagogue did not connect the Day of Atonement with the concept of creation." *Colossians*, p. 46.

[48]Käsemann, "A Primitive Christian Baptism Liturgy," pp. 154-59.

[49]Robinson, "A Formal Analysis of Col. 1:15-20," pp. 277-78

doctrine.[50] Jack Sanders sees the passage along with the other Christ-hymns in the New Testament as a stage of development in the Wisdom speculation of pre-Christian Judaism.[51]

The preceding survey of hypotheses concerning the origin of the Colossian hymn leads to two observations. One is that most of the studies see Jewish Wisdom motifs as one of the sources of influence on the hymn.[52] But the other is more important. Form critical analysis can move along with reasonable sure-footedness when dealing with structural, stylistic, and linguistic matters. It can classify the types of literary forms with a high degree of probability, but it faces a very complicated and complex task when it attempts to identify sources. Vawter well says: "There were no taps marked 'Jewish: Aramaic-speaking' or 'Jewish: Hellenist' or 'Hellenist: non-Jewish' which writers and thinkers could turn on to supply themselves with ideas and categories; what may have once been separate tributaries had long flowed into a common stream."[53]

Syncretism is a powerful force that is always active. It operates wittingly or unwittingly. It can take words and ideas from one ideology and turn them into something entirely different from another.[54]

All of this may appear as a nice way to avoid making a decision about the origin of the hymn. It is not intended to be. As has already

---

[50]Hegermann, *Die Vorstellung vom Schöpfungsmittler im Judentum und Urchristentum.* See F. B. Craddock, "All Things in Him: A Critical Note on Col. 1:15-20," *NTS* 12 (1966): 78-80, for a critique of Hegermann.

[51]Sanders, *The New Testament Christological Hymns: Their Historical Religious Background,* p. 136.

[52]W. D. Davies, after summarizing the appeals to Stoicism and the Logos doctrine of Philo as the provenance of the Colossian hymn, says: "But there is clearly one figure in the Old Testament which bears a striking resemblance to the Christ here depicted by Paul. Judaism had ascribed to the figure of Wisdom a pre-cosmic origin and a part in the creation of the world. It becomes probable, therefore, that Paul has here pictured Christ as the image of Wisdom." *Paul and Rabbinic Judaism,* p. 151.

[53]B. Vawter, "The Colossian Hymn and the Principle of Redaction," *CBQ* 33 (1971): 73.

[54]One is reminded of A. Schweitzer's criticism of Reitzenstein's analysis of Paul. "Before the poor apostle can get in a word he has overwhelmed him with a shower of parallel passages from the Hellenistic literature." *The Mysticism of St. Paul the Apostle,* trans. by William Montgomery (London: A & C Black, 1931), p. 27. It is not a very helpful procedure to assign certain ideas to Hellenistic provenance and others to Jewish when the facts of history indicate that Judaism had been

been suggested, it may be that the *Vorlage* was already well known by the readers and that the writer wants to get on good terms with the readers by using it. He, therefore, "corrects" the hymn by adding words and phrases which would be readily recognized as corrections. It seems to me, however, that there is something incongruous about a writer taking material which he regarded as "fascinating and dangerous" (to use Schweizer's words) and using that material in his letter to call his readers to walk in the light of the received Christological traditions (Colossians 2:6, 7). That he would use a tradition which he regarded as needing correction seems doubtful. Would not an erroneous tradition (in the writer's mind) be put in the category of "according to the tradition of men," against which he warns? It is not hard to see why a writer would use a hymn based upon a primitive Christian baptismal liturgy, but it is difficult to understand how material regarded as erroneous could become the basis for a Christian hymn.

Once the question of the source of the hymn is postulated in terms of Judaism or Gnosticism (or Christian or non-Christian), the resultant methodology will invariably stress the similarities of the hymn with the position taken and stress the differences with the position rejected. It seems reasonable to accept Colossians 1:15-20 in terms of what it professes to be.[55] By form, content, and use it professes to be a poetic celebration of Christ developed out of the experience of Christian worship. It contains a theology that squares with the confession of the church in other parts of the New Testament. It may not be the way the writer usually expresses his Christology, but it is not really incompatible with it. The writer may want to stress certain matters by

---

thoroughly Hellenized and the Graeco-Roman world had also assimilated Jewish ideas. It would be convenient for analytical purposes if all Palestinian Jews were nomistic and provincial and all Diaspora Jews were not. But in Jerusalem, according to Acts, it was the Diaspora Jews who stoned Stephen for speaking against the temple and Moses (Acts 6:8-14) and it was Diaspora Jews who sought Paul's life when he returned to Jerusalem at the conclusion of his missionary journeys (Acts 21:27ff., 24:18ff.).

Craddock's criticism of Hegermann ("All Things in Him," pp. 79, 80) is appropriate for this point. Because in Stoicism the Logos had a relationship to all things, Hegermann saw the Stoic Logos as a source for Col. 1:15-20. However, in Stoicism the Logos is in all things. But, in the hymn all things are in Christ. The form may be similar, but the content directly contradicts the Stoic schema.

[55] B. Vawter, "The Colossian Hymn and the Principle of Redaction," p. 73.

redacting the hymn, but he nevertheless finds the hymn to be useful for his purpose.

The Theology of Colossians 1:12-20

On the basis of the investigation we have made of 1:12-14 and 1:15-20, let us now turn to the entire passage (1:12-20) and attempt to discover its theological concerns.

Redactions in Colossians 1:15-20. Let us first observe the probable redactional statements in verses 15-20. As can be seen from the sample structural arrangements given previously (pp. 19-23), Norden in his early study was primarily interested in the hymnic structure of the passage. Later studies drew attention to the materials marked by awkward syntax which interrupted the discernible flow of the passage. When we observe Schweizer's analysis (p. 22), it is quite clear that he regards the following four phrases as redactions:

(1) v. 16a "things visible and invisible whether thrones or principalities or powers."

(2) v. 18a "the church."

(3) v. 18c "in order that he might be preeminent in everything."

(4) v. 20b,c "making peace by the blood of his cross, through him whether things upon the earth or in heaven."

It would be overly optimistic to say that there is general agreement with Schweizer on this. E. Käsemann is persuaded that the phrases "the church" (18a) and "through the blood of his cross" (20b) were added to make the hymn suitable for Christian use.[56] R. P. Martin believes that there are three redactional elements: "the church" (18a), "whether on earth or in heaven" (20c), and "making peace through the blood of his cross' (20b).[57] He cogently argues for the middle one on syntactical grounds. "It is far removed from its antecedent (τα πάντα)."[58] Just as cogently, he argues for the other two on theological grounds. By adding "the church" and "making peace through the blood of his cross," the author radically transforms a (Hellenistic?) hymn about cosmic restitution to one celebrating Christ's lordship over the church and reconciliation based upon his death.

---

[56]Käsemann, *N. T. Essays*, pp. 154-56.

[57]Martin, "Reconciliation and Forgiveness," pp. 112-13.

[58]Ibid., p. 112.

The arguments of Käsemann and Martin are strong and persua- sive. But as I have stated previously, it seems to me unlikely that the author would admonish his readers to walk in the light of the received Christological tradition (which I assume he would regard as "accord- ing to Christ") and then use a tradition which was obviously in need of drastic alteration. In any event, the phrases about the church and about the cross are commonly accepted as additions to the original hymn and Professor Martin's argument for the redactional character of the phrase "whether things on earth or in the heavens" is convincing. These three redactional phrases will help us focus on the theological concerns of the writer in his use of the hymn.

The Eschatological Implications of the Redactions. An important and debated observation should be made before looking at the theological emphases introduced into the hymn by these redactions. If the hymn was already in use by the Christian community, it already had an eschatological meaning. Since the term "eschatology" has been used with such a wide and confusing variety of meanings, it is necessary for me to explain how I will use it in the forthcoming discussion.

I use the term "eschatology" in connection with the earliest procla- mation of the Gospel. The Gospel itself is an eschatological announce- ment. The announcement was made against the backdrop of the Jewish hope related to the teaching of the "two ages": "this age" and "the age to come." "This age" can be described as an evil one which is under the rule of the evil powers. The "age to come" is related to the promised eschatological day of salvation that will be marked by the rule or "kingdom" of God. The Gospel announces that the promised reign (kingdom) of God has become present in Jesus, the Messiah (Mark 1:1-15). The Gospel, therefore, announces the fulfillment of that which God promised in the Old Testament through the prophets. Jesus is the promised Son of David and Son of God of the last days (Romans 1:2-4). He is the promised Messiah who came into history as the warrior who wages a war against the evil powers and defeats them. The beginning and ending of that warfare is related to the "already" of his death and resurrection and the "not yet" of his *Parousia* (1 Corinthians 15:20-28). The cross and resurrection event mark the beginning of the eschatological day. The *Parousia* marks its climax and culmination. Eschatology has to do with salvation and redemption and the day of salvation began with the Christ-event.

It is on these grounds that I make the statement that the hymn already has eschatological meaning. Regardless of what structure of the hymn one may be disposed to follow, it begins with a protological statement about Christ as the preexistent Creator and Lord of all and comes to a climax with an eschatological proclamation which celebrates Christ as the Reconciler of all. The hymn does not need the redactional statement about "making peace through the blood of the cross" to indicate the eschatological significance of the cross-resurrection event. It is already present in the description of Christ as the πρωτότοκος ἐκ τῶν νεκρῶν.[59] It is the cross-resurrection event that makes Christ the agent of God in the new creation (eschatology) just as in his preexistence he was the agent of God in the original creation (protology).

Let us now return to the three probable redactional phrases we have noted above: (1) "the church," (2) "making peace through the blood of his cross," and (3) "whether things on the earth or in the heavens." The following observations can be made: Redaction (3) indicates that the writer of the letter wanted to assert the lordship of Christ over everything, things in the heaven as well as things on earth. It is interesting to observe that both Robinson's and Schweizer's analyses of the hymn regard the phrases "things visible and invisible, whether thrones or dominions or rulers or authorities" (16b) and "that in everything he might become preeminent" (18c) as redactions which break up the symmetry of the passage. If these phrases also were regarded as redactional statements, the stress would be on Christ's lordship over *everything*, including the invisible powers. It is not our purpose at this time to discuss the nature of the Colossian heresy, but it is clear that the "powers" were in some way a threat to the Colossians. Whether they were evil in and of themselves (which seems likely to me) or were evil because the Colossians attributed to them an authority which they did not possess, they were evidently hostile forces that

---

[59] Käsemann asserts that "even the title 'Firstborn from the dead' can no longer be put into this (Christian) category by anyone who has to some extent familiarized himself with gnostic terminology." *Primitive Christian Baptismal Liturgy*, p. 154. But even though it is his opinion that the hymn came from pre-Christian gnostic circles, it is also his opinion that it came to be part of the primitive Christian liturgy of baptism and was therefore already in the hymn used by the author of Colossians. Thus *in the church* it already had eschatological meaning.

influenced the readers to a way of life that was not befitting the Christian community.

In redaction (2) "making peace by the blood of his cross," it is clear that the writer sought to stress Christ's triumph over the hostile powers by virtue of his death on the cross. The cross was the way in which he triumphed over them. By his death he "died out" on the authorities and stripped them of their power.[60] In 2:11-15 the author describes the significance of the death of Christ in terms of circumcision, which in turn is related to baptism. What Christ has done in his flesh-body on the cross is reproduced in Christians by their solidarity with him demonstrated in baptism.

Probably the most important redaction from the writer's point of view is the addition of the words "the church" in verse 18. By its addition, a protological-cosmological statement becomes an eschatological-ecclesiological one. The eschatological reconciliation which was brought about by the cross, demonstrated in the resurrection, and declared in the title "firstborn from the dead," has already begun in the church. The writer stresses the "already" of reconciliation in the application of the hymn to his readers in verses 21 and 22 through the forceful contrast of ποτὲ (v. 21) and νυνὶ δὲ (v. 22). Christ the Cosmocrator-Redeemer has already "made peace through the blood of his cross" (v. 20) and defeated the evil powers (2:15). The cosmic redemption will ultimately affect τὰ πάντα but it has already begun in the church. The Colossians are to know this indicative reality (1:9) and walk accordingly (1:10, 11; 3:1-4:6.)

---

[60]See J. A. T. Robinson, *The Body*, Studies in Biblical Theology 5 (London: SCM Press, 1963), pp. 32-48. His statement on p. 40 is especially appropriate:

The only way evil wins victories is by making a man retort by evil, reflect it, pay it back, and thus afford it a new lease on life. Over one who persistently absorbs it and refuses to give it out, it is powerless. It is in this kind of way that Paul sees Christ dealing with the forces of evil—going on and on and on, triumphantly absorbing their attack by untiring obedience, till eventually there is nothing more they can do. Or, rather, there is one thing more—and that is to kill Him. This they do. But in the very act they confess their own defeat. For all they achieve thereby is to deprive Him, still inviolate, of the flesh, through which alone they have the power of temptation over Him. He thus slips their grasp and renders them impotent. The Resurrection is the inevitable consequence of this defeat; death could have no grip on Him. It was impossible that He should be holden of it.

The Relationship of 1:15-20 to 1:12-14

It would be well to make some comment on the relationship of
1:15-20 to 1:12-14. Norden regarded it as a part of the total hymn.
Käsemann takes the same view because he believes that the whole unit
(1:12-20) was part of a baptismal liturgy but that baptismal language is
present only in verses 12-14.[61] Lohse regards 1:12-14 as a confessional
"introit" by which the writer introduced the hymn into the letter.[62]
Robinson, reasoning on the basis of the Christian use of the Jewish
hodayoth (thanksgivings) formulae, believes that 1:15-20 forms the
reason for the thanksgiving in 1:12-14.[63]

If the conclusion drawn from our analysis of 1:12-14 is correct, then
the unit consists of traditional materials which were already extant for
the writer to use. The character of the pericope is creedal or confessional. On the other hand 1:15-20 is marked by distinct poetic or
hymnic qualities. It does not seem to me that they were originally
together. But were they together when the writer used them? It is
impossible to tell for certain, but, in my opinion, they probably were
not. I say this for the following reasons: (1) It seems likely that the
writer knew that the statements in verses 12-14 were based upon a
baptismal confession. He used the hymn in verses 15-20 to assert that
the Christ into whom they were baptized was the Creator-Redeemer
who was Lord over *all*, including the στοιχεῖα and the heavenly
authorities. (2) The ethical injunctions in 3:1-13 are clearly based on
the readers' experience of baptism. Indeed it is possible, though
unlikely, that all of the paraenetic material in Colossians (from 3:1 to
4:6) is based upon baptismal catechetical material. The reminder concerning the Colossians' relationship to Christ through their experience
of baptism (2:11ff.) is obviously based upon a Christological declaration (2:9, 10) which itself refers to the Christ-hymn in 1:15-20. It seems
likely, then, that just as the writer connected the baptismal teaching
and paraenesis in 2:11-4:6 to the Christological proclamation of 2:9,

---

[61]E. Käsemann, "Primitive Christian Baptismal Liturgy," p. 152-54.

[62]E. Lohse, *Colossians*, p. 33.

[63]J. M. Robinson, "Die Hodajot-Formel in Gebet und Hymnus des Frühchristentums," *Apophoreta, Festschrift für Ernst Haenchen*, ed. W. Eltester and F. H. Kettler,
BZNW 30 (Berlin: Verlag Alfred Topelmann, 1964), pp. 231-33.

10, so also he connected the Christ-hymn of 1:15-20 to the baptismal confession in 1:12-14.

THE TRADITIONAL CHARACTER
OF COLOSSIANS 2:9-15

The third passage with which we are concerned in this chapter is Colossians 2:9-15. This great Christological proclamation also contains characteristics which point to the author's use of materials which were already at hand. The importance of this section within the letter can be seen by its setting and general structure.

As the verses immediately preceding this passage (2:6-8) make clear, the author regarded the Christological traditions which had been received by the community to be extremely important to them. This is substantiated by the fact that his first concern after the standard salutation and thanksgiving (1:1-8) was to express his desire (in prayer form) that his readers be filled with the knowledge of the will of God and that they walk worthily of the Lord (1:9-23). As we have shown, the heart of this section consists of traditional materials which set forth Christ as Creator, Redeemer, and the One who is preeminent over all (1:12-20). This is followed by a section in which the author sought to establish his right to address them (1:24-2:5). This, in turn, is followed by a second momentous proclamation about Christ which is obviously related to the Christ-hymn in 1:15-20 and which is given in the context of the admonition to walk in the light of the received Christological tradition (2:6-15). It should be noted that these two important Christological passages are separated only by the writer's description of his ministry which established his credentials for writing to them. The first Christ-passage follows the order of first celebrating the Father (1:12-14) and then the Son (1:15-20). The second Christ-passage reverses the order and first celebrates the Son (2:9-13) and then the Father (2:14, 15—though the contents of these verses are concerned primarily with the Son).

Although G. Schille believes that a single baptismal hymn underlies 2:9-15, he surely goes beyond that which the data will allow.[64] Verses 9

---

[64]G. Schille, *Frühchristliche Hymnen* (Berlin, 1962), pp. 31-37. See Deichgräber's critique of Schille in *Gotteshymnus und Christushymnus*, pp. 167ff. and E. Lohse, *Colossians*, pp. 99, 100, fn. 43.

and 10 are clearly references to 1:19 of the Christ-hymn and are not part of a unified hymn. F. Zeilinger thinks that a baptismal hymn underlies verses 11-15 and divides that hymn into two strophes with subsections (verses 11, 12 and 13-15).[65] K. Wengst thinks that just verses 13-15 are based on a formal traditional hymn.[66] R. Deichgräber believes that formal hymnic material may underlie 13c-15, beginning with the participle χαρισάμενος.[67] R. P. Martin limits the formal composition of the pre-Pauline hymn to verses 14 and 15.[68] From all of this, it can be seen that the problem area with regard to the use of traditional materials has to do with verses 9-13. I shall attempt to show that although no single formal hymn lies behind these verses, the influence of pre-Pauline or para-Pauline traditions is present. Let us divide our discussion into three sections dealing with verses 9, 10; 11-13; and 14, 15.

Colossians 2:9, 10

Verses 9 and 10 consist of three predications:

(1) ὅτι ἐν αὐτῷ κατοικεῖ πᾶν τὸ πλήρωμα τῆς θεότητος σωματικῶς
(2) καὶ ἐστε ἐν αὐτῷ πεπληρωμένοι
(3) ὅς ἐστιν ἡ κεφαλὴ πάσης ἀρχῆς καὶ ἐξουσίας

It is clear that ἐν αὐτῷ stands in an emphatic position. The admonitions in the preceding context (2:6-8) begin with an injunction to walk according to the Christ of the received tradition and end with a warning against the "philosophy" and "empty deceit" which is "according to the tradition" of men and the "*stoicheia*" and not "according to Christ." Both the injunction and the warning are concerned with the tradition about Christ. The emphatic position of ἐν αὐτῷ shows that the predications in verses 9 and 10 are all based on the Christ of the

[65]Franz Zeilinger, *Der Erstgeborene der Schöpfung: Untersuchungen Formalstruktur und Theologie des Kolosserbriefes* (Wien: Verlag Herder, 1974), p. 54.

[66]K. Wengst, *Christologische Formeln und Lieder des Urchristentums*, Studien zum Neuen Testament 8d.7 (Guetersloher Verlaghaus, 1972), pp. 186-94.

[67]Deichgräber, *Gotteshymnus und Christushymnus*, pp. 167-68.

[68]Martin, "Reconciliation and Forgiveness," pp. 117-24.

apostolic tradition (and, by implication, not on the Christ of the "heresy").[69]

It is equally clear that the assertion about Christ made in the first predication is based on 1:19 of the Christ-hymn: ὅτι ἐν αὐτῷ εὐδόκησεν πᾶν τὸ πλήρωμα κατοικῆσαι. The second predication is related to the first by conjunction καί. The repetition of ἐν αὐτῷ and the use of πεπληρωμένοι indicates that the author intended to apply the Christ-hymn to his readers. The third predication was also derived from the Christ-hymn in 1:15-20 and parallels the assertions made there about Christ's sovereignty over the heavenly powers. This can be seen, first of all, by the affirmation in 1:18 that Christ is the κεφαλὴ τοῦ σώματος, which, as we have previously surmised, had a cosmic meaning in the *Urhymnus* and was redacted to bring about an ecclesiological meaning. Secondly, it can be seen from the declaration in 1:16 that Christ is the one who created all things, including the ἀρχαί and the ἐξουσίαι.

The traditional character of Colossians 2:9, 10 is made evident in the fact that practically all of its ideas and vocabulary are drawn directly from the traditional Christ-hymn in 1:15-20.

Colossians 2:11-13

Of the entire Christological passage in 2:9-15, verses 11-13 are the most difficult to handle with respect to their traditional character. The baptismal features in these verses are obvious. However, to say that they are based on a single underlying baptismal hymn, as P. Zeilinger tentatively suggests, seems to me to go beyond the evidence.[70] There are at least three difficulties which stand in the way of this hypothesis. First, it is nearly impossible to reconstruct a formal hymnic pattern from these verses. There is a great deal of difference, for example, between the pattern observable in 1:15-20 and (as we shall show further on) in 2:14, 15. Second, there is a change of subject from "you" to "he" in verse 13. Third, the application of the baptismal statements change from the second person plural to the first person plural in the final

---

[69]I use the word "apostolic" because the readers received their instruction from Epaphras who in 1:7, 8 is closely associated with Paul the apostle as a "faithful servant of Jesus Christ on behalf of us (ὑπερ ἡμῶν)." (ὑμῶν, however, has strong manuscript support.)

[70]Zeilinger, *Der Erstgeborene der Schöpfung*, p. 54.

participial phrase in verse 13c. This last difficulty loses its point if 13c belongs to a formally-structured unit consisting of 13c-15 as Deichgräber and Lohse believe.[71] But 13c breaks up the remarkable grammatical parallelism of verses 14 and 15 and probably should not be included with the latter verses.

Nevertheless there are a number of features present in verses 11-13 that give credence to the theory that the section is constructed from baptismal materials that were already at hand. The following tentative reconstruction will help make this clear:[72]

(1) Verses 11-12b

ἐν ᾧ καὶ περιετμήθητε περιτομῇ ἀχειροποιήτῳ
ἐν τῇ ἀπεκδύσει τοῦ σώματος τῆς σαρκός
ἐν τῇ περιτομῇ τοῦ Χριστοῦ συνταφέντες αὐτῷ
ἐν τῷ βαπτισμῷ

(2) Verse 12c-e

ἐν ᾧ καὶ συνηγέρθητε
διὰ τῆς πίστεως τῆς ἐνεργείας τοῦ θεοῦ
τοῦ ἐγείραντος αὐτὸν
ἐκ νεκρῶν

(3) Verse 13

καὶ ὑμᾶς νεκροὺς ὄντας τοῖς παραπτώμασιν
καὶ τῇ ἀκροβυτίᾳ τῆς σαρκὸς ὑμῶν
συνεζωοποίησεν ὑμᾶς σὺν αὐτῷ
χαρισάμενος ἡμῖν πάντα τὰ παραπτώματα

The striking accumulation of relative pronouns, prepositional phrases, and participial constructions are at once noticeable and point to the possibility of a hymnic background for the passage. The structural and thematic elements in the section point in the same direction. Although the structure does not consist of strictly formal elements, it is clear that the author used more than a little care in its construction. He

---

[71]Deichgräber, *Gotteshymnus und Christushymnus*, pp. 167ff. and E. Lohse, *Colossians*, p. 99, fn. 43.

[72]See Zeilinger, *Der Erstageborene der Schöpfung*, p. 55 for a different reconstruction.

almost seems to be creating a hymn out of standard baptismal motifs. No doubt the ἐν ᾧ καὶ which begin strophes 1 and 2 were evoked by the double use of ἐν αὐτῷ in verses 9 and 10. In strophe 1 the use of ἐν with the article seems deliberate, whereas in strophe 2 the format is more loosely arranged. Strophe 3 departs from the prepositional structure but clearly has two movements, each of which contains ὑμᾶς, παράπτωμα, and a participle.

The development of the theme in verses 11-13 also indicates that the section was carefully and artistically composed. Strophe 1 declares participation in the death of Christ; strophe 2 asserts participation in the resurrection of Christ; and strophe 3 (by the emphatic position of καὶ ὑμᾶς in verse 13) stresses the readers' participation in both the death and the resurrection of Christ. There are obvious parallels between 2:11-13 and the Christ-hymn and its application in 1:15-23. The hymn includes statements about the death and resurrection of Christ in verses 18 and 20 and it is applied to the readers by the use of καὶ ὑμας in 1:21. It is also noteworthy that the phrase "body of his flesh" occurs in both 1:22 and 2:11. As was true of verses 9 and 10, verses 11-13 are an application of the Christ-hymn to the readers. The basic (three strophe) structure and the thematic relationship of 2:11-13 and 1:15-23 point to the author's own creative manner of expression, but the grammatical features of the substructure and the presence of the baptismal motif seem to indicate the presence of material that the writer already had at hand.

One other factor should be considered before a firmer conclusion may be drawn. Is there any evidence of the presence of traditional modes of expression and traditional phraseology in verses 11-13? One of the striking features of this passage is the linking of circumcision with baptism. Such a comparison is made nowhere else in the New Testament. Lohse assumes that "the author of Colossians adopted the term 'circumcision' (περιτομή) from the 'philosophy.' "[73] That may be so, but the term is used in Colossians with regard to participation in the death of Christ in baptism and a manner of life befitting that new relationship (1:22 and 2:20-3:17). Even though a comparison of baptism with circumcision is not directly stated anywhere else in the New Testament, the idea is an obviously useful one and was likely already

---

[73]Lohse, *Colossians*, pp. 101-102.

present in the early church. The moral application of circumcision was already in use in the Old Testament (Deuteronomy 10:16; Jeremiah 4:4; Ezekiel 44:7) and the instruction given to the Qumran fellowship that the men of truth in the community "shall circumcise the foreskin of evil inclination and stiffness of neck" (1QS 5:5 [Vermes' translation]) shows that the Old Testament rite was spiritualized in Palestinian Judaism in New Testament times. Paul describes a real Jew and true circumcision as a spiritual matter of the heart in Romans 2:28, 29.

Perhaps more significantly, both circumcision and baptism function aptly as covenant signs. Circumcision was a sign of the people of the Covenant in the Old Testament (Genesis 17:11) and baptism is an effective sign of the eschatological people of the Covenant. A contrast between the people of the Old Covenant and the people of the New Covenant is present in Paul's emphatic statement in Philippians 3:3 that "*we* are the (true) circumcision who worship God in Spirit and glory in Christ Jesus, and put no confidence in the flesh." His own testimony in the succeeding verses in Philippians was that he gladly gave up all of the prestigious Jewish things that were associated with the exclusivism of the Old Covenant in order to be found in Christ, share in his sufferings by becoming like him in his death, and ultimately attain the resurrection of the dead. Though baptism is not expressly stated, the ideas associated with baptism are abundantly present and the eschatological implications of being in Christ are clear. It should also be pointed out that Philippians 3:3-11 closely parallels the Christ-hymn and its application in Philippians 2:1-11. The Christ-hymn in Philippians 2 and the one in Colossians 1 both connect the death of Christ with his authority over all the heavenly and earthly powers.

The same cluster of ideas associating the death of Christ and baptism is also present in 1 Peter 3:18-22, thus showing their possible traditional character. There Christ's death is related to his "flesh" (as in Colossians 2:11-13), is associated with baptism, and is connected with the authority of Christ over "angels, principalities, and powers." A similar statement is made about baptism in 1 Peter 3:21 as is made about circumcision in Colossians 2:11. It is generally recognized that the term "made without hands" (ἀχειροποιήτῳ) which modifies "circumcision" in Colossians 2:11 is a negative term meaning something which God, not man, has done.[74] In 1 Peter 3:21 baptism is described as

---

[74]Ibid., pp. 102-103; Martin, *Colossians*, p. 82.

not a "removal of dirt from the body, but as an appeal to God for a clear conscience through the resurrection of Christ." Neither circumcision (Colossians 2:11) or baptism (1 Peter 3:21) are to be regarded as merely external human acts.

All of these things (the spiritual meaning of circumcision in the Old Testament and in the Judaism of New Testament times, the appropriateness of circumcision and baptism as covenant signs, and the association of the death of Christ with his "flesh") make it easy to accept the notion that an association of baptism with circumcision was a common theological idea in the early church.

Besides the circumcision-baptism mode of expression which underlies strophe 1 of this passage, there are some words and phrases in the section which were apparently "stock" or traditional words and phrases. The first one is ἀπεκδύσις in 2:11. The verb form of the word is used in a clearly hymnic passage (as we shall show) which celebrates Christ's triumph over the "rulers" and "authorities" (2:15). The verb form is used again in 3:9 in the context of a catalogue of vices associated with baptismal paraenesis and calling for the stripping off of the "old man." The phrase συνταφέντες αὐτῷ ἐν τῷ βαπτισμῷ in 2:12 is very similar in wording to Romans 6:4, another baptismal passage which contains a reference to the "old man" (Romans 6:6). The phrase διὰ τῆς πίστεως τῆς ἐνεργείας τοῦ θεοῦ τοῦ ἐγείραντος αὐτὸν ἐκ νεκρῶν in 2:12 closely parallels τοῖς πιστεύουσιν ἐπὶ τὸν ἐγείραντα Ἰησοῦν τὸν κύριον ἡμῶν in Romans 4:24 which in turn is modified by a phrase regarded by many as coming from a traditional confession.[75] A remarkably similar expression is found in 1 Peter 1:21, a writing well known for its probable use of traditional baptismal materials. Finally, the last phrase in Colossians 2:13 (χαρισάμενος ἡμῖν πάντα τὰ παραπτώματα) seems to be a standard expression. In the baptismal command that follows the Pentecostal sermon in Acts 2, Peter admonishes: "Repent and be baptized, every one of you, in the name of Jesus Christ for the forgiveness of your sins" (v. 38). The idea is also included in the Lord's Prayer pericope in Matthew 6:9-15 and parallels. Furthermore, the participial construction as well as the change from the

---

[75]Wegenast, *Das Verständnis der Tradition bei Paulus und in den Deuteropau-linen*, pp. 80-83; Popkes, *Christus Traditus*, pp. 258-65.

second to the first person would seem to indicate that the phrase was a well-known traditional one in use in the early church.

To summarize: Although Colossians 2:11-13 is probably not based upon an already existing unified hymn, the passage does bear a large number of features which leads to the conclusion that this passage was carefully constructed by the author of Colossians from materials already at hand. The grammatical constructions in the section, the structural and thematic elements which give it shape, the presence of traditional phraseology, and the probable standard theological association of baptism with circumcision confirm this view. Verses 9 and 10 are directly based on the Christ-hymn in 1:15-20 and verses 11-13 are made up of traditional concepts and phrases related to baptism.

Colossians 2:14, 15

I shall now seek to establish that Colossians 2:14, 15 is a redacted quotation from a previously existing hymn which celebrated the death of Christ as a victory over sin and the hostile powers. The presence of the Christ-hymn in chapter one shows that the author regarded hymns to be a helpful way of reminding his readers of what they had been taught. His instruction in 3:16 further confirms this: "Let the word of Christ dwell in you richly in all wisdom, teaching and admonishing one another in psalms and hymns and spiritual songs, with grace reigning in your hearts to God."

Although in previous times writers tried to show distinction in meaning between "psalms and hymns and spiritual songs" the present consensus is that exact differentiations cannot be made and that the New Testament writers did not intend rigid distinctions to be made.[76] In current discussions a wide variety of terms are used to designate various kinds of liturgical materials and no consensus has been reached. In general the term "hymn" has been used to designate poetic material consisting of prayer, praise, thanks, or liturgical narrative.[77] Sanders, in commenting on Kroll's statement that the common mark of early Christian hymnody was an "ardor of enthusiasm," writes: "It

---

[76]See J. Kroll, *Die christliche Hymnodik bis zu Klemens von Alexandreia. Verzeichnis der Vorlesungen an der Akademie zu Braunsberg im Sommer 1921* (Königsberg, 1921; reprinted Darmstadt, 1968), pp. 4ff.; Deichgräber, *Gotteshymnus und Christushymnus*, pp. 22ff., 47; Delling, *TWNT* 8:502, and others.

[77]See Sanders, *The New Testament Christological Hymns*, pp. 1-5.

may be noted here, however, that this is not merely a stylistic or formal observation, but refers to the *content* of the hymns, since early Christian hymnody tends to deal with a divine *drama*, a cosmic redemption, thus with an 'exalted' subject."[78] As we shall notice, Colossians 2:14, 15 contains the enthusiastic tone, stylistic features, and contents of the hymns of the early church to a marked degree.

Before an analysis of 2:14, 15 can be made, a word about verse 13 is in order. As we previously noted, some believe that verse 13 belongs with verses 14 and 15. I will briefly explain why I do not think that is so and then seek to show the traditional hymnic character of verses 14 and 15.

Lohse says of Colossians 2:13-15: "The piling up of participial clauses shows that in these verses the author takes up formulations that were already at hand and incorporates them into his argument."[79] At first glance that seems correct. Verses 13-15 could be divided into three strophes, each of which contains an identical grammatical arrangement: a participial construction, a full verb construction, another participial construction. The following arrangement will show this:

(1) Verse 13

καὶ ὑμᾶς νεκροὺς ὄντας [ἐν] τοῖς παραπτώμασιν
    καὶ τῇ ἀκροβυστίᾳ τῆς σαρκὸς ὑμῶν
συνεζωοποίησεν ὑμᾶς σὺν αὐτῷ
χαρισάμενος ἡμῖν πάντα τὰ παραπτώματα

(2) Verse 14

ἐξαλείψας τὸ καθ᾽ ἡμῶν χειρόγραφον (τοῖς δόγμασιν
    ὃ ἦν ὑπεναντίον ἡμῖν)
καὶ αὐτὸ ἦρκεν ἐκ τοῦ μέσου
προσηλώσας αὐτὸ τῷ σταυρῷ

(3) Verse 15

ἀπεκδυσάμενος τὰς ἀρχὰς καὶ τὰς ἐξουσίας
ἐδειγμάτισεν ἐν παρρησίᾳ
θριαμβεύσας αὐτοὺς ἐν αὐτῷ

---

[78]Ibid., p. 5.

[79]E. Lohse, *Colossians*, p. 92.

There are two factors which make it unlikely that verse 13 originally belonged to the *Urhymnus* in verses 14 and 15. The first one is
thematic. Verse 13 belongs with verses 11 and 12 as a summary
statement of the participation of Christians in the death and resurrection of Christ. It does not belong thematically with verses 14 and 15
which declare the significance of Christ's death as a triumph over evil.
Secondly, as pointed out above (pp. 39-40), the change of pronouns in
verse 13 makes it unlikely that even all of verse 13 was originally a unit.

However, with the exception of the phrase τοῖς δόγμασιν ὅ ἦν
ὑπεναντίον ἡμῖν, verses 14 and 15 take the shape of a formally structured unit.[80] Whether God or Christ is the subject referred to in the
participles is debatable, but the parallel structure of the passage is
clear. Each strophe deals with a saving effect of Christ's death. The
participle-full verb-participle construction of verse 14 is exactly repeated in verse 15. The first participial phrase in each strophe sets forth an
act of God in Christ. The full verb statement in each verse indicates the
manner or result of that act. The final participial phrase in each strophe
has a reference to the cross. It is clear that verses 14 and 15 are carefully
and formally structured in hymnic fashion.

The only phrase which interrupts the flow of the section is τοὶς
δόγμασιν ὅ ἦν ὑπεναντίον ἡμῖν in verse 14. This phrase adds a remark
that seems redundant in the light of the expression τὸ καθ᾽ ἡμῶν which,
in turn, modifies χειρόγραφον. It is likely that the phrase is a redactional comment added by the author because of the situation in Colossae. Verse 16 indicates concern about food laws and calendar
observations. Verse 20 uses the verb form of the word δόγμα to refer to
prohibitions which probably were demanded by the proponents of the
false teaching. It is interesting to observe that verses 16 and 20 introduce practices which portray an exclusivistic tendency. This sensitivity
to exclusiveness is also present in 3:11.[81] The author's theological
concern about the incompatibility of exclusivism with the gospel and
the obvious tendencies towards exclusivism in the Colossian community are ample reasons for the author to define the "certificate of

---

[80]I am indebted to Professor Martin for his very clear structural and theological
analysis of these verses in "Reconciliation and Forgiveness," pp. 116-24.

[81]"Here there cannot be Greek and Jew, circumcised and uncircumcised, but Christ
is all and in all."

indebtedness" in terms of regulations which stood in a hostile relationship to his readers.

With the exception of the redactional phrase just noted, verses 14 and 15 form a highly structured hymnic unit. But there is still another feature which points to its hymnic character: the contents of the unit. James M. Robinson sought to demonstrate the existence of an early Christian thanksgiving formula which was related to the Jewish *hodayoth* and *berachoth* formulae. He noted that the formula "I thank thee Lord for . . ." was followed by two liturgical lines giving the reasons for the thanksgiving.[82] It would not be difficult to surmise that Colossians 2:14, 15 may have been the liturgical conclusion to an early Christian *hodayoth* formula used in connection with baptism. Whether this is true or not, the verses clearly indicate reasons for giving thanks in two liturgical strophes. Furthermore, the strophes celebrate a divine redemptive drama with a cosmic perspective. God or Christ has cancelled the "certificate of indebtedness" which was against us and has stripped off the evil powers which were hostile to us. Both of these liturgical declarations of redemptive acts find their climax in the event of the cross. In style, contents, and emotional depth Colossians 2:14, 15 contains the qualities of an early Christian hymn.

Summary

The following reconstruction and review will help make the hymnic character of Colossians 2:9-15 clear:

(1) Verses 9 and 10

ὅτι ἐν αὐτῷ κατοικεῖ πᾶν τὸ πλήρωμα τῆς
      θεότητος σωματικῶς
καὶ ἐστὲ ἐν αὐτῷ πεπληρωμένοι
ὅς ἐστιν ἡ κεφαλὴ πάσης ἀρχῆς καὶ ἐξουσίας

(2) Verses 11-13

ἐν ᾧ καὶ περιετμήθητε περιτουῇ ἀχειροποιήτῳ
ἐν τῇ ἀπεκδύσει τοῦ σώματος τῆς σαρκός
ἐν τῇ περιτομῇ τοῦ Χριστοῦ συνταφέντες αὐτῷ
ἐν τῷ βαπτισμῷ

---

[82]Robinson, "Die Hodajot Formel in Gebet und Hymnus," pp. 194-235.

ἐν ᾧ καὶ συνηγέρθητε
    διὰ τῆς πίστεως τῆς ἐνεργείας τοῦ θεοῦ
    τοῦ ἐγείραντος αὐτὸν
    ἐκ νεκρῶν
καὶ ὑμᾶς νεκροὺς ὄντας ἐν τοῖς παραπτώμασιν
    καὶ τῇ ἀκροβυστίᾳ τῆς σαρκὸς ὑμῶν
συνεζωοποίησεν ὑμᾶς σὺν αὐτῷ
    χαρισάμενος πάντα τὰ παραπτώματα

(3) Verses 14 and 15
ἐξαλείφας τὸ καθ' ἡμῶν χειρόγραφον
    καὶ αὐτὸ ἦρκεν ἐκ τοῦ μέσου
    προσηλώσας αὐτὸ τῷ σταυρῷ
ἀπεκδυσάμενος τὰς ἀρχὰς καὶ τὰς ἐξουσίας
    ἐδειγμάτισεν ἐν παρρησίᾳ
    θριαμβεύσας αὐτοὺς ἐν αὐτῷ

Verses 9 and 10 consist of words and ideas drawn from verses 1:16, 18, and 19 of the Christ-hymn. Verse 9 cites the proclamation about the "fullness" dwelling in Christ and verse 10 applies that proclamation to the readers. The repetition of ἐν αὐτῷ in each verse and the ideas drawn from the Christ-hymn tie the two verses together.

Verses 11-13 relate the application of the Christ-hymn to baptism. The grammatical features as well as the thematic arrangement indicate that the passage was carefully constructed by the writer. Verse 12, by the use of the "circumcision" motif and the "body of flesh" phrase drawn from 1:22 as well as phraseology found in the baptismal passages in Romans and 1 Peter, asserts participation in the death of Christ. Verse 13, using both circumcision language and traditional phraseology, provides a summary to the baptism proclamation.

Verses 14 and 15 contain the formal stylistic features, the dramatic redemptive content, and an "ardor of enthusiasm" that seem to indicate that they were cited from a previously existing form of thanksgiving. The concluding proclamation of Christ's victory over the heavenly powers is parallel to the celebration of his sovereignty over those powers in the Christ-hymn (1:16, 20).

The entire passage (2:9-15) seems to fall into three strophes. The first and third strophes restate Christological affirmations made in 1:15-20 and the middle strophe repeats the main idea presented in the application of the Christ-hymn in 1:21, 22 by the use of baptismal materials. The impression one receives from all of this is that the author, who was keenly aware of the usefulness of the hymn for teaching and admonition (3:16), created a hymn for the Colossians out of existing materials in order to stress the significance of the hymn in 1:15-20 for the Colossian situation.

CONCLUSION

Our conclusion can be brief. We started out in this chapter to show that the central Christological passages in Colossians (1:12-14; 1:15-20; and 2:9-15) are based upon hymnic and confessional materials already known to the author and his readers. The author is obviously concerned that his readers remember those traditions and conduct their behavior in the light of them (2:6-8).

Our investigation of each of these passages has drawn attention to their liturgical nature. On the grounds of style, language, contents, and their praise or thanksgiving-like character, the traditional nature of these passages seems to be firmly established. Based upon the United Bible Societies' text of Colossians, of the 114 lines of text in the first two chapters, thirty-four (or thirty percent) of them are drawn from traditional material and twenty-five of them are careful applications of the traditional material. This means that over fifty percent of the first two chapters of Colossians are influenced by words, ideas, and modes of expression that were already existing in the early church. Any judgment made about the authorship of the letter must keep this important factor fully in mind. It should also be noted that the theological perspectives set forth in these passages in their redacted form are not in conflict with the theology of the undisputed letters of Paul. We will have more to say about this in the last chapter.

3

Traditional Paraenetic Materials: The Vice and Virtue Catalogues

In this chapter and the next we shall be dealing with an entirely different kind of material from that which we discussed in chapter 2. The passages dealt with there were confessional and hymnic in character and Christological and cosmological in content. We shall now investigate a literary product that is hortatory in nature and ethical in content. Whereas the previous chapter considered passages marked by participles, prepositions, relative pronouns, genitive constructions, and ideas presented in parallel and rhythmic patterns, these will deal with passages made up of imperative verbs followed by lists of vices and virtues or of admonitions which can be classified into identifiable groups. My purpose in this chapter will be to show that the vice and virtue catalogues in Colossians 3:5-12 are based on materials already existing and which were derived from a standard type of baptismal instruction.

PRELIMINARY OBSERVATIONS

Let us turn our attention first of all to the lists of vices and virtues in 3:5-12. In seeking to demonstrate the traditional character of this passage we come face to face with the crucial problem of our task.

Though there are many such lists in the New Testament and subsequent early Christian literature, there is no *Urkatalog* that has been found or which can be reconstructed that can adequately account for the diversified structures and variegated contents of these lists. Indeed, we are forced to ask whether lists of vices and virtues belong to a distinct literary form at all and whether they are related to the heritage of traditions from the primitive Christian church. N. J. McEleney states the problem skillfully:

> Although the virtue and vice lists of the New Testament have been the objects of several special studies, many matters relating to the nature and origins of such lists need further clarification. As interpreters, are we confronted with fully distinct and univocal literary forms here? If so, if the New Testament virtue and vice lists exemplify ancient and clearly identifiable literary forms with their own purposes, structures, and rhetorical devices, then obviously, the search for the origins of these forms will take us in a particular direction and will yield additional information to illuminate the New Testament passages in which the lists occur. If not, if the lists are simply the result of fortuity (fortuitousness?), their total explanation will lie within their immediate contexts, and we cannot connect them with any literary form or its origins. If the New Testament lists lie somewhere on the spectrum between form and fortuity, what have we?[1]

Even though this problem must be kept in mind, we shall seek to establish the traditional character of the vice and virtue catalogues in 3:5-12 and attempt to discover the writer's purpose for including them in his letter. Our procedure will be (1) to examine the problem of "form" and fortuitousness posed by McEleney by observing the relationship of the Colossian catalogues to the other vice and virtue lists in the New Testament and early Christian writings, (2) to show the connection of the lists to the established paraenetic tradition in the New Testament and to the central baptismal motif of the letter, and (3) to suggest a source for the provenance of the lists.

Form and Content of Colossians 3:5, 8 and 12

Traditions tend to fall into distinct patterns or forms in order that they might be remembered and easily transmitted. The following diagrams will help us to see the structure and content of the vice and

---

[1]N. J. McEleney, "The Vice Lists of the Pastoral Epistles," *CBQ* 36 (1974): 203. McEleney concludes that the vice lists in the Pastorals cannot "be reduced to a single, hard and fast genre" (p. 216).

virtue catalogues and compare them with similar lists in the New Testament and other early Christian literature.

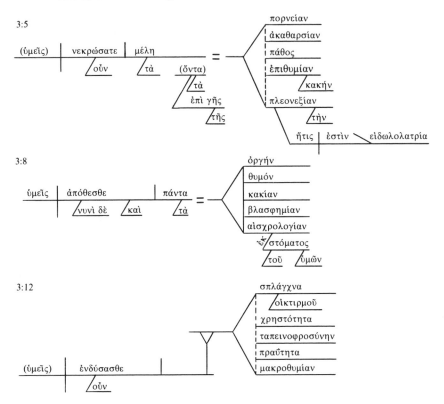

All of the lists contain second person plural aorist imperatives as the main verbs of the commands. Both the first and last lists are related to their contexts with οὖν and the subjects are included in the verb endings. The middle list (3:8) is introduced by νυνὶ δὲ and the emphatic personal pronoun ὑμεῖς stresses the subject. In the vice catalogues, the vices function as appositives. In 3:5 they are in apposition to μέλη and in 3:8 to πάντα. In the virtue catalogues, all of the virtues function as the direct object of the verb.

Probably the most striking feature of the catalogues is that each list contains a series of five vices or five virtues[2] and each series seems to be

---

[2]Because of this Lohse follows Bornkamm in tracing the origin of the lists to

related to a central theme. The vices listed in 3:5 are all associated with sexual sins and bring to mind the "Holiness Code" in Leviticus 18.³ The vices in the second list are centered on the kinds of attitudes and practices which are destructive to interpersonal relationships. The virtues in the third list are all "other-centered" traits which are so Christ-like in nature that one is tempted to wonder whether they were associated with ways in which Christ was remembered in the Gospel tradition.⁴

The Colossian Catalogues Compared with Other New Testament Catalogues

Vice Lists.

Matthew 15:19 and Mark 7:21, 22. These texts are from parallel accounts of the parable of defilement. It is not that which goes into the stomach that defiles a man, but that which comes out of the heart. In both lists the vices function as appositives with evil thoughts (διαλογισμοὶ πονεροί in Matthew and οἱ διαλογισμοὶ οἱ κακοί in Mark). The lists are as follows:

Matt. 15:19	Mk. 7:21,22	Parallels in Col. 3
φόνος	πορνεία	πορνεία
μοιχεία	κλοπή	βλασφημία
πορνεία	φόνος	πλεονεξία
κλοπή	μοιχεία	
φευδομαρτυρία	πλεονεξία	
βλασφημία	πονηρία	
	δόλος	
	ἀσέλγεια	
	ὀφθαλμος πονηρός	
	βλασφημία	
	ὑπερηφανία	
	ἀφροσύνη	

Iranian influence. "Five good and five evil deeds are mentioned in every instance in the Iranian tradition." *Colossians*, p. 137.

³Πλεονεξία seems to be an exception in the list of social vices. However, it is modified by the relative clause ἥτις ἐστὶν εἰδωλολατρία, a sin associated with unfaithfulness to Yahweh or adultery in the Old Testament.

⁴In 2 Cor. 10:1 the Corinthians are entreated on the basis of the "meekness and

Of thirteen vices, only three are paralleled in the Colossian lists.
Romans 1:24, 26. It is difficult to know how many items make a list.
Perhaps the following three should not be included but they are
connected with the formula that introduces the longest list of vices in
the New Testament. All three of the vices are found in the list of sexual
vices in Colossians 3:5. They are objects of the prepositions which
modify the verb in the formula "God abandoned them." Explicitly,
they are ἐν ταῖς ἐπιθυμίαις, εἰς ἀκαθαρσίαν, and εἰς πάθη.
Romans 1:29-31. This is the longest list of vices in the New Testament. It too is associated with the thrice repeated formula "God
abandoned them." The syntax of the sentence in which the list occurs is
complicated. The sentence contains sixty-nine words and lists twenty-
one different vices. All of them describe those whom God abandons.
Of the twenty-one, only two (πλεονεξία and κακία) are found in the
Colossian lists.
Romans 13:13. Chapter 13 occurs in the context of a long series of
paraenetic admonitions. The chapter ends with a reminder that the
eschatological climax is at hand. In the light of this crisis there are three
pairs of vices which should be avoided by the people of God: revelling
and drunkenness (κώμοις και μέθαις), sexual intercourse and
debauchery (κοίταις και ἀσελγείαις), and strife and envy (ἔριδι και
ζήλῳ). Though the kinds of evils listed are similar to those mentioned
in Colossians 3:5 and 8, none of the vices explicitly occurs in the
Colossian lists.
1 Corinthians 5:10, 11. In seeking to correct a misunderstanding
brought about by a former letter, the apostle admonishes his readers
not to keep company with a brother who is called πόρνος or πλεονέκτης or εἰδωλολάτρης or λοίδορος or μέθυσος or ἅρπαξ. All of the
vices function in a predicate nominative relationship with ἀδελφός and
three of them are cognates of vices in Colossians 3:5 (πόρνος, πλεονέκτης, and εἰδωλολάτρης).
1 Corinthians 6:9, 10. Here is a rather lengthy list of those who will
not enter the kingdom of God: πόρνοι, εἰδωλολάτραι, μοιχοί, μαλα-
κοί, ἀρσενοκοῖται, κλέπται, πλεονέκται, μέθυσοι, λοίδοροι,
ἅρπαγες. Of the ten vices listed in this passage, the same three cognates

---

gentleness of Christ." Such language seems to point to traditions about his earthly
ministry. Some have hypothesized that 1 Cor. 13 was based on an earlier description of
Christ.

mentioned above appear in the Colossians 3:5 list (πόρνοι, εἰδωλολά-τρι, and πλεονέκται).

2 Corinthians 12:20. Paul expressed his concern that on his third trip to Corinth he would not find his readers in a satisfactory condition. The following eight vices function as predicate nominatives to a supplied verb: ἔρις, ζῆλος, θυμοί, ἐριθεῖαι, καταλαλιαί, ψιθυρισμοί, φυσιώσεις, and ἀκαταστασίαι. All of these evils are specifically related to the divided conditions of the Corinthian church. Only θυμός occurs in the Colossian lists.

Galatians 5:19-21. One of the most well-known catalogues of vices and virtues in the New Testament is the list of the works of the flesh and the fruit of the Spirit. The former list contains fifteen evils: πορνεία, ἀκαθαρσία, ἀσέλγεια, εἰδωλολατρία, φαρμακεία, ἔχθρα, ἔρις, ζῆλος, θυμός, ἐριθεία, διχοστασία, αἵρεσις, φθόνος, μέθη, and κῶμος. Four of them are also found in the Colossian catalogues (πορνεία, ἀκαθαρσία, εἰδωλολατρία, and θυμός.

Ephesians 4:31. We would expect to find similarities in Ephesians and Colossians and we are not disappointed. Of the five evils in Colossians 3:8, four of them appear in Ephesians 4:31. Only αἰσχρολογία is missing in Ephesians 4:31. This text, which contains six evils, has two which do not occur in Colossians 3:8 (bitterness [πικρία] and clamor [κραυγή]). Both lists are associated with aorist imperative verbs and the verbs are synonymous (ἀποτίθημι [Colossians 3:8] and αἴρω [Ephesians 4:31]).

Ephesians 5:3-5. In 5:3 three vices, which also occur in Colossians 3:5 (πορνεία, ἀκαθαρσία and πλεονεξία), function as the subject of a present imperative passive verb (ὀνομαζέσθω). In 5:4 there are three more (αἰσχρότης, μωρολογία, and εὐτραπελία). The latter two (foolish talking and coarse jesting) parallel in thought the αἰσχρολογία of Colossians 3:8. In 5:5 cognates to the list in Colossians 3:5 occur again (πόρνος, ἀκάθαρτος, and πλεονέκτης). It is interesting, but not unexpected, to find that πλεονέκτης is identified with idolatry as is πλεονεξία in Colossians 3:5.

1 Timothy 1:9, 10. The evil people for whom the law was given are described in four pairs of vices, which in turn are followed by a list of six additional ones. The law is for the lawless and disobedient (ἀνόμοις δὲ καὶ ἀνυποτάκτοις), the ungodly and sinners (ἀσεβέσει καὶ ἁμαρτωλοῖς), the unholy and profane (ἀνοσίοις καὶ βεβήλοις), those who commit patricide and matricide (πατρολῴαις καὶ μητρολῴαις), immoral persons (πόρνοις), sodomites (ἀρσενοκοίταις), kidnappers (ἀνδραποδισταῖς), liars (φεύσταις), perjurers (ἐπιόρκοις), and anything else contrary to sound teaching. Only the cognate πόρνος is similar to the πορνεία in Colossians 3:5.

1 Timothy 6:4, 5. One who teaches a different doctrine and does not hold to the sound words is puffed up (τετύφωται), knowing nothing (μηδὲν ἐπιστάμενος), has a morbid craving for controversy and word battle (νοσῶν περὶ ζητήσεις καὶ λογομαχίας), from which come envy (φθόνος), strife (ἔρις), blasphemies (βλασφημίαι), evil suspicions (ὑπόνοιαι πονηραί), and wranglings of men (διαπαρατριβαὶ ἀνθρώπων) who are depraved in mind (διεφθαρμένων τὸν νοῦν) and bereft of the truth (ἀπεστερημένων τῆς ἀληθείας). The list is similar in spirit to Colossians 3:8 but βλασφημία is the only vice the two lists have in common.

2 Timothy 3:2-5. The author lists nineteen classic faults that characterize the godless of the last days. As is the case in 1 Timothy 6:4, 5 only one of them (βλασφημία) is common to the Colossian lists though the spirit is similar to the catalogue in Colossians 3:8.

Titus 3:3. Less villifying of the offenders than the other lists in the Pastorals is this catalogue of evils which describes the readers in their pre-Christian days. They were, at one time, foolish (ἀνόητοι), disobedient (ἀπειθεῖς), led astray (πλανώμενοι), slaves to various lusts and pleasures (δουλεύοντες ἐπιθυμίαις καὶ ἡδοναῖς), passed their days in malice and envy (κακίᾳ καὶ φθόνῳ), were hated by men (στυγητοί) and hated one another (μισοῦντες ἀλλήλους). Only ἐπιθυμία, which is found in Colossians 3:5, and κακία, which is found in Colossians 3:8, are common to both the Titus and Colossian lists.

1 Peter 2:1. The vices function as direct objects of the same verb found in Colossians 3:8 (ἀποτίθημι). As in the Colossian lists, this text also contains five evils, but only κακία occurs in Colossians 3:8. The vices in 1 Peter 2:1 are κακία, δόλος, ὑπόκρισις, φθόνος, and καταλαλία.

1 Peter 4:3, 4. The author of 1 Peter provides information about the dissipations of the heathen environment by listing a series of vices to which his readers had previously succumbed. The evils are all objects of the preposition ἐν and include licentiousness (ἀσελγείαι), lusts (ἐπιθυμίαι), winebibbings (οἰνοφλυγίαι), carousing (κῶμοι), drinking bouts (πότοι), and unlawful idolatries (ἀθέμιτοι εἰδωλολατρίαι). Only one of them (ἐπιθυμία) occurs in the Colossian lists. Εἰδωλολατρία is associated with πλεονεξία in Colossians 3:5.

Jude 8, 16. The ungodly men who crept into the church are described by Jude in verse 8 as dreamers who defile the flesh (σάρκα μιαίνουσιν), reject authorities (κυριότητα ἀθετοῦσιν), and defame glories (δόξας βλασφημοῦσιν). In verse 16 they are described as murmurers (γογγυσταί), fault-finders (μεμψίμοιροι), those who walk according to their lusts (ἐπιθυμίας), those whose mouths speak haughty things (τὸ στόμα αὐτῶν λαλεῖ ὑπέρογκα), and those showing respect of persons for gain (θαυμάζοντες πρόσωπα ὠφελείας χάριν). Though the general ideas of immorality and alienated attitudes are present in both Jude and Colossians, they are in the main quite different from one another.

Revelation 9:20, 21. Those who were not killed by the plagues which followed the sounding of the sixth trumpet are described as idolaters in terms of Psalms 115:4-7 and 135:15-17 (LXX). They did not repent of their murders (ἐκ τῶν φόνων αὐτῶν), of their sorceries (ἐκ τῶν φαρμάκων αὐτῶν), of their fornications (ἐκ τῆς πορνείας αὐτῶν), nor of their thefts (ἐκ τῶν κλεμμάτων αὐτῶν). Only πορνεία parallels the list in Colossians 3:5.

Revelation 21:8. In antithesis to the overcomers are the cowardly (δειλοί), faithless (ἄπιστοι), abominable (ἐβδελυγμένοι), murderers (φονεῖς), fornicators (πόρνοι), sorcerers (φάρμακοι), idolaters (εἰδωλολάτραι), and all liars (ψευδαί). Πόρνος and εἰδωλολάτρης are cognates of vices listed in Colossians 3:5, but the emphasis is upon sexual sins in Colossians and on idolatry in Revelation. The two are often related in the Bible and are stated as the consequence of refusing God in Romans 1:18-20.

Revelation 22:15. In this verse, also, the list of vices refers to people rather than deeds or attitudes. Those outside are dogs (κύνες), sorcerers (φάρμακοι), fornicators (πόρνοι), murderers (φονεῖς), idolaters (εἰδωλολάτραι), and everyone who practices falsehood (ψεῦδος). There are some general conceptual parallels to the Colossian lists (πόρνοι and εἰδωλολάτραι) but nothing that would point to a common *Urkatalog.*

Summary and Conclusion. With the exception of the lists in Ephesians (Ephesians 4:31 and 5:3-5 parallel Colossians 3:5 and 3:8 respectively) there are few similarities between the lists in Colossians and the other New Testament writings. The main likeness lies in the penchant for making lists of vices. The most common evils are fornication (eight times) and idolatry (five times).[5] Nearly all of the catalogues describe either the people or the traits of people who live outside the eschatological kingdom, are in darkness, and are Gentiles. The vices are clearly characteristics which are not befitting the people of God.

Virtue Lists.
Matthew 5:3-11. The most famous list of virtues in the New Testament is found in the Beatitudes. Of the eight virtues listed there, none is identical to the virtues in the Colossian list (though πραΰς and πραΰτης are nearly equivalent). Indeed, none of the virtues listed in the Beatitudes appears in any other New Testament list.

2 Corinthians 6:6, 7. Paul described his ministry in Corinth by citing seven virtues: purity (ἁγνότης), knowledge (γνῶσις), longsuffering (μακροθυμία), kindness (χρηστότης), genuine love (ἀγάπη ἀνυπόκριτος), in the word of truth (λόγος ἀληθείας), and in the power of God (δυνάμει). Only two (μακροθυμία and χρηστότης) are also present in Colossians 3:12.

Galatians 5:22, 23. Among the nine virtues described as the "fruit of the Spirit" (ἀγάπη, χαρά εἰρήνη, μακροθυμία, χρηστότης, ἀγαθωσύνη, πίστις, πραΰτης, and ἐγκράτεια), three are included in Colossians 3:12 (μακροθυμία, χρηστότης, and πραΰτης).

Ephesians 6:14-17. This catalogue lists the six items that make up the "Panoply of God." It appears to follow the steps which a soldier would follow in putting on his armor. The wording seems influenced by Isaiah 11:5; 59:17; and 52:7 (LXX). The first four pieces of armor are included in four participial phrases and the last two are the objects of an imperative verb (δέξασθε). There are no linguistic or conceptual parallels with Colossians 3:12.

Philippians 4:8. None of the virtues listed in this text (ἀληθῆ, σεμνά, δίκαια, ἀγνά, προσφιλῆ, and εὔφημα) are found in Colossians 3:12.

1 Timothy 3:2, 3. The qualifications for a bishop are that he must be irreproachable, the husband of one wife, temperate, prudent, respectable, hospitable, skillful in teaching, not a drunkard, not belligerent,

---

[5]In Judaism fornication and idolatry were especially regarded as Gentile sins which led to base forms of immorality such as are described in the other vices in the lists.

gentle, peaceable, and not a lover of money (ἀνεπίλημπτον, μιᾶς γυναικὸς ἄνδρα, νηφάλιον, σώφρονα, κόσμιον, φιλόξενον, διδακτικόν, μὴ πάροινον, μὴ πλήκτην, ἐπιεικῆ, ἄμαχον, and ἀφιλάργυρον). This list also differs entirely from Colossians 3:12.[6]

1 Timothy 6:11. Timothy is admonished to follow righteousness (δικαιοσύνη), godliness (εὐσέβεια), faith (πίστις), love (ἀγάπη), steadfastness (ὑπομονή), and gentleness (πραϋπαθίαν). Only the latter even remotely resembles any of the virtues listed in Colossians 3:12.

Titus 1:7, 8. This passage contains a list of thirteen qualifications for a bishop. There are no similarities to the Colossian list.

James 3:17. The "wisdom from above" is pure (ἀγυή), peaceable (εἰρηνική), gentle (ἐπιεικής), full of mercy and good fruits (μεστὴ ἐλέους καὶ καρπῶν ἀγαθῶν), impartial (ἀδιάκριτος), and sincere (ανυπόκριτος). Though the "other-centered" attitude which characterizes the list in Colossians 3:12 is present, there are no exact parallels.

2 Peter 1:5-7. In the sphere of their faith, the readers are admonished to supply six moral principles, which have a Stoic ring to them. They are: virtue (ἀρετή), knowledge (γνῶσις), self-control (ἐγκράτεια), steadfastness (ὑπομονή), piety (εὐσέβεια), brotherly love (φιλαδελφία), and love (ἀγάπη). There are no verbal parallels, though the latter two are in the same spirit as the Colossian list.

Summary and Conclusion. As with the vice lists, there are very few similarities between the virtue catalog in Colossians and the other New Testament lists. Only in 2 Corinthians 6:6, 7 and Galatians 5:22, 23 are three of the virtues listed in Colossians to be found. They are πραΰτης χρηστότης and μακροθυμία.

Colossian Catalogues Compared with the Catalogues in Early Christian Literature

The Epistle of Barnabas.[7] The writer of the Epistle of Barnabas was persuaded that he was living in the last days. He sought to explain to

---

[6]B. S. Easton, drawing upon a reference in Dibelius' *Pastoralbriefe*, shows a striking parallel of the qualification of a bishop to those of a general. Tacitus Osander made the following statement about the traits needed by a general: "I say, then, that the general should be chosen . . . soberminded, self-controlled, temperate, frugal, hardy, intelligent, no lover of money, not (too) young or old, if it may be, the father of children, able to speak well, of good repute." "New Testament Ethical Lists," *JBL* 51 (1932): 10.

[7]I have used the text in J. B. Lightfoot, *The Apostolic Fathers*, ed. and completed by J. R. Harmer (London: MacMillan and Co., 1907), pp. 262-64.

his readers the true and spiritual meaning of certain Old Testament passages. The passages deal with such cultic matters as sacrifice, fasting, the Sinaitic Covenant, the Day of Atonement, circumcision, and the like.

Chapters 18 and 19 contain the notable teaching of the Two Ways. The way of light in chapter 18 contains a list of virtues. In a long series of apodictic laws essentially based on the Decalogue, the writer lists fifty-two commandments in the "thou shalt" and "thou shalt not" forms. Thirteen of them are in the "thou shalt" form. Only two of them are to be found in the Colossian virtue list: ταπεινόφρων and πραΰς.

Chapter 19 deals with the "Black One" and includes a list of thirty-five vices. In this case also, only two of them are present in the Colossian vice lists: κακία and πλεονεξία.[8]

The Didache.[9] The *Didache* or *The Teaching of the Twelve Apostles* in its redacted form appears to be a church manual written near the beginning of the second century A.D. It consists of three or possibly four main sections. The first six chapters contain moral instruction based on the same tradition of the Two Ways that we noted in *Barnabas.* Chapters 7-10 consist of instructions concerning prayer, baptism, and what seems to be the eucharist. Chapters 11-15 deal with matters about various kinds of ministers and show a special concern with prophecy. Chapter 16 is an apocalypse similar to Matthew 24. In 5:1 a catalogue of vices occurs. Twenty-two evils are associated with the "way of death." Among them are five included in the Colossian list: ἐπιθυμία, πορνεία, κακία, πλεονεξία, and αἰσχρολογία. Εἰδωλολατρία is connected with πλεονεξία in Colossians but is regarded as a separate sin in the *Didache.*

1 Clement.[10] With the exception of the New Testament writings themselves, probably the earliest Christian document which we possess is an anonymous letter from the church of Rome to the church at Corinth. It is known to us as 1 Clement. The Corinthian church was torn by the same factious spirit which Paul encountered there some forty years earlier. A list of vices occurs in 1 Clement 35:5. Thirteen

---

[8]In Colossians, πλεονεξία and εἰδωλολατρία are regarded as one vice, whereas in Barn, they are listed as two separate vices.

[9]Lightfoot, *Apostolic Fathers*, pp. 217-25.

[10]Ibiḏ., pp. 23, 24.

evils are listed, but only one of them is also in the Colossian list (πλεονεξία).

Polycarp to the Philippians.[11] This early second century A.D. letter from the bishop of Smyrna to the church at Philippi contains several catalogues of vices and one list of virtues. In 2:2 the readers in general are admonished to refrain from all wrongdoing (ἀδικίας), covetousness (πλεονεξία), love of money (φιλαργυρία), slander (καταλαλιά), and false witness (ψευδομαρτυρία). Similar lists of sins are forbidden for widows in 4:3, deacons in 5:2, and presbyters in 6:1. With the exception of πλεονεξία in 2:2 and ὀργῆς in 6:1, there are no parallels to the Colossian lists.

Unfortunately the Greek text of the last six chapters of the letter has been lost.[12] Chapters 10-15 are preserved in an old Latin manuscript. A catalogue of virtues is found in Chapter 12. Polycarp pronounces the following benediction on the Philippians: "May the God and Father of our Lord Jesus Christ, and the eternal High Priest Himself, the Son of God, Jesus Christ, build you up in the faith and truth in all avoidance of wrath (*sine iracundia*) and in forebearance *patientia*) and in longsuffering (*longanimatate*) and in patient endurance (*tolerentia*) and purity (*chastitate*)." It is plain that *patientia, longanimitate, and tolerantia* belong in the same category as μακροθυμία in Colossians 3:12. The same is true for *mansuetudo* and πραΰτης. However, in Polycarp's letter to the Philippians the virtues are descriptions of the desired results of God's activity, whereas in Colossians they are commanded of the readers.

Observations and Conclusions

We began this section by raising the question of form. Does the form and content of the various catalogues indicate a distinct literary form? Our investigation would lead us to conclude that the lists fall somewhere on the spectrum in between form and fortuitousness. Most of the lists contain goods and evils that are general in character and do not necessarily apply to the concrete situation addressed by the writer. However, many of the vices and virtues clearly do apply to the histori-

---

[11]Ibid., pp. 168-81.

[12]A portion of chapter 13 is preserved in Greek by Eusebius in his *Ecclesiastical History*.

cal and social setting of the letters. It is also clear that they are not based on some *Urkatalog* of goods and evils at large in Christian circles. The catalogues have far too many differences in literary structure and contents to hypothesize such a list or even to conjecture a distinct literary form. However, all the lists are given for the purpose of contrasting the true people of God with outsiders or sinners.

The vice lists tend to fall into general categories. Some of them seem to show a special interest in the Decalogue. One would expect that the ten commandments would exert a large influence on them. It is surprising to note that such an influence seems only to occur in Mark 7:20, 21 (and its parallels in Matthew 15:19); 1 Corinthians 5:9, 10; 1 Timothy 1:9, 10;[13] and Barnabas 19. Several of the lists are especially concerned with paganism and idol worship (Romans 1:24, 26, 29-31; 13:13; 1 Corinthians 5:9, 10; Galatians 5:19-21; 1 Peter 4:3, 4; Revelation 9:20, 21). They show overtones of the Old Testament polemic against idol worship. B. S. Easton was persuaded that "Hellenistic Judaism had developed a regular 'form' for denouncing Gentiles, in which idolatry was linked with the habitual perpetration of various grossly atrocious deeds and was often made their cause."[14]

Another category consists of those vices which describe heretics (1 Timothy 6:4, 5; 2 Timothy 3:2-5: Jude 8, 16). The intention of these lists is apparently not merely to describe false teachers but to vilify them. A modern reader could easily take offense at the name-calling tactics of the writer of the Pastorals.

A fourth category includes those lists which are hortatory in nature. Just a few catalogues belong in this category and it may be significant that Colossians 3:5-12 is one of them. With the exception of 1 Peter 2:1, 11 only the lists in Colossians and Ephesians are hortatory in nature.[15] It seems almost certain that the lists in Ephesians are expansions of the catalogues in Colossians.[16] It is significant to observe

---

[13]See McEleney, "Vice Lists of the Pastoral Epistles," pp. 204-10 for a thorough discussion of the influence of the Decalogue on 1 Tim. 1:9, 10.

[14]B. Easton, "New Testament Ethical Lists," p. 4. See also fn. 5.

[15]E. Selwyn relates 1 Pet. 1:21 to primitive Christian catechetical teachings used in connection with baptism. *The First Epistle of Peter*, pp. 98ff., 153, 393-400.

[16]Not only are most of the vices in Colossians repeated in Ephesians, but only in these two letters is πλεονεξία identified as εἰδωλολατρία (Col. 3:5 and Eph. 5:5).

that all three of these letters (1 Peter, Colossians, and Ephesians) have been associated with baptismal traditions.

Even though the vice lists seem to fall into general categories, there is no clear evidence of "stock" lists for each category. The writers seem to have drawn upon their own general knowledge in each of the categories. The "idolatry" and "false teacher" categories seem to focus on basic themes of hostility to these two ways of life and seem to draw on generally shared descriptions and prejudices.

The virtue lists are fewer in number than the vice lists. Even the *Didache* in its setting forth of the doctrine of the Two Ways does not include an actual list of virtues.[17] The virtues are often more general in nature than the vices. They are related to traits or characteristics more than to deeds.

Where do the catalogues in Colossians fit into all of this? Although we have been unable to demonstrate a distinct literary form for the catalogues, we have been able to observe that such lists were commonly used by the early Christian writers. In addition to this, there are some distinctive features about the catalogues in Colossians which are important for our investigation. In the first place, the vice and virtue lists in Colossians 3:5-12 have the most tightly structured literary form of any of the lists we have considered.[18] Secondly, each of the three lists of five vices or virtues has a central focus. I have already mentioned that the vices in 3:5 are basically related to sexual sins which call to mind that part of the Holiness Code found in Leviticus 18. Furthermore, the sins listed in 3:8 are especially the kinds of vices which produce and foster intensely alienated personal and social relationships. On the other hand, the list of virtues in 3:12 are noticeably other-centered and so Christ-like in character that they may be based on ways in which the early church remembered the earthly Jesus.[19] Thirdly, the lists are included in a letter which places special emphasis on the importance of the received traditions which are according to Christ. Lastly, and most importantly, the Colossian catalogues belong to that small category of vice and virtue lists that are hortatory in

---

[17]The "way of life" consists of loosely related apodictic and casuistic laws which are probably based on Matthew and the Old Testament.

[18]See the diagram above, p. 53.

[19]See above, fn. 4.

nature and which are connected with baptism. Only Ephesians, which is probably based on Colossians, and 1 Peter contain catalogues which are hortatory in nature and come in contexts which refer to baptismal ideas. In addition, the vice lists in Colossians and 1 Peter are introduced by the same verb: ἀποτιθέναι.

Let me summarize by drawing attention to two significant and related observations. The first one is that in our investigation of the vice and virtue catalogues in the New Testament and other early Christian writings, we found no evidence for a distinct literary "catalogue" form or for the existence of any prototypical lists or *Urkatalog*. It is clear, however, that such lists are frequently used by the writers of the early Christian period and that they primarily served to contrast the true people of God with pagans. Such a function was, as we shall see, appropriate for reminding new Christians of their identity as the unique people of God at the time of their baptism.

The second observation is that the Colossian catalogues are the most carefully structured of any that we have investigated and belong to that small category of "hortatory" lists which are found only in 1 Peter, Colossians, and Ephesians. All three of these letters are known for their inclusion of baptismal motifs and are regarded by many to include or to be based on primitive Christian baptismal instructions.

THE NEW TESTAMENT PARAENETIC TRADITION AND THE BAPTISMAL MOTIF IN COLOSSIANS

We shall now seek to demonstrate the relationship of the catalogues in Colossians 3 to the established paraenetic tradition in the New Testament and the central baptismal motif of the letter. Our examination will deal primarily with Colossians 3:5.

New Testament Paraenetic Tradition

A. M. Hunter defines paraenesis as "moral instruction with a dash of exhortation."[20] There were at least two kinds of instruction in Rabbinic Judaism: *haggadah*, which dealt with doctrinal matters, and

---

[20]A. Hunter, *Paul and His Predecessors*, p. 52.

halakah, which dealt with moral and cultic matters.[21] The early church also circulated traditions about doctrine and conduct. It is the latter which we call "paraenetic tradition." Let us examine some of the New Testament evidence for this moral tradition and see how the vice and virtue catalogues in Colossians are related to it. A brief examination of three passages will help us achieve this goal.

Acts 15:29. One of the earliest and most serious controversies in the primitive church had to do with the status of Gentile Christians in the Jewish church. The seriousness of this controversy is everywhere evident in the letters of Paul. The author of Acts, for his own good reasons, chose to minimize the controversy. Nevertheless, even in a work stressing the unity of the earliest Christian community, the author gave a prominent position to an Apostolic Council held in Jerusalem which draws attention to the problem. Preserved for us in the passage about the Council is a document that promulgates a decision attributed to the apostles and elders concerning the status of Gentile Christians (Acts 15:23-29; 21:25). The decision does away with circumcision and other ritualistic requirements for Gentile Christians but demands that certain minimal standards of ritual purity be maintained. The text of the decree reads: ἀπέχεσθαι εἰδωλοθύτων καὶ αἵματος καὶ πνικτῶν καὶ πορνείας.[22] This decree, according to Acts, was sent to the churches of the Gentile mission and was regarded as authoritative paraenesis traceable to the original apostles of Christ. It demands abstention from ritual uncleanness, idolatry, and fornication.

1 Thessalonians 4:1-8. In 2 Thessalonians 2:15 the readers are exhorted to "stand fast and hold the traditions which you were

---

[21]See C. S. Montefiore and H. Loewe, *A Rabbinic Anthology*, pp. xviff. and xciiiff. for a treatment of *haggadah* and *halakah*.

[22]The many problems connected with the text and with the exegesis of Acts 15:20-29 and 21:25 are discussed by B. M. Metzger (*A Textual Commentary on the Greek New Testament*, pp. 429-34). The Western text, by omitting πνικτός and adding a negative form of the Golden Rule, moralizes the Decree so that it refers to idolatry, unchastity, and murder rather than to ritualistic matters. The relationship of Jewish ritualism and the gospel in Pauline theology is a significant issue which will be discussed later. For an excellent treatment of the Decree and its relationship to the Holiness Code, the Noachian Commandments, and its use in the church in apostolic and postapostolic times see M. Simon, "The Apostolic Decree and its Setting in the Ancient Church." *BJRL* 52 (1970): 437-60.

taught."[23] That those traditions included matters of conduct (paraenesis) is evident from the admonition in 2 Thessalonians 3:6: "Now we command you, brothers, in the name of our Lord Jesus Christ, that you keep away from every brother who walks disorderly, and not after the tradition which they received from us (μὴ κατὰ τὴν παράδοσιν ἥν παρελάβοσαν[24] παρ' ἡμῶν)." An example of that paraenetic tradition is found in 1 Thessalonians 4:18:

> Finally, then, brothers, we beseech you and exhort you in the Lord Jesus that as you received (παρελάβετε) from us how you ought to walk and to please God—even as you are walking—that you abound more and more. For you know what instructions we gave you through the Lord Jesus. For this is the will of God, your sanctification (ἁγιασμός), that you abstain from fornication (ἀπέχεσθαι ὑμᾶς ἀπο τῆς πορνείας), in sanctification (ἁγιασμῷ) and honor, not in the passion of lust (πάθει ἐπιθυμίας) as the Gentiles do who do not know God; that no one transgress and defraud (πλεονεκτεῖν) his brother in this matter, because the Lord is the avenger concerning all of these things even as we forewarned and testified. For God did not call us to uncleanness (ἀκαθαρσίᾳ) but in holiness. Therefore, he that neglects this does not neglect man but God, who gives his Holy Spirit to you.

Evidently the apostle had previously delivered some instructions concerning behavior which he regarded to be vitally important to the Thessalonians. He traced the authority for those instructions to the Lord Jesus Christ. Therefore, those who refused to heed them would be accountable to the Lord Himself. These authoritative instructions were not too difficult for them because God had given them His Holy Spirit to enable to keep them.[25] The object of the paraenesis was to produce a community characterized by holiness (ἁγιασμός). It is significant to note that the entire passage has the same kind of cultic tone that is present in the Apostolic Decree in Acts 15:29 and contains several identical words.

Romans 6:17. There is one other Pauline text which we shall consider before we observe the relationship of the Colossian catalogues to all of this. It is Romans 6:17. This passage is found in a context in which the apostle announces the good news that one can be

---

[23]I accept that 2 Thessalonians is an authentic Pauline letter and that it may have been written before 1 Thessalonians.

[24]Various mss. read παρέλαβον, παρέλαβεν, or παρελάβετε.

[25]I draw attention to the gift of the Holy Spirit because the reception of the Spirit is associated with baptism in the New Testament.

transferred out of a solidarity relationship with the first Adam and the ruinous consequences of that relationship to a new solidarity connection with Christ, the *eschatos Adam* (1 Corinthians 15:45) and the saving consequences of that new solidarity (Romans 5:12-21). Paul describes the new relationship in terms of baptism. Baptism into Christ and into the consequences of his death and resurrection brings freedom from the tyranny of sin (6:1-14). Freedom from sin's enslaving power, in turn, brings about a new obligation (6:15-23). In the same way that a person at one time presented his members (μέλη)[26] as servants to uncleanness (ἀκαθαρσίᾳ) and iniquity, he must now present them "as servants of righteousness unto sanctification (εἰς ἁγιασμόν)." The result of the new obedience to the new master is "fruit unto sanctification (καρπὸν εἰς ἁγιασμόν)."[27] Verse 17 comes in the heart of this section and is an expression of thanksgiving over the fact that the new freedom from sin's tyranny and the new obligation to serve righteousness came about because his readers were "obedient from the heart to that pattern of teaching unto which you were delivered (ὑπηκούσατε ἐκ καρδίας εἰς ὃν παρεδόθητε τύπον διδαχῆς)." To use the words of Professor Hunter, "What didactic pattern is this if it is not the catechesis we have been discussing—or something very like it?"[28] The basic significance of this verse, for our investigation, is that it draws attention to a pattern of teaching about conduct and is found in a setting dealing with baptism. Furthermore, "holiness" and "uncleanness" terminology is used.

The Relationship of Colossians 3:5 to the
New Testament Paraenetic Tradition

One of the features which we observed about the majority of early Christian vice catalogues is that the vices tend to be general in nature and often have little to do with the context in which they occur. In the three passages just considered, however, the things forbidden are quite specific. All of them forbid "uncleanness" and "fornication" and two of them prohibit matters related to idolatry. There is a distinctly Jewish or Old Testament "ring" to them.

---

[26]Note Col. 3:5 where the same term is used.

[27]Romans 6:19, 22.

[28]Hunter, *Paul and His Predecessors*, p. 131.

B. S. Easton agrees that most of the New Testament vice lists are conventional in character.[29] He includes the lists in Colossians 3:5 and 8 in this category of general vices. His treatment of the troublesome phrase "covetousness, which is idolatry" is thought-provoking,[30] but Easton has failed to notice that all of the rest of the vices in Colossians 3:5 are associated with sexual sins and those in 3:8 are those which bring about social disruption. The two lists bring to mind the specific stresses of the Holiness Code in Leviticus 18 and 19 respectively. It does not seem to me that these vices belong in the sphere of conventional sins which characterize the majority of the lists. The sins belong to specific groupings and in this respect resemble the three passages discussed above.

There is a more direct way of showing the relationship of Colossians 3:5 to the above discussed paraenetic passages in Acts, Thessalonians, and Romans. That is by noting the rather clear verbal and conceptual parallels that exist among them. We have already noted the cultic tone with its emphasis on holiness in these passages. Each of the paraenetic texts calls for abstinence from any practice that would produce ἀκαθαρσία rather than ἁγιασμός.

'Απέχεσθαι, which occurs in both the Apostolic Decree in Acts 13:20, 29 and 21:15 and in the call to abound more and more in the traditions learned from Paul in 1 Thessalonians 4:1-8 does not occur in Colossians 3:5, but the imperative νεκρώσατε does (as well as ἀπόθεσθε in Colossians 3:8) and it conveys the same idea. The baptismal context with its reference to the death of Christ (2:12) and the death of the Christian in and with Christ (2:13, 20) make νεκρώσατε so appropriate that it does not seem too speculative to think that the demands of the context led the writer to substitute νεκρώσατε for ἀπέχεσθε. If that should be so, then 1 Thessalonians 4:3 and Colos-

---

[29]B. S. Easton, "New Testament Ethical Lists," *JBL* 51 (1932): 8.

[30]Ibid., p. 6. Easton believes that Paul was citing from a formula which ended with "covetousness *and* idolatry" (emphasis his). Easton states: "It suddenly occurred to him that the Colossians were in no need for a warning against idolatry, and so he changed the wording, producing a phrase that, no doubt, lacks clarity but which teaches an excellent moral lesson." I am not inclined to accept Easton's reason. There is evidence in late Jewish and early Christian writings that covetousness and idolatry were associated. (See C. F. D. Moule, " 'The New Life' in Colossians," *Review and Expositor* 70 [1973]: 487, and Polycarp, *Letter to the Philippians*, 11:1.) Besides, it is by no means certain that the Colossians did not need to be warned against idolatry.

sians 3:5 would both begin the paraenesis with "abstain from fornication." However, even if it is not so, one cannot fail to be impressed with both the conceptual and verbal similarities in the lists of vices which are forbidden.

Acts 15:29	1 Thessalonians 4:3-8	Colossians 3:5
εἰδωλόθυτον	πορνεία	πορνεία
πνικτός	πάθος ἐπιθυμίας	ἀκαθαρσία
αἷμα	ἀκαθαρσία	πάθος
πορνεία		ἐπιθυμία
		πλεονεξίαν ἥτις
		ἐστιν εἰδωλολατρία

Of the six vices listed in Acts and 1 Thessalonians, five occur in Colossians 3:5. Only πνικτός and αἷμα are missing.[31]

One final observation will pave the way for our next item of discussion. The reference in Romans 6:17 to the "pattern of teaching unto which you were delivered" comes in a context related to baptism. The admonition to "present your members as servants to righteousness unto sanctification" is based upon the indicative of their union with Christ in baptism.[32] In the next section we will show that the vice and virtue catalogues in Colossians are directly connected with baptism. It is this connection plus the verbal and conceptual parallels with the New Testament paraenetic traditions discussed above which points to the traditional character of the Colossian catalogues.

The Contextual Connection of the Catalogues with Baptism

There is little doubt that the author makes a strong appeal to the significance of baptism in the letter. In chapter 2 it was argued that 1:12-14, which contains terms associated with the Exodus from Egypt, functions as an introit by which the writer introduces the Christ-hymn (1:15-20) and was probably originally a creedal or confessional unit that

---

[31]Πλεονεξίαν, which is missing in Acts and 1 Thessalonians, is defined as idolatry in Col. 3:5, which is mentioned in Acts.

[32]It could be noted that both baptismal passages (Rom. 6 and Col. 3) refer to the "members" of the readers. However, the μέλη in Rom. 6:13, 19 are morally neutral and can be used for good or evil, whereas the μέλη in Col. 3:5 are metaphorically identified with the vices.

belonged in a baptismal liturgy.[33] Even more to the point, the paraenetic section from 2:14-4:6 is based upon the believer's experience of
baptism. In discussing 3:1-11, Professor Moule makes a significant
statement about New Testament ethics:

> [New Testament ethics] are sacramentally, as well as doctrinally involved.
> When the listeners on the day of Pentecost were cut to the heart and cried,
> "Brethren, what shall we do?" Peter's answer was not, "Try harder to be
> good," but "Repent and be baptized . . ."(Acts 2:37f.). The Christian's gospel
> is, in any case, statement before it is exhortation; but also its exhortation is a
> sacramental one before it becomes an ethical one—logically, if not always
> chronologically. Not only does guidance for Christian conduct spring out of
> belief in Jesus as God's Son; the will-power to implement it springs from
> organic union with God through Jesus Christ.[34]

The veracity of Moule's assertion that ethics are based upon the reality
signified and actualized in baptism is substantiated by the way in which
the writer of Colossians links paraenesis with baptism. Let us observe
three of the ways in which he makes this connection.

First, in 2:11-13 the writer describes his reader's relationship to
Christ in terms of a "circumcision not made with hands" which he
associates with baptism. As in Romans 6:3-11, the believer participates
in the power and consequences of Christ's death and resurrection
through baptism. By the repeated use of the conjunction οὖν the writer
links a series of admonitions to his readers who share in the mighty
triumph of Christ through baptism. "Let no man *therefore* judge you in
meat or drink" (2:16). "If you were *therefore* raised together with
Christ" (3:1). "Put to death *therefore* your members which are upon
the earth" (3:5). "Put on *therefore* as the elect of God . . ." (3:12).

Second, the deliberate use of death and resurrection language by
the writer in the paraenetic sections indicates his intention to relate the
paraenesis with baptism. In 2:20 and 3:1 the phrases εἰ ἀπεθάνετε σὺν
Χριστῷ and εἰ οὖν συνηγέρθητε τῷ Χριστῷ have an obvious connection with baptism. We have previously noted the appropriateness of
νεκρώσατε in 3:5 to the baptismal motif.

Third, and most importantly the expressions "putting off the old
man (ἀπεκδυσάμενοι τὸν παλαιὸν ἄνθρωπον)" and "putting on the

---

[33]See above, "The Baptismal Motif in 1:12-14," chapter 2, pp. 16-19.

[34]C. F. D. Moule, "The New Life in Colossians," *Review and Expositor* 70 (1973):
483-84.

new (ἐνδυσάμενοι τὸν νέον), which occur in the heart of the vice and
virtue catalogues, clearly belong in a baptismal setting.[35] Lohse regards
the participles ἀπεκδυσάμενοι and ἐνδυσάμενοι as participial imperatives because they occur in a list of commands, thus making them
additional commands which do not refer to the past experience of
baptism.[36] However, the references to the old and new man hark back
to the Adam-Christ typology such as is set forth in Romans 5:12-6:14
which are related to baptism. It is possible that the participles ἀπεκδυσάμενοι and ἐνδυσάμενοι may function as adverbial modifiers of
φεύδεσθε in 3:9, thereby giving the reason why the readers should not
lie to one another.[37] Furthermore, the imagery of "stripping off" and
"putting on" was in all likelihood evoked by the practice of nude
baptism.[38] It also seems significant to note that ἀπεκδύομαι is a rare
verb in the New Testament and occurs only in Colossians 3:9 and 2:15.
Its use in 2:15 is difficult to interpret but it is associated with the death

---

[35]P. W. van der Horst has an interesting history-of-religions approach to the
participles for "putting off" and "putting on." He objects to finding the origins of the
metaphor in the mystery religions or gnosticism. Parallels cited from such sources are
chronologically too late and they do not have *man* as the object of the putting off or on.
He thus draws attention to a fragment written by Antigonus of Carystus (third century
B.C.) preserved by Eusebius in *Ecclesiastical History* (18:26). In it is an anecdote about
Pyrrho, the founder of the Skeptic school. When Pyrrho was attacked by a dog, he
found refuge in a tree, thus demonstrating a behavior quite inconsistent with his
convictions. When he was mocked by those standing by for his inconsistency, Pyrrho,
in shame, admitted his failure but excused himself by saying, "χαλεπόν ἐστιν τὸν
ἄνθρωπον ἐκδῦναι (it is difficult to put off the man)." It is an amusing story but there is
no way of knowing whether the writer of Colossians had heard it. It does indicate that
the metaphor was not limited to use in the primitive church. There is a more obvious
source for the expression in Colossians and that is baptism. (P. W. van der Horst,
"Observations on a Pauline Expression," *NTS* 19 [1973]: 181-87.)
  Van der Horst does not deny that the writer connects the expression with baptism,
but traces the origin of the expression to Pyrrho. It is doubtful, however, that either the
writer of Colossians or the early church thought of Pyrrho's response to his critics
when they heard or used the metaphor.

[36]Lohse, *Colossians*, p. 141.

[37]See Jacob Jervell, *Imago Dei: Gen 1, 26f im Spätjudentum, in der Gnosis und in
den paulinischen Briefen*, FLRANT 58 (Göttingen, 1960): 236. "Auf die grund legende
Handlung, die Taufe, greift Paulus immer wieder zurück, und er benutzt immer Aorist
Indikativ oder Partizip, um dies zu zeigen.—Demnach ist es auch natürlich, die
Partizipien in 3, 9 und 10 als echte Partizipien zu verstehen."

[38]See G. R. Beasley-Murray, *Baptism in the New Testament* (London: Macmillan
and Co., 1962), p. 148.

of Christ in the baptism pericope (2:11-15)[39] and occurs in a formal hymnic unit.[40] The noun form, ἀπεκδύσις is found only in Colossians 2:11 in the same pericope in which it is related to circumcision and baptism.

Enough has been said to indicate with reasonable certainty that the Colossian vice and virtue catalogues are found in a baptismal setting. What bearing does this have on the traditional character of the catalogues? It is to this issue that we now turn.

A Primitive Christian Baptismal Catechism

I am inclined to agree with D. Schroeder that it is problematic to trace the origin of the New Testament catalogues to an early Jewish proselyte catechism.[41] In the first place, as Vögtle has pointed out, there is no firm proof of the existence of such a catechism[42] and in the second place, most of the New Testament catalogues are too conventional to be related to a specific setting. However, even though there is no extant documentary evidence for an early Jewish proselyte catechism, it is extremely likely that such instruction was given and that it provided a basis for early Christian baptism instruction.[43] As for tracing the origin of the New Testament catalogues to such baptismal instruction, it seems to me that this is not likely for the majority of the catalogues, but it is very likely for those "hortatory" lists such as are found in Acts 15, 1 Thessalonians 4, 1 Peter 4, and Colossians 3 and Ephesians 4, 5.

Probably the most influential work which seeks to link Jewish proselyte baptism instruction with early Christian baptism instruction is Philip Carrington's famous volume, *The Primitive Christian Catechism*. Though some have reacted negatively to Carrington's book, an examination of his hypothesis and its relationship to the Colossian catalogues may be helpful.

---

[39]See R. P. Martin, "Reconciliation and Forgiveness," fn. 2, p. 118.

[40]See pp. 65-70.

[41]D. Schroeder, "Ethical Lists," *Interpreters Dictionary of the Bible*, supplementary volume, p. 546.

[42]A Vögtle, *Die Tugend- und Lasterkataloge: exegetisch, religions- und formgeschichtlich Untersucht* (Münster: Aschendorff, 1936).

[43]See below, pp. 74-79.

Carrington's Hypothesis. Bishop Philip Carrington's work on *The Primitive Christian Catechism* was published in 1940. If his thesis about the origin and content of such a catechism is true, it will have an important bearing on the traditional character of the Colossian catalogues. Let us note some of the reasons which Carrington presents for his thesis.

He begins by pointing out that the "religious instruction among the Jews in the New Testament times was oral, traditional, and semi-ritual."[44] The word *torah* means instruction and was mainly concerned with behavior. It was passed on orally in traditional form by fathers, elders, and eventually by professional teachers. The principal occasions for oral instruction were Passover, synagogue assembly, and the rabbinic schools. *The Wisdom of Ben Sirach* (Ecclesiasticus) provides a cross section of the instruction in the schools. The materials of chapters 1-7 are used again and again by later writers. This is especially true in the Two Ways (embodied in the *Didache* and *Barnabas*), the *Mandata* (commandments) of Hermas and the Epistle of James. Many of the phenomena of the New Testament are best understood by the assumption that the elementary education of converts concerning religious duties was not given in the form of books, but rather from oral catechisms such as we find in the above mentioned writings. The Sermon on the Mount is a "transcript of the *torah* of the Lord as it was taught by the elders of the Christian community."[45]

The system of oral instruction by elders was also used for proselytes. It was essentially the same as that which was given to the children when they were initiated into full membership in the community. The Greek word "proselyte" represents the Hebrew word *ger*. Both the Book of the Covenant (Exodus 12-14) and the Holiness Code (Leviticus 17-26) have sections dealing with the status of the *ger*. He was initiated into full membership in the Israelite community by baptism, circumcision, and the offering of a sacrifice. Baptism was originally "a preliminary rite which cleansed him from defilements due to the neglect of the taboos of Leviticus xvii and xviii, in which chapters the

---

[44]P. Carrington, *The Primitive Christian Catechism* (Cambridge: University Press, 1940), p. 2.

[45]Ibid., pp. 5, 94, 95.

ceremony of total immersion (*tebilah*) is prescribed."[46]

Although Christian baptism had meaning beyond Jewish proselyte baptism, both rites signified entrance into a new community. It was natural that the latter would influence the former. The early church controversy which is discussed in Acts 15 had to do with the status of non-Jews who had received Christian baptism. Should they also be required to be circumcised? The decision of the Jerusalem Council dispensed with circumcision but required abstention from things offered to idols, fornication, and blood-elements which were treated in the introductory chapters of the Holiness Code (Leviticus 17, 18). The emphasis on holiness and the call for abstention from certain practices set forth in several of the Pauline letters, 1 Peter, and James (all of which recall the Levitical Holiness Code) led Dr. Carrington to see the church as a neo-Levitical community. He, therefore, posits the following outline of a Christian Holiness code based on Leviticus 17-19 which forms the basis for the baptismal catechesis.

(1) Not to walk as the gentiles: Leviticus xviii, 1-5.
(2) To avoid the (three) major sins: Leviticus xvii-xviii.
(3) The reception of the Spirit is a call to holiness: Leviticus xix, 2.
(4) Love one another: Leviticus xix, 18.[47]

After examining parallels in 1 Peter, the Pauline letters and James, Carrington looked for a common catechetical pattern in these New Testament documents. He found "four phrases which occur with but little variation of diction or order" and gave Latin headings to the phrases. They are (1) wherefore putting off all evil (*Deponentes*); (2) submit yourselves (*Subiecti*); (3) watch and pray (*Vigilate*); and (4) resist the devil (*Resistite*)[48] The following chart will show the distribution of the pattern.

---

[46]Ibid., p. 14.

[47]Ibid., p. 12.

[48]Ibid., p. 31. Selwyn finds another category which he calls "The Children of Light" (*Filii Lucis*). *The First Epistle of Peter*, pp. 375-82. C. H. Dodd finds a seven-fold pattern: (1) lay aside pagan vices; (2) put on the "new man" with all his virtues; (3) order your family relations on a proper Christian basis; (4) respect your leaders or elders; (5) deal prudently with "outsiders"; (6) be law-abiding citizens and pay your taxes; and (7) in view of the times, be vigilant. *The Gospel and Law: The Relations of Faith and Ethics in Early Christianity* (New York: Columbia University Press, 1968), pp. 20-21.

	Col.	Eph.	I Pet.	Jas.	Heb.
Deponentes	3:8-17	4:25-32	2:1	1:21	12:1, 2
Subiecti	3:18—4:1	5:21—6:9	2:13-18 3:17; 5:5	4:7	12:9
Vigilate	4:2-6	6:18-20	4:7; 5:8	----	13:7
Resistite	----	6:11-17	5:9	4:7	----

Although Carrington was interested in the presence of catechetical materials in all of the New Testament, he tended to focus on 1 Peter.[49] The importance of Colossians seemed to force itself upon him as he progressed in his study. In reconstructing the four-fold pattern of the baptismal catechism he wrote, "On attempting this task it was found necessary to include Colossians."[50] Later on he thought it necessary to include a special discussion of the Colossian catechism in an appendix.[51]

Since Carrington's hypothesis has not found unanimous acceptance, it would be well to observe the kind of arguments that are used against it. To do this, I shall comment on Victor Furnish's indirect refutation of the hypothesis.

Critique of Victor Furnish's Criticism of Carrington's Hypothesis.[52] To begin with, it must be stressed that Carrington's hypothesis is precisely that—a hypothesis. It is a theory based upon probability. Because of the striking parallel concerns and ideas in Jewish proselyte baptism and Christian baptism, it is likely that Jewish proselyte catechesis served as a useful model for Christian baptismal catechesis.[53] The ethical sections of the various New Testament letters contain a series of formulae, usually in the same order, that indicate a common

---

[49]It was this that so deeply influenced Selwyn's great commentary on 1 Peter.

[50]Carrington, *The Primitive Christian Catechism*, p. 31. It seems to me that there was a bit of reluctance in his decision.

[51]Ibid., pp. 92, 93.

[52]Victor P. Furnish, *Theology and Ethics in Paul* (Nashville and New York: Abingdon Press, 1968), pp. 38-44.

[53]See David Daube, *The New Testament and Rabbinic Judaism* (University of London: The Athlone Press, 1956), pp. 106-40.

catechetical tradition. Upon these grounds, Bishop Carrington hypothesizes the existence of a Christian baptismal procedure modeled after Jewish proselyte baptismal instructions.

Professor Furnish indirectly takes issue with Carrington by criticizing W. D. Davies, who was dependent upon Carrington, G. Klein, and D. Daube.[54] Davies accepts Carrington's hypothesis that the ethical sections of the Pauline letters reveal a common tradition of catechesis which may have been used in the instructing of converts at baptism and which was probably influenced by the Jewish practice of instruction at the time of baptizing proselytes. Furnish finds fault with Davies on two issues.

First, he criticizes Davies for saying that Romans 1 and 2 reflect the same concerns as the Noachian Commandments. Davies admits that the form of Paul's argument in Romans 1 and 2 is Hellenistic and only wanted to state that the Noachian Commandments were but a part of the wider background of Paul's teaching (a point with which Furnish agrees).[55] Furnish strangely faults Davies for showing no "evidence that the Noachian Commandments exerted any 'normative' influence on Paul's ethical teaching."[56] Furnish criticizes Davies for making a statement with which he basically agrees. He seems to accept the argument based on probability and then to reject it.

Second, Furnish takes issue with Davies for drawing upon David Daube's investigation of the imperatival use of the participle (which Daube traces to the influence of Tannaitic Hebrew) and for using the Jewish tractates *Derek 'Eretz Rabba* and *Derek 'Eretz Zuta* to show Jewish influence on Christian catechesis. Admittedly the latter is late ninth century A.D.), but the former is commonly dated in the second century A.D.[57] Furnish agrees that "both (tractates) doubtless have

---

[54]W. D. Davies, *Paul and Rabbinic Judaism* (London: S.P.C.K., 1962), pp. 111-46. G. Klein, *Der älteste Christliche Katechismus und die Jüdische Propoganda-Literatur* (Berlin, 1909). D. Daube, "Forms of Old Testament Legislation," *Proceedings of the Oxford Society of Historical Theology* (1944-1945): 36ff., and "Appended Note" to E. G. Selwyn, *The First Epistle of Peter*, pp. 456ff.

[55]Davies, *Paul and Rabbinic Judaism*, p. 116.

[56]Furnish, *Theology and Ethics in Paul*, p. 39.

[57]See the articles on these two tractates by Louis Ginzberg in *Jewish Encyclopedia* (New York and London: Funk and Wagnells,) 1901-1916.

assembled and incorporated earlier traditions."[58] Davies does not claim that the *derek 'eretz* material is a *source* for Jewish ethical teaching. In fact he criticizes Klein for saying that "the *derek 'eretz* literature formed a *point d' appui* for Judaism in its missionary work."[59] All Davies claims is that the *derek 'eretz* literature supplied "precedents for the early Christian leaders in their work of moral education."[60] Furnish charges Davies with claiming more than he actually does.

In a rather surprising way Furnish refutes Davies' dependence on Daube's explanation of the Rabbinic form of instruction by quoting Daube out of context. Furnish writes:

> The questionableness of describing Paul's ethical teaching as rabbinic may be underscored by noting Daube's perceptive description of the *Sitz im Leben* of the rabbinic form of instruction, specifically the Tannaitic form of the participial imperative. The teacher or lawgiver who employs it "addresses an elite among whom the right thing, provided only it is known, is done—or at least is supposed to be done—as a matter of course. There is no need of exhortation or warning. He appeals to the self-respect of his public." Indeed, "this form of legislation is a result of the change from revelation to interpretation and stabilization of custom, from prophet to scholar and compiler."[61]

Daube's point was certainly not to limit rabbinic instruction to the scholar or the elite. Rather it was to show the derivative nature of rabbinic instruction, especially (but not solely) as it related to the participial form. He says:

> The Rabbis did not feel entitled to lay down "judgments," "statutes," or "commandments." Leaving out of account the *taqqana* (in Aramaic *taqqanta*), the "putting straight," "amendment," "reform in an emergency," their main task was a subordinate one: to interpret, elaborate, protect by a "fence" and order the traditional material—chiefly material contained in the Pentateuch, but also usages that had grown up without any such basis. In other words, they had carefully to work out the proper course to take in any set of circumstances, the *halakhah*, the walking expected of a man who desired to do the right thing. It is easy to see that this is exactly the milieu, the setting in life, which we postulated for the participles of the correct practice. They are the form of legislation corresponding to the notion of *halakhah*.[62]

---

[58]Furnish, *Theology and Ethics in Paul*, p. 40.

[59]Davies, *Paul and Rabbinic Judaism*, p. 134.

[60]Ibid., p. 135.

[61]Furnish, *Theology and Ethics in Paul*, p. 41.

[62]Daube, *The New Testament and Rabbinic Judaism*, p. 97.

Furthermore, rabbinic instruction was by no means limited to the elite within the community. Daube concludes his section on *halakhah*, or "the walking of a man who desired to do the right thing" with the following observation:

> There is preserved a Tannaitic summary of the procedure to be adopted for proselyte baptism. The participle-form is use throughout, and its legislative quality is rather more in evidence than in the Sectarian Manual. None the less, the two cases are essentially parallel. In the Manual we read "And the priests are narrating the exploits of God and the Levites are narrating the iniquities of Israel and those who enter are confessing after them;" similarly among the Rabbinic rules we find "And two scholars are standing by him and are telling him some of the lighter commandments and some of the weightier commandments."[63]

These new converts might be regarded elite because they belong to the community of God, but they were certainly not elite members of the community.

Furnish is probably right in reacting to Davies' implication that Paul regarded himself to be a "Christian Rabbi" who instructed a neo-Levitical community. However, his irritation over that implication seemed to lead him to an unwarranted rejection of two arguments based upon probability and which lend support to Carrington's hypothesis.

Although Carrrington's hypothesis is a theory, it is a theory based on probability. It seems to me most unlikely that the Pauline churches thought of themselves as neo-Levitical communities, but Carrington's association of the ethical sections of the letters with Christian baptismal instruction patterned after Jewish proselyte instruction has not been successfully refuted and seems firmly established. With his hypothesis in mind, let us pursue the matter of the presence of catechetical materials in Colossians a little further.

Colossians and the Catechism. Three observations can be made with regards to the relationship of Colossians to a primitive Christian catechism. One has to do with the influence of the Holiness Code, another with the pattern of the Colossian instructions, and the third with the position of the vice and virtue catalogues in the structure of Colossians.

---

[63]Ibid., pp. 101, 102.

(1) Whether or not the early church thought of itself as a kind of neo-Levitical community (as Carrington suggests) is a difficult question. For reasons to be stated later, it is very unlikely that the Pauline churches would take that view. It is most likely, however, that the early church would regard itself as the unique people of God and as such the Holiness Code could serve as an appropriate model.

Is there any evidence of the influence of the Holiness Code in Colossians? The central themes of the Code are "You shall be holy, for I the Lord am holy" and "You shall not be like the Gentiles" (Leviticus 18:2, 3; 19:2; 20:22-26). The introit to the Christ-hymn (1:12-14) celebrates the new status of the "saints in light" and the text immediately following it applies the reconciling work of the cosmic Redeemer to the readers who had been delivered from their former way of life to be a holy people (Colossians 1:21, 22). The same reminder about the former pagan behavior of the readers follows the vice list in 3:5-7.

We have already drawn attention to the sexual orientation of the vices listed in 3:5. The Holiness Code contains an unusually long series of prohibitions against various kinds of sexual relationships (Leviticus 18:6-23; 19:20-23; 20:10-21). The sins of wrath, anger, malice, slander, and foul talk listed in the catalogue in 3:8 are all the sorts of vices that produce severely alienated relationships. Such alienation is forbidden in Leviticus 19:11-18. "You shall not lie to one another." "You shall not go up and down as a tale bearer among your people." "You shall not oppress your neighbor or rob him." "You shall not hate your brother in your heart." "You shall not take vengeance or bear any grudge."

The Holiness Code is also reflected in the virtue list. The admonition to put on mercy, kindness, humility, meekness, long-suffering, and love (3:12-14) parallels the concern of Leviticus 19:11-18, which reaches its climax with "You shall love your neighbor as yourself." The same is true about the laws concerning the treatment of the debtors and the poor in the instructions about the Sabbath Year and Jubilees in Leviticus 25.

Although there is no evidence of direct reference to the explicit text of the Holiness Code, the same concerns are clearly stressed in the vice and virtue catalogues. It seems justifiable to conclude that Colossians does show the indirect influence of the Holiness Code.

(2) When one examines the chart (above) showing the common pattern of the primitive Christian instructions in Colossians, Ephesians, 1 Peter, James, and Hebrews, two things stand out: (a) The

pattern in Colossians follows through without interruption. This is a unique feature in the New Testament letters. (b) A higher percentage of the total text of Colossians consists of paraenetic materials which are included within the catechetical pattern evidenced by the chart than is so in any other New Testament letter.

(3) The final observation has to do with the position of the catalogues within the structure of Colossians. They immediately follow the warnings and admonitions which are directly related to the situation in Colossae and which are based on the Colossians' union with Christ through baptism. After warning the readers about the false teaching based on false traditions (2:6-8), the writer refers to the Christological tradition which they had received and which was set forth in the Christ-hymn (2:9, 10) and in hymnic baptismal materials (2:11-15). This is followed by a series of warnings and exhortations particularly related to the false teaching at Colossae (2:16-3:4). These admonitions are connected to the readers' identification with Christ in baptism by the οὖν in 2:16 and the indicative statements "since you died with Christ" (2:20) and "Since you were raised together with Christ" (3:1).

Then comes the paraenetic section which Carrington believes is based on the baptismal catechism. It is connected with the preceding context not only by οὖν (which may belong to the tradition itself), but also by the baptismal setting to which the paraenesis clearly belongs—a fact which the readers would have recognized immediately. Its function in the letter was to remind the readers of the *halakhah* (note 2:6b) which they had received when they first became Christians. The section begins with the catalogue of vices and virtues and takes the following pattern:

1. *The Levitical Prologue.* "Put to death fornication, uncleanness, passion, evil desire and covetousness which is idolatry, for which things' sake comes the wrath of God upon the sons of disobedience among whom you also at one time walked (3:5-7)."
2. *Deponentes.* The "put off" and "put on" lists of vices and virtues followed by admonitions to forebearance, love, thankfulness, all of which are reminiscent of Leviticus 19 (3:8-17).
3. *Subiecti.* A code of subordination concerning the basic relationships in the Christian household (3:18-4:1).
4. *Vigilate.* The admonition to watch and continue steadfastly in prayer and to walk in wisdom toward those without (4:2-6).[64]

---

[64]See Carrington's treatment of the pattern, *Primitive Christian Catechism*, pp. 59-65.

Summary: The vice and virtue catalogues in Colossians are associated with baptism contextually (both grammatically and conceptually). By virtue of their position in the letter they appear to be a part of a baptismal catechesis. It is the similarity of the catalogues to the wording and concerns of the established New Testament paraenesis along with their setting in a baptismal context that point to their traditional character.

THE PROVENANCE OF THE VICE AND VIRTUE CATALOGUES

As we pointed out above, the Colossian vice and virtue catalogues belong to that small category of "hortatory" lists that are found elsewhere only in 1 Peter and Ephesians and which are associated with baptismal motifs. A discussion of the origin of the New Testament catalogues in general is therefore not as directly related to our investigation of the use of traditional materials in Colossians as is the baptismal background of the "hortatory" lists. Nevertheless, such an inquiry will enable us to consider our investigation from a broader perspective and to shed some light on the more specific use of the lists in baptismal instruction.

Survey of Research on the Origins of the Vice and Virtue Catalogues

Although some special studies of the New Testament ethical lists have been made during the past half-century, it cannot be said that there has been a major interest in this subject. Not many advances have been made since B. S. Easton's presidential address to the Society of Biblical Literature in 1931.[65]

Prior to Easton's address there was general agreement that the catalogues were derived ultimately from the ethical teachings of the Stoa. In 1928 H. Lietzmann summarized the Stoic influence on the lists in his treatment of the vice catalogue set forth in Romans 1:29-31.[66] Easton's presidential address in 1931 sought to carry the discussion further by showing the influence of Hellenistic Judaism and "pure"

---

[65]Easton, "New Testament Ethical Lists," pp. 1-12.

[66]Hans Lietzmann, *An die Römer*, Handbuch zum Neuen Testament, ed. Hans Lietzmann and Günther Bornkamm (Tübingen: 1933), pp. 35-36.

Hellenism on the ethical lists. Using Wisdom 14:25, 26 as a model, he affirmed that the vice lists, though conventional in character, were influenced by Hellenistic Judaism.[67] The lists of virtues, on the other hand, contain words that are practically absent from the Septuagint and are more related to the catalogues in use among the contemporary Stoic teachers.

In 1936 A. Vögtle sought to trace the origin of the New Testament vice and virtue lists to the popular preaching of Hellenistic philosophy.[68] Twenty years later S. Wibbing became interested in the findings at Qumran and wrote a dissertation for the University of Heidelberg on *Die Tugend- und Lasterkataloge im Neuen Testament*.[69] His study consisted of three parts: (1) an investigation of the virtue and vice lists in the Stoa and late Jewish literature, (2) an examination of the lists in the "recently discovered manuscripts of Qumran by the Dead Sea," and (3) a study of the form, structure, content, and meaning of the lists in the New Testament. On the basis of the dualistic anthropology of the Qumran sectarian writings, Wibbing finds the roots of the New Testament catalogues in the Jewish doctrine of the two spirits.[70]

In 1964 E. Kamlah, who had much appreciation for Wibbing's work on the catalogues, published a study concerning the form of the New Testament paraenetic catalogues.[71] He begins and ends his study by examining the New Testament catalogues. In chapter one he divides the catalogues into two groups: descriptive catalogues and catalogues with a paraenetic function. In chapter two he discusses a history of religions approach to the origins of the catalogues and traces their

---

[67]Easton cites Philo's monstrous list of vices in the *Sacrifices of Cain and Abel*, section 32. It is interesting to observe that of the 147 vices listed, not one occurs in the lists in Colossians.

[68]Anton Vögtle, *Die Tugend- und Lasterkataloge: exegetische, religions- und formgeschichtlich Untersucht* (Münster: Aschendorff, 1936).

[69]Siegfried Wibbing, *Die Tugend- und Lasterkataloge im Neuen Testament und ihre Traditionsgeschichte unter besonderer Berücksichtigung der Qumran-Texte*, BZNW 25 (Berlin: Topelmann, 1959).

[70]Ibid., pp. 108-17.

[71]Erhard Kamlah, *Die Form der katalogischen Paränese im Neuen Testament*, WUNT 7 (Tübingen, 1964).

immediate background to Jewish and Iranian sources. In the last chapter he sets forth general characteristics of the New Testament paraenetic catalogues by discussing their patterns, composition, and their familiarity to the catalogue tradition in Paul and the later apostolic catalogues. He locates the origin of the catalogue genre in Iranian dualism.[72]

In 1974 N. J. McEleney assessed the current status of the study of the New Testament virtue and vice lists as unsettled. There are "many matters relating to the nature and origin of such lists that need further clarification."[73] In his own study of the vice lists in the Pastoral epistles he really did not break any new ground on the subject. "The vice lists of the Pastorals," he wrote, "have been influenced by more or less of these elements":

> (1) Reference to the Decalogue or other commands of the law; (2) polemic against immoral pagan idolaters; (3) Hellenistic conceptions of virtue and vice as qualifications of a man; (4) moral dualism due to various inclinations or spirits in a man causing him to walk in one of two ways; (5) the theme of eschatological punishment.[74]

More recently (1978) D. Schroeder rejected Kamlah's conclusion that the paraenetic catalogues originated from Iranian dualism and declared that:

> The NT catalogues manifest, rather, the sort of ethical dualism implicit in Israel's expectation of the DAY OF THE LORD which will bring salvation for some and judgment for others, and in such OT passages as Deuteronomy 27ff., where a catalogue of curses and blessings has been incorporated into a hortatory setting.[75]

It seems to me that Schroeder's major contribution to the study of the origins of the catalogues is the attention he draws to the eschatological expectation of salvation and judgment in Judaism and and Old Testament teaching of the Two Ways, especially as the latter is related to the expression of God's covenant with His people. I will attempt to show later that these matters were of great importance in Paul's understand-

---

[72]Ibid., pp. 214, 215.

[73]McEleney, "Vice Lists in the Pastorals," p. 203.

[74]Ibid., p. 218.

[75]D. Schroeder, "Ethical Lists," p. 546.

ing of the Gospel and the church and that materials traceable to such theological sources would be of special significance to him.

The Influence of the "Two Ways" Teaching as Set Forth in the Didache and Barnabas

It has long been known that the teaching of the Two Ways in the *Didache* 1-6 and *Barnabas* 18-20 are related to one another. Either one was dependent upon the other or else they both drew from a common source. Is there any evidence in these two writings of a tradition common to one known and used by the author of Colossians?

It is clear that the lists of vices and virtues in Colossians 3:5-17 have some noticeable resemblances to the teaching of the Two Ways in the *Didache* and *Barnabas*. If the teaching of the Two Ways was created by either of the authors of those two ancient writings, the catalogues in Colossians obviously have no relationship of dependence on them. However, if the teaching of the Two Ways springs from a source independent from and known by both the Didachist and Barnabas, the whole picture would be changed. Furthermore, if the teaching of the Two Ways came from a source predating the New Testament period and was known and used by the author of Colossians, it would indicate that it was a very important and useful tradition that maintained its power from pre-apostolic to post-apostolic times.[76]

The literary history of the relationship of the teaching of the Two Ways in the *Didache* and *Barnabas* is an interesting and complicated one. At the time of the closing of the nineteenth century the issue was in a state of flux. Bryennios the Metropolitan of Nicomedia discovered a manuscript of the *Didache* in the Convent of the Holy Sepulchre of Constantinople in 1873. He believed that the teaching of the Two Ways was indirectly traceable to the twelve apostles of the Lord and was therefore authoritative and binding.[77] A. Harnack and O. Gebhardt

---

[76]Besides being present in the *Didache* and *Barnabas*, the teaching of the Two Ways is also found in *Doctrina Apostolorum*, the *Shepherd of Hermas*, the *Epitome*, the *Ecclesiastical Canons*, the *Syntagma Doctrinae* attributed to Athanasius, the *Faith of the 318 Fathers*, the *Arabian Life of Schedoudi*, the *Didascalia Apostolorum*, the *Apostolic Constitutions*, the *Anastasian Fragments* and the *Collection of Sentences* attributed to Isaac the Syrian. See S. Giet, *L'Enigme De La Didache* (Paris, 1970), pp. 15-26 and 121-52 for summary backgrounds and treatments of the Two Ways in these post apostolic documents.

[77]P. Bryennios, *Didache Ton Dodeka Apostolon,* (Constantinople, 1883).

were convinced that the Two Ways in the *Didache* was dependent upon *Barnabas*;[78] and T. Zahn was just as persuaded that the opposite was true.[79] B. Warfield and C. Taylor were inclined to believe that there was no literary dependence between *Barnabas* and the *Didache*, but that a common source was behind them both.[80]

During the first fifty years of the twentieth century J. Armitage Robinson and R. H. Connolly dominated the discussion. They held that the Two Ways in the *Didache* was clearly dependent upon *Barnabas* and *Hermas* and that the literary affinities between *Barnabas* 1-17 and 18-20 proved that the author of *Barnabas* was the creator of the teaching of the Two Ways. The tendency in this period was to date the *Didache* late in the second century and to associate it with Montanism.[81]

Since 1950 there has been a nearly complete "about face" in discussions concerning the literary relationships between the *Didache* and *Barnabas*. The period has been marked by the discovery of new sources of information and the development of more refined methods for investigating the early Christian documents. The finding of the Gnostic Nag Hammadi documents and the Qumran scrolls has greatly enriched our knowledge of early Christianity and late Judaism. Fragments of the *Didache* in Greek, Ethiopic, Coptic, and Georgian have been found. The latter is believed to be based upon a fifth-century document.[82] All of this has produced a renewed interest in the *Didache* and

---

[78]A. Harnack, *Die Lehre der Zwölf Apostel* (Leipzig, 1884).

[79]T. Zahn, "Lehr der Zwölf Apostel," *Forschungen zur Geschichte des neutestamentlichen Kanons und der altkirchlichen Literatur* 3 (1884).

[80]B. Warfield, "Text, Sources, and Content of the 'Two Ways' of First Section of the Didache," *Bibl. Sacra* 43: 100-61. C. Taylor, *The Teaching of the Twelve Apostles, with Illustrations from the Talmud* (Cambridge, 1886).

[81]J. Robinson, "The Problem of the *Didache*," *JTS* 13 (1912): 339-56. "The Epistle of Barnabas and the Didache" published posthumously by R. Connolly in *JTS* 35 (1934): 113-46 and 225-48. R. Connolly, "New Fragments of the Didache," *JTS* 24 (1923): 151-53 and "The Didache in Relation to the Epistle of Barnabas," *JTS* 32 (1932): 237-53. J. Muilenburg, *The Literary Relations of the Epistle of Barnabas and the Teaching of the Twelve Apostles* (Marburg, 1929).

[82]See F. Vokes, "The Didache—Still Debated," *Church Quarterly* (July 1970): 57-62.

at the same time has seriously challenged the view that the teaching of the Two Ways was created by the author of *Barnabas.*

Without doubt the dominating figure in the study of the *Didache* in recent years is Father Jean-Paul Audet. His monumental work, published in 1958, has been the major influence on recent studies of this ancient document and has largely established the direction which these studies have taken.[83] Audet believes that the *Didache* went through three stages of development. The first stage (D1) consisted of 1:1-11:2 (minus a few passages). This was later enlarged by the Didachist with the addition of 11:3-16:8 (D2). Still later, in the third stage, interpolations were added by a different person. These consisted of 1:3b-2:1; 6:2ff.; 7:2-4; 13:3; and 13:5-7 (I). The main criterion for determining the work of the interpolator is the use of the second person singular verb form. The original author (the Didachist) regularly used the second person plural except in the Two Ways section.[84]

Was the *Didache* dependent on the New Testament Gospels? Audet answers in the negative. By means of a very thorough investigation he sought to demonstrate that there is no dependence on any of the Gospels in D1 and that though both D2 and I were acquainted with written Gospel material, there is no reason for identifying this material with any of the present Gospels.[85] By concluding that the *Didache* is not dependent upon Matthew or any of the New Testament Gospels, but on common sources that lie behind them, Audet is able to posit a date for the *Didache* that makes it contemporary with some of the New Testament documents and consequently a very important source of knowledge of the primitive church and an important resource for

---

[83]J. P. Audet, *La Didachè: Instructions des Apôtres* (Études Bibliques: Paris, 1958). Three years after Audet's work was published, it was reviewed by J. N. D. Kelly (*JTS* 12 [1961]: 329-33). He disagrees with some of the key features in Audet's book but expresses his gratitude to Audet for "breaking the deadlock which has immobilized criticism of the *Didache* since the thirties" and said that "even those who disagree with him most sharply must concede that his edition marks an epoch in the study of early Christian literature." Scarcely an article on the *Didache* or the teaching of the Two Ways written since 1958 fails to mention Audet.

[84]Ibid., pp. 104-20.

[85]Ibid., pp. 167-86. Concerning the use of Gospel material in D2, he says: "Tout ce qu'il est permis de dire, c'est donc, de nouveau, que la *Didachè* hérite, pour une part dont la mesure est fixée par les textes, d'une tradition évangélique nettement apparentée à celle de *Mt.*, sans cependant connaître *Mt.* lui-même" (p. 182).

investigating early Christian traditional materials. Few would propose as early a date as he (50-70 A.D.), but his investigation of sources makes his study pertinent for our investigation.

With reference to the source behind the Two Ways in the *Didache* and *Barnabas*, Audet takes to task Robinson's hypothesis that the Two Ways of *Barnabas* (chapters 18-20) is the creation of Barnabas himself because of the literary affinities that exist between chapters 1-2 and 18-20. What do literary affinities prove about sources? "Very little," he says, "if they prove anything at all."[86] Indeed, one should expect them. One should also notice the literary ruptures between these two parts of *Barnabas*.[87] After a thorough investigation, he concludes that both the *Didache* and *Barnabas* depend on a Jewish Two Ways document best represented by the Latin *Doctrina Apostolorum*, published by Schlecht in 1900.

Since 1950 the general consensus is that the teaching of the Two Ways came from a Jewish background and went through many alterations and transformations. The Two Ways thus predates the New Testament documents and was an influence upon the literature of late Judaism and early Christianity.

A further word about the Jewish antecedents to the teaching of the Two Ways is necessary for our discussion. Shortly after the discovery of the Bryennios manuscript some rabbinic scholars hypothesized that the Two Ways sections in *Barnabas* and the *Didache* were based upon a Jewish manual which may have been used in the instruction of catechumens and proselytes. The main reasons why this theory did not gain wide acceptance are that such a written manual has never been discovered and the data are much too complicated to make a satisfactory reconstruction of it. However, the works of G. Klein, P. Carrington, E. Selwyn, and D. Daube have shown that behind the New Testament epistles lies the use of common catechetical or paraenetic material which circulated in the early church in both oral and written form. Since the earliest gospel was based on the Jewish eschatological teaching about the two ages and since the earliest Christians regarded

---

[86]Ibid., p. 124.

[87]The most apparent "est celle du passage abrupt de la deuxième personne du pluriel à la deuxième personne du singulier, au ch. 19, avec retour à la deuxième personne du pluriel pour le ch. 21 . . . ," ibid., p. 126.

themselves as the New Israel, the powerful influence of Jewish thought is to be expected. That influence was especially evident in matters dealing with social and ethical instruction.

We know that some Jewish rabbis had great respect for the oral *Torah*. It is not difficult to suppose that the Two Ways pattern of instruction existed in oral form and was adapted by the rabbis for various groups and occasions. Sometimes it was probably written down. This background was certainly inherited by the early church. Thus, behind the version of the Two Ways in the *Doctrina*, the *Didache*, *Barnabas*, and other documents may lie several written or oral versions of the original Jewish oral pattern of the Two Ways. Whatever the circumstances may have been, one thing is certain. The idea of two ways—the one good and the other evil—is found throughout the Old Testament and later Jewish writings (for example, Deuteronomy 30:15, 16; Jeremiah 21:8; Psalms 1:6; Proverbs 2:12, 13; 4:18, 19; 4 Maccabees 14:5; 1 Enoch 94:1-4; 2 Enoch 30:15; *Pirke Aboth* 2:1, among others).

More important than the several references to the Two Ways in Jewish literature is the central importance of this motif in the cultic life of Israel. Everyone who reads the Two Ways in *Barnabas* and the *Didache* and the *Doctrina* can immediately see that much of it takes the form of apodictic commands and has a large amount of material from the Old Testament Decalogue. Some of the most important research of this century has dealt with the central importance of the Decalogue in cultic worship.[88] G. Mendenhall has traced the origin and form of the Sinaitic covenant to the Hittite suzerainty treaty and, by making a careful examination of the biblical material concerning the covenant at Sinai, has concluded that the covenant was the central historical element in the life and worship of Israel.[89] Most importantly, A. Alt and G. von Rad have shown that the Decalogue was of major importance in the highly significant festival of the covenant renewal.[90]

---

[88]Sigmund Mowinckel, *La Decalogue* (Paris, 1927).

[89]G. Mendenhall, "Covenant Forms in Israelite Tradition," *The Biblical Archeologist* 17 (1954): 50-76.

[90]Albrecht Alt, "The Origins of Israelite Law," in *Essays on Old Testament History and Religion*, trans. R. A. Wilson (Oxford, 1966), pp. 81-132; G. von Rad, *Old Testament Theology*, vol. 1, trans. D. M. Stalker (New York: Harper & Row, 1962), pp. 192ff.; *The Problem of the Hexateuch and Other Essays*, trans. E. W. Dicher

Their evidence is based mainly on an examination of the liturgical materials in Exodus 19-24, Joshua 24, and the entire book of Deuteronomy. The cultic worship of Israel was not centered in abstract or mythical ideas, but in an historic event. God liberated His people from Egyptian bondage and made a solemn and gracious covenant with them. That event was remembered and reactualized in the repeated experience of covenant renewal celebrated in the Feast of Tabernacles.[91] Connected with the celebration were instructions concerning the religious and ethical obligations of the covenant and the solemn pronouncement of blessings on those who keep the covenant and curses on those who do not. Such a setting is clearly appropriate for the use of the Two Ways motif. It is expressed in Deuteronomy 30:15, 16:

> See, I have set before you this day life and good, death and evil. If you obey the commandments of the Lord your God which I command you this day, by loving the Lord your God, by walking in his ways, and by keeping his commandments and his statutes and his ordinances, then you shall live and multiply, and the Lord your God will bless you in the land which you are entering to take possession of it.

The Two Ways reached quite full expression in the *Testaments of the Twelve Patriarchs* which date from the second century B.C:

> God has appointed two ways to the sons of men; two inclinations, two kinds of activity, two dispositions and two outcomes. Therefore all things are by two, each opposing the other. The ways are two: one good, one evil, in regard to which the two inclinations in our breasts make their choice. (Testament Asher 1:3-5.)
>
> Choose for yourselves either the light or the darkness, either the law of the Lord or the works of Beliar. (Testament Levi 19:1.)
>
> Know, then, my children, that two spirits are active in man, the one of truth and the one of error. And between them is that of the mind's insight, whose function is to incline as it may choose. Indeed, the things of truth and those of error have been written upon the breast of man; and the Lord is aware of each one of them. And there is no time in which men can hide their works; because on their very breast bones they have been inscribed in the Lord's sight. And the spirit of truth testifies about all things and makes accusation about all things; and the sinner is set afire out of his own heart, and cannot raise his face in the presence of the judge. (Testament Judah 20:1-5.)

(Edinburgh and London, 1966), pp. 1-78; *Deuteronomy, A Commentary*, trans. Dorothea Barton (Philadelphia: Westminster Press, 1975), p. 12.

[91]See Brevard Childs, *Memory and Tradition in Israel*, Studies in Biblical Theology 37 (London: SCM Press, 1962), pp. 45-89, for a significant treatment of the meaning of cult in Israel's worship.

Another Jewish pre-Christian document which reflects the Two Ways is the Qumran writing known as the *Manual of Discipline* (DSD).[92] This document is of special value to our discussion because it is the first *written* manual based on the Two Ways motif. In some ways it more closely resembles the Two Ways in *Barnabas* than in the *Didache*. However, neither of the Christian documents shows a direct acquaintance with the *Manual of Discipline*. Yet all three of the documents contain a Two Ways teaching that is related to a common conceptual background.

The *Manual* opens by describing itself as "the ordinances for the whole assembly . . . as (God) commanded through Moses and all his servants, the prophets" (1QS 1:1-3). The similarities of this statement to the title and first verse of the *Didache* are obvious. More importantly, these "ordinances" are specifically related to the cultic worship of the Qumran community. *Manual of Discipline* (1QS) 1:21-3:12 describes the liturgy of the covenant renewal ceremony. It begins with the priests recounting God's righteous deeds (1:21-2:1) and continues with the priestly bestowal of blessings on those who walk in God's ways (2:2-4) and curses on those who do not (2:5-18)—a practice clearly related to the Two Ways motif.

It is in the section which gives instructions concerning the moral nature of man that the teaching of the Two Ways surfaces most clearly (1QS 3:13-4:26). These instructions are "for the wise man's use, that he may instruct and teach all the sons of light" (3:13). They explain that God "assigned two spirits by which to walk"—the "spirit of truth" and the "spirit of perversion" which spring from the realms of light and darkness (3:17-19). The "prince of light" rules over the "sons of righteousness" and the "angel of darkness" rules over the "sons of perversion." God loves the activities of the good spirit, but "as for the other, He has loathed its counsel, and all its ways He has hated forever" (4:1). The "way of the spirit of truth" is then described with a catalogue of virtues (4:2-8) and the "way of the spirit of perversion" is depicted with a catalogue of vices (4:9-14). It is precisely these kinds of catalogues that describe the ways of light and darkness in *Barnabas* and the ways

---

[92]For an extended treatment of this subject see J-P. Audet, "Les Affinities litteraires et doctrinales du Manual de Discipline," *Revue Biblique* 59 (1952): 219-38; 60 (1953): 41-82. See also L. W. Barnard, *Studies in the Apostolic Fathers and Their Background* (New York: Schocken Books, 1966), pp. 97-107.

of life and death in the *Didache.* As we have stressed in this chapter, similar catalogues appear in Colossians and other New Testament writings.

People have thought in categories of good and evil from the beginning. The metaphor of the Two Ways was present among the Greeks as well as the Jews. But for the latter this was not just a dialectical way of thinking. It was a central part of their cultic worship. The Two Ways became a way of expressing the contrast between the people of the covenant and those outside the covenant. It was not only useful at the festival of covenant renewal, but for the instruction of children and proselytes. It was a way of proclaiming and teaching what manner of men the people of God ought to be. Such a concept was bound to have an influence upon those who regarded themselves as the people of the New Covenant.

Conclusion

There is no doubt much is to be learned by a history of religions approach to the origins of the vice and virtue lists in the New Testament. The basic issue, however, is not the source from which the church borrowed the lists. The earliest Christian communities were probably not conscious of "borrowing." They simply used what had become their own in the process of culturization and created forms which met their immediate needs. A more important question, in my opinion, is: What was the decisive impulse which led to the creation of their paraenetic forms? What theological and liturgical needs led them to connect the cultic drama of baptism with moral and social instruction?

Since the primitive Christian church understood itself as a new Israel on a new Exodus and bound to God by a new covenant, it seems appropriate to look to the Old Testament counterparts of these motifs as a probable source for the theological and religious impulse that led to the combining of baptism and paraenesis. These themes permeate the Pentateuch.

It seems to me that Dr. Carrington was on the right track when he traced the influence on the New Testament paraenetic tradition to the Levitical Holiness Code. Our comparison of Colossians with the Holiness Code (pages 80-82) seems to confirm this. The initiation of Gentiles into full membership of the Israelite community by baptism and circumcision after receiving instruction in the traditions clearly calls to mind the presence of those same motifs in the letter to the Colossians. A baptismal catechism was as appropriate and necessary for converts to the new Israel as it was for the old.

The Holiness Code and proselyte baptism probably provide the immediate background for the New Testament paraenetic tradition in general and the "put off" and "put on" motif of the Colossian vice and virtue lists in particular. Connected with the Holiness Code (but further in the background of influence on the Colossian catalogues) may lie the cultic connection between the covenant and the Decalogue in the Pentateuchal tradition as Mowinckel, Alt, and von Rad have expressed it. The Two Ways motif and catalogues of vices and virtues are clearly appropriate for all of these theological and liturgical needs and are consequently present in materials dealing with them.

SUMMARY AND CONCLUSION

We began our investigation of the vice and virtue catalogues by raising the question of form or fortuitousness and concluded that the catalogues fall somewhere on the spectrum in between the two. Most of the vice lists are conventional in character and are related to familiar issues. They tend to fall into general categories describing immorality, idolatry, and heretics. But there is one category that stands out from the others. It has to do with the lists that are hortatory in nature and are associated with baptismal ideas. Only Colossians, Ephesians, and 1 Peter belong in this category. In Colossians the catalogues are more highly structured and more directly related to baptism than either of the other two. Since the hortatory catalogues appear in a setting in which walking in the light of the received tradition is the major admonition and in which the readers are reminded of important Christological and baptismal elements of those traditions, it is most likely that the highly structured catalogues with their hortatory "put off" and "put on" baptismal introductions are themselves derived from traditional baptismal paraenesis.

Carrington's hypothesis based on a common paraenetic pattern in the New Testament letters may not be the final word on a primitive Christian catechism for candidates for baptism, but it has not been adequately refuted. It is firmly based on probability and it tends to confirm our conclusion about the traditional character of the vice and virtue catalogues in Colossians.

Research on the origins of the New Testament catalogues has shown that a variety of backgrounds doubtless had an influence on them, but the primary influence seems to have come from the Old Testament and Judaism. Whether or not the New Testament catalogues were directly or indirectly drawn from the Jewish teaching of the Two Ways cannot be established for certain. However, the conceptual similarities between the catalogues and the Two Ways is obvious and the ways in which both of them are used in the Old Testament and late Judaism have undeniable theological and liturgical affinities with the use of the catalogues in Colossians.

4

Traditional Paraenetic Materials: The Household Code

We shall now turn our attention to the so-called Household Code in Colossians 3:18-4:1.[1] Unlike the catalogues of vices and virtues which have sparked only modest interest in the last two decades, the New Testament Household Codes have received considerable attention.[2]

---

[1]Since the time of Luther, the scheme of household duties found in Col. 3:18ff. has been called a *Haustafel*, a list of rules or duties for the household.

[2]Karl Rengstorf, "Die neutestamentlichen Mahnungen an die Frau, sich dem Manne unterzuorden," in *Verbum Dei manet in aeternum*, Festscrift für Otto Schmitz, ed. Werner Foerster (Witten, 1953), pp. 131-45; H. D. Wendland, "Zur sozialethischen Bedeutung der neutestamentlichen Haustafeln," *Festgabe A. Körberle* (Hamburg, 1959), pp. 34-46; David Schroeder, *Die Haustafeln des Neuen Testaments. Ihre Herkunft und ihr theologischer Sinn* (Hamburg: unpublished dissertation, 1959); Lohse, *Colossians*, pp. 154-63; W. Munro, "Col. 3:18-4:1 and Eph. 5:1-6:9: Evidence of a Late Literary Stratum?" *NTS* 18 (1972): 434-47; James E. Crouch, *The Origin and Intention of the Colossian Haustafel*, Forschungen zur Religion und Literatur des Alten und Neuen Testaments (Göttingen: Vanderhoek and Ruprecht, 1972); E. G. Hinson, "The Christian Household in Colossians 3:18-4:1," *Review and Expositor* 70 (1973): 495-507; Marcus Barth, *Ephesians*, vol. 2, The Anchor Bible Series 34a (Garden City: Doubleday & Co., 1974), pp. 608-10, 617-19, 660-62, 754-58; W. Lillie, "The Pauline House-tables," *Expository Times* 86 (1975): 179-83; W. Schrage, "Zur

On 16 February 1949, E. J. Goodspeed wrote the following in a personal letter to F. W. Beare:

> As for the haustafeln idea, we at Chicago were never able to find any such 'haustafeln' as it had been claimed anciently existed. Most scholars simply accept Weidinger's say-so, but the natural explanation seems to be a germ in Col. expanding in Eph., and then in 1 Peter.[3]

In this chapter I shall take issue with the position of Professor Goodspeed and seek to show the probable traditional character of the Colossian *Haustafel.* In seeking to accomplish this objective, the form, the source, and the purpose of the Colossian *Haustafel* will be considered.

THE FORM OF THE COLOSSIAN HAUSTAFEL

An examination of the form of the Colossian *Haustafel* in 3:8-4:1 will indicate the unlikelihood of this section of the letter being written on the spur of the moment. It is more likely that we are dealing with a paraenetic arrangement which existed before the Colossian letter was written. With the ultimate goal of establishing the probability of this conclusion, let us discuss the form of the Household Code in Colossians by taking the following steps: (1) analyzing the structure of the Colossian *Haustafel*, (2) making a general investigation of the sources of the early Christian *Haustafeln*, and (3) summarizing the evidence that points to the likelihood that the Colossian *Haustafel* is an independent, pre-Colossian, traditional paraenetic unit.

Ethik der neutestamentlichen Haustafeln," *NTS* 21 (1975): 1-22; David Schroeder, "Lists, ethical," *The Interpreters Dictionary of the Bible,* supplementary volume (Nashville: Abingdon, 1976), pp. 546-47; Eduard Schweizer, "Die Weltlichkeit des Neuen Testaments: Die Haustafeln," in *Beiträge zur alttestamentlichen Theologie, Festschrift für W. Zimmerli* (1977); Ralph P. Martin, "Haustafeln," in *New International Dictionary of New Testament Theology,* vol. 3, ed. Colin Brown (Grand Rapids: Zondervan, 1975), pp. 928-32; E. Schweizer, "Traditional ethical patterns in the Pauline and post-Pauline letters and their development (lists of vices and housetables)," in *Text and Interpretation: Studies in the New Testament Presented to Matthew Black,* ed. Ernest Best and R. McL. Wilson (Cambridge: University Press, 1979), pp. 195-209.

[3]Quoted with approval by Francis W. Beare, *The First Epistle of Peter* (Oxford: B. Blackwell, 1947), p. 195.

A Structural Analysis of Colossians 3:18-4:1

The following arrangement of the text shows the schematic nature of the Colossian Household Code:[4]

(18) Αἱ γυναῖκες, ὑποτάσσεσθε τοῖς ἀνδράσιν, ὡς ἀνῆκεν ἐν κυρίῳ.

(19) Οἱ ἄνδρες, ἀγαπᾶτε τὰς γυναῖκας καὶ μὴ πικραίνεσθε πρὸς αὐτάς.

(20) Τα τέκνα, ὑπακούετε τοῖς γονεῦσαν κατὰ πάντα, τοῦτο γὰρ εὐάρεστόν ἐστιν ἐν κυρίῳ.

(21) Οἱ πατέρες, μὴ ἐρεθίζετε τὰ τέκνα ὑμῶν, ἵνα μὴ ἀθυμῶσιν.

(22) Οἱ δοῦλοι, ὑπακούετε κατὰ πάντα τοῖς κατὰ σάρκα κυρίοις, μὴ ἐν ὀφθαλμοδουλίαις ὡς ἀνθρωπάρεσκοι, ἀλλ' ἐν ἁπλότητι καρδίας φοβούμενοι τὸν κύριον.

(1) Οἱ κύριοι, τὸ δίκαιον καὶ τὴν ἰσότητα τοῖς δούλοις παρέχεσθε, εἰδότες ὅτι καὶ ὑμεῖς ἔχετε κύριον ἐν οὐρανῷ.

(23) ὁ ἐάν ποιῆτε, ἐκ φυχῆς ἐργάζεσθε ὡς τῷ κυρὶῳ ~~καὶ οὐκ ἀνθρώποις,~~

(24) εἰδότες ὅτι ἀπὸ κυρίου ἀπολήμφεσθε τὴν ἀνταπόδοσιν τῆς κληρονομίας.

(25) τῷ κυρίῳ Χριστῷ δουλεύετε. ὁ γὰρ ἀδικῶν κομίσεται ὅ ἠδίκησεν, καὶ οὐκ ἔστιν προσωπολημφία.

Several observations can be made which point to the intrinsically formal structure of the *Haustafel* unit. First, the basic structure of the

---

[4]Taken from J. E. Crouch, *The Origin and Intention of the Colossian Haustafel*, p. 9.

passage consists of three sets of reciprocal exhortations. Second, the groups mentioned have a general relationship to the household but appear in a context which has a broader application. It is hardly likely that the exhortations to the household would be included in a letter to a church unless those admonitions had a bearing upon the total life of the church. It is striking that those letters in which the *Haustafel* form is most pronounced (Colossians, Ephesians, and 1 Peter) it is the relationship of the church to those outside of the church that is stressed. Third, the groups are arranged in an order beginning with the closest relationship (wives and husbands) and ending with the least close (slaves and masters). Fourth, in terms of a first century cultural setting, the first party addressed in each set is subordinate to the second one and the first party is exhorted to submission or obedience to the other. Fifth, the formal structure of each individual segment consists of an address ("wives"), admonition ("submit yourselves to your husbands"), and a motive or reason ("as is fitting in the Lord"). Sixth, with the single exception of the masters, only the subordinate members of the sets are addressed with theologically oriented motives or reasons. For the husbands and fathers the admonitions are suprisingly general in nature and the motives are either absent or extremely obvious. Furthermore, even though the admonition to the master is based on a theological motive ("knowing that you also have a Master in heaven"), it is miniscule in comparison to the theological motive given to slaves, which consists of more than three verses of the text.[5] Seventh, and perhaps most importantly, the entire unit can be lifted from the context without making an awkward break. Indeed, 4:2-6, which consists of an exhortation to prayer and thanksgiving, is more closely related to the theme of singing and thanksgiving in 3:16, 17 than is the intervening Household Code. Finally, with the exception of the segment dealing with slaves, the reciprocal admonitions in each set are of approxi-

---

[5]It is possible that 3:25 ("For the wrong doer will be paid back for the wrong he has done, and there is no partiality") applies to both slaves and masters. It immediately precedes the admonition to the masters and really seems more applicable to the masters than the slaves. Martin, following A. Schlatter and G. Schrenk, believes that it refers solely to the masters (*Colossians*, pp. 123-24). If so, it breaks the pattern of the *Haustafel* in which the motive statement *follows* the admonition in the other reciprocal pairs. It is interesting to observe that in Eph. 6:8, 9, the first part of Col. 3:25 is applied to both slaves and masters and the last part ("there is no partiality") is applied to the masters.

mately the same length. The exhortation to slaves and masters (3:22-4:1) is so greatly out of proportion with the others that one gets the impression that either the slave-master relationship was an especially acute one in the early church or else that the unit has been expanded by the author of the letter to deal with a special situation in the Colossian church.[6]

General Investigation of the Early Christian Haustafeln

The Colossian *Haustafel* is one of several such Household Codes in the New Testament and early Christian literature. It must be admitted, however, that there is no general agreement on what passages should be classified as *Haustafeln*. One reason for this lack of consensus is that scholars differ in assessment of the extent of the *Haustafel* genre. W. Lillie, for instance, believes that the term "house-table" should not only be limited to admonitions addressed to members of the household, but that it also should include the principle of reciprocity.[7] Consequently, he limits the *Haustafeln* to Colossians 3:18-4:1, Ephesians 5:21-6:9, and 1 Peter 3:1-7. J. Sampley seems to agree that the genre should be limited to the household but does not insist upon reciprocity. Hence he includes Colossians 3:18-4:1, Ephesians 5:21-6:9, 1 Peter 2:17-3:9, 1 Timothy 2:8-15, 6:1-10, and Titus 2:1-10.[8] M. Dibelius, however, believes that the primary feature of the *Haustafel* genre is the exhortation to submit to others. Thus he includes Romans 13:1-7 and Titus 3:1ff.[9] On this ground 1 Peter 2:13-17 should also be included. J. Crouch is representative of scholars who take a broad view of the extent of the *Haustafeln*. He includes duties related to church

---

[6]John Knox believes that Col. 3:25 contains an allusion to the case of Onesimus the runaway slave for whom an appeal is made in Philemon and that the longer admonition to slaves in Col. 3:22-25 is related to Paul's concern about the social consequences of the favor shown to Onesimus. "Philemon and the Authenticity of Colossians," *JR* 18 (1939): 154-57.

[7]Lillie, "The Pauline House-tables," p. 180.

[8]J. Paul Sampley, "*And the Two Shall Become One Flesh*" (Cambridge: University Press, 1971), p. 19.

[9]Martin Diebelius and Heinrich Greeven, *An die Kolosser, Epheser, an Philemon*, ed. Hans Lietzmann and Günther Bornkamm, Handbuch zum Neuen Testament (Tübingen, 1953), p. 48. Philip Carrington uses the same criterion to posit a "Code of Subordination" in an early Christian catechism. *The Primitive Christian Catechism* (Cambridge: University Press, 1940), pp. 30ff.

order as well as to the household. Consequently, he includes instructions related to bishops, deacons, presbyters, old and young men, old and young women, widows, and the state.[10] All of these are found in the Pastoral Epistles.

In order to make our investigation of the *Haustafel* form as broad as possible, we shall follow the example of Crouch. One of the main reasons for doing this is that the use of the *Haustafel* in the New Testament is not limited to the internal affairs of the households themselves but are more broadly applied to the concerns of the church. It would not be wrong to affirm that the Household Code serves a more ecclesiological than sociological function. Let us, therefore, proceed in our investigation by examining three groupings of *Haustafeln*: those in Colossians, Ephesians, and 1 Peter; those in the Pastoral Epistles; and those in non-canonical early Christian literature.

The Haustafel in Colossians, Ephesians, and 1 Peter[11]

WIVES

Colossians 3

18 Αἱ γυναῖκες, ὑποτάσσεσθε τοῖς ἀνδράσιν, ὡς ἀνῆκεν ἐν κυρίῳ.

Ephesians 5

22 Αἱ γυναῖκες τοῖς ἰδίοις ἀνδράσιν ὡς τῷ κυρίῳ, 23 ὅτι ἀνήρ ἐστιν κεφαλὴ τῆς γυναικὸς ὡς καὶ ὁ Χριστὸς κεφαλὴ τῆς ἐκκλησίας, αὐτὸς σωτὴρ τοῦ σώματος. 24 ἀλλὰ ὡς ἡ ἐκκλησία ὑποτάσσεται τῷ Χριστῷ, οὕτως καὶ αἱ γυναῖκες τοῖς ἀνδράσιν ἐν παντί.

1 Peter 3

1 Ὁμοίως [αἱ] γυναῖκες ὑποτασσόμεναι τοῖς ἰδίοις ἀνδράσιν, ἵνα καὶ εἴ τινες ἀπειθοῦσιν τῷ λόγῳ διὰ τῆς τῶν γυναικῶν ἀναστροφῆς ἄνευ λόγου κερδηθήσονται 2 ἐποπτεύσαντες τὴν ἐν φόβῳ ἁγνὴν ἀναστροφὴν ὑμῶν. 3 ὧν ἔστω οὐχ ἔξωθεν ἐμπλοκῆς τριχῶν καὶ περιθέσεως χρυσίων ἢ ἐνδύσεως ἱματίων κόσμος, 4 ἀλλ᾽ ὁ κρυπτὸς

---

[10]Crouch, *Origin and Intention*, pp. 12-13. Hinson, "The Christian *Haustafel*," p. 496, fn. 5, also takes the broad view. It should be noted, however, that those who take the broad view do not usually include the admonitions concerning church officers.

[11]For a good summary treatment of the N. T. *Haustafeln* see J. Sampley, "*And the Two Shall Become one Flesh*," pp. 18-28.

τῆς καρδίας ἄνθρωπος ἐν τῷ ἀφθάρτῳ τοῦ πραέως καὶ ἡσυχίου πνεύματος, ὅ ἐστιν ἐνώπιον τοῦ θεοῦ πολυτελές. 5 οὕτως γάρ ποτε καὶ αἱ ἅγιαι γυναῖκες αἱ ἐλπίζουσαι εἰς θεὸν ἐκόσμουν ἑαυτὰς, ὑποτασσόμεναι τοῖς ἰδίοις ἀνδράσιν, 6 ὡς Σάρρα ὑπήκουσεν τῷ Ἀβραάμ, κύριον αὐτὸν καλοῦσα· ἧς ἐγενήθητε τέκνα ἀγαθοποιοῦσαι καὶ μὴ φοβούμεναι μηδεμίαν πτόησιν.

HUSBANDS

Colossians 3

19 Οἱ ἄνδρες, ἀγαπᾶτε τὰς γυναῖκας καὶ μὴ πικραίνεσθε πρὸς αὐτάς.

Ephesians 5

25 Οἱ ἄνδρες, ἀγαπᾶτε τὰς γυναῖκας, καθὼς καὶ ὁ Χριστὸς ἠγάπησεν τὴν ἐκκλησίαν καὶ ἑαυτὸν παρέδωκεν ὑπὲρ αὐτῆς, 26 ἵνα αὐτὴν ἁγιάσῃ καθαρίσας τῷ λουτρῷ τοῦ ὕδατος ἐν ῥήματι, 27 ἵνα παραστήσῃ αὐτὸς ἑαυτῷ ἔνδοξον τὴν ἐκκλησίαν, μὴ ἔχουσαν σπίλον ἢ ῥυτίδα ἤ τι τῶν τοιούτων, ἀλλ᾽ ἵνα ᾖ ἁγία καὶ ἄμωμος. 28 οὕτως ὀφείλουσιν καὶ οἱ ἄνδρες ἀγαπᾶν τὰς ἑαυτῶν γυναῖκας ὡς τὰ ἑαυτῶν σώματα. ὁ ἀγαπῶν τὴν ἑαυτοῦ γυναῖκα ἑαυτὸν ἀγαπᾷ, 29 οὐδεὶς γάρ ποτε τὴν ἑαυτοῦ σάρκα ἐμίσησεν, ἀλλὰ ἐκτρέφει καὶ θάλπει αὐτήν, καθὼς καὶ ὁ Χριστὸς τὴν ἐκκλησίαν, 30 ὅτι μέλη ἐσμὲν τοῦ σώματος αὐτοῦ. 31 ἀντὶ τούτου καταλείψει ἄνθρωπος τὸν πατέρα καὶ τὴν μητέρα καὶ προσκολληθήσεται πρὸς τὴν γυναῖκα αὐτοῦ, καὶ ἔσονται οἱ δύο εἰς σάρκα μίαν. 32 τὸ μυστήριον τοῦτο μέγα ἐστίν, ἐγὼ δὲ λέγω εἰς Χριστὸν καὶ εἰς τὴν ἐκκλησίαν. 33 πλὴν καὶ ὑμεῖς οἱ καθ᾽ ἕνα ἕκαστος τὴν ἑαυτοῦ γυναῖκα οὕτως ἀγαπάτω ὡς ἑαυτόν, ἡ δὲ γυνὴ ἵνα φοβῆται τὸν ἄνδρα.

1 Peter 3

7 Οἱ ἄνδρες ὁμοίως συνοικοῦντες κατὰ γνῶσιν, ὡς ἀσθενεστέρῳ σκεύει τῷ γυναικείῳ ἀπονέμοντες τιμήν, ὡς καὶ συνκληρονόμοις χάριτος ζωῆς, εἰς τὸ μὴ ἐγκόπτεσθαι τὰς προσευχὰς ὑμῶν.

CHILDREN

Colossians 3

20 Τὰ τέκνα, ὑπακούετε τοῖς γονεῦσιν κατὰ πάντα, τοῦτο γὰρ εὐάρεστόν ἐστιν ἐν κυρίῳ.

Ephesians 6

1 Τὰ τέκνα, ὑπακούετε τοῖς γονεῦσιν ὑμῶν ἐν κυρίῳ, τοῦτο γὰρ ἐστιν δίκαιον. 2 τίμα τὸν πατέρα σου καὶ τὴν μητέρα, ἥτις ἐστὶν ἐντολὴ πρώτη ἐν ἐπαγγελίᾳ, 3 ἵνα εὖ σοι γένηται καὶ ἔσῃ μακροχρόνιος ἐπὶ τῆς γῆς.

FATHERS

Colossians 3

21 Οἱ πατέρες, μὴ ἐρεθίζετε τὰ τέκνα ὑμῶν, ἵνα μὴ ἀθυμῶσιν.

Ephesians 6

4 Καὶ οἱ πατέρες, μὴ παροργίζετε τὰ τέκνα ὑμῶν, ἀλλὰ ἐκτρέφετε αὐτὰ ἐν παιδείᾳ καὶ νουθεσίᾳ κυρίου.

SLAVES

Colossians 3

22 Οἱ δοῦλοι, ὑπακούετε κατὰ πάντα τοῖς κατὰ σάρκα κυρίοις, μὴ ἐν ὀφθαλμοδουλίᾳ ὡς ἀνθρωπάρεσκοι, ἀλλ᾽ ἐν ἁπλότητι καρδίας, φοβούμενοι τὸν κύριον. 23 ὅ ἐὰν ποιῆτε, ἐκ ψυχῆς ἐργάζεσθε, ὡς τῷ κυριῳ καὶ οὐκ ἀνθρώποις, 24 εἰδότες ὅτι ἀπὸ κυρίου ἀπολήμψεσθε τὴν ἀνταπόδοσιν τῆς κληρονομίας. τῷ κυριῳ Χριστῷ δουλεύετε· 25 ὁ γὰρ ἀδικῶν κουίσεται ὅ ἠδίκησεν, καὶ οὐκ ἔστιν προσωπολημψία.

Ephesians 6

5 Οἱ δοῦλοι, ὑπακούετε τοῖς κατὰ σάρκα κυρίοις μετὰ φόβου καὶ τρόμου ἐν ἁπλότητι τῆς καρδίας ὑμῶν ὡς τῷ Χριστῷ, 6 μὴ κατ᾽ ὀφθαλμοδουλίαν ὡς ἀνθρωπάρεσκοι ἀλλ᾽ ὡς δοῦλοι Χριστοῦ ποιοῦντες τὸ θέλημα τοῦ θεοῦ ἐκ ψυχῆς, 7 μετ᾽ εὐνοίας δουλεύοντες, ὡς τῷ κυρίῳ καὶ οὐκ ἀνθρώποις, 8 εἰδότες ὅτι ἕκαστος, ἐάν τι ποιήσῃ ἀγαθόν, τοῦτο κομίσεται παρὰ κυρίου, εἴτε δοῦλος εἴτε ἐλεύθερος.

1 Peter 2

18 Οἱ οἰκέται ὑποτασσόμενοι ἐν παντὶ φοβῳ τοῖς δεσπόταις, οὐ μόνον τοῖς ἀγαθοῖς καὶ ἐπι-

εικέσιν ἀλλὰ καὶ τοῖς σκολιοῖς. 19 τοῦτο γὰρ χάρις εἰ διὰ συνείδησιν θεοῦ ὑποφέρει τις λύπας πάσχων ἀδίκως. 20 ποῖον γὰρ κλέος εἰ ἁμαρτάνοντες καὶ κολαφιζόμενοι ὑπομενεῖτε; ἀλλ᾽ εἰ ἀγαθοποιοῦντες καὶ πάσχοντες ὑπομενεῖτε, τοῦτο χάρις παρὰ θεῷ. 21 εἰς τοῦτο γαρ ἐκλήθητε, ὅτι καὶ Χριστὸς ἔπαθεν ὑπὲρ ὑμῶν, ὑμῖν ὑπολιμπάνων ὑπογραμμὸν ἵνα ἐπακολουθήσητε τοῖς ἴχνεσιν αὐτοῦ·
22 ὅς ἁμαρτίαν οὐκ ἐποίησεν οὐδὲ εὑρέθη δόλος ἐν τῷ στόματι αὐτοῦ· 23 ὅς λοιδορούμενος οὐκ ἀντελοιδόρει, πάσχων οὐκ ἠπείλει, παρεδίδου δὲ τῷ κρίνοντι δικαίως, 24 ὅς τὰς ἁμαρτίας ἡμῶν αὐτὸς ἀνήνεγκεν ἐν τῷ σώματι αὐτοῦ ἐπὶ τὸ ξύλον, ἵνα ταῖς ἁμαρτίαις ἀπογενόμενοι τῇ δικαιοσύνῃ ζήσωμεν· οὗ τῷ μώλωπι ἰάθητε. 25 ἦτε γὰρ ὡς πρόβατα πλανώμενοι, ἀλλὰ ἐπεστράφητε νῦν ἐπὶ τὸν ποιμένα καὶ ἐπίσκοπον τῶν ψυχῶν ὑμῶν.

MASTERS

Colossians 4

1 Οἱ κύριοι, τὸ δίκαιον καὶ τὴν ἰσότητα τοῖς δούλοις παρέχεσθε, εἰδότες ὅτι καὶ ὑμεῖς ἔχετε κύριον ἐν οὐρανῷ.

Ephesians 6

9 Καὶ οἱ κύριοι, τὰ αὐτὰ ποιεῖτε πρὸς αὐτούς, ἀνιέντες τὴν ἀπειλήν, εἰδότες ὅτι καὶ αὐτῶν καὶ ὑμῶν ὁ κύριός ἐστιν ἐν οὐρανοῖς, καὶ προσωπολημψία οὐκ ἔστιν παρ᾽ αὐτῷ.

In terms of the principle of reciprocity and the household classes addressed, the *Haustafel* form in Colossians and Ephesians is unsurpassed. In both of these letters three sets of classes are addressed: wives and husbands, children and fathers, and slaves and masters. Furthermore, the sets occur in exactly the same order. In 1 Peter the situation is somewhat different. The order is changed. Slaves are addressed first and wives and husbands are addressed last. Some of the classes are missing. Masters, children and fathers are not addressed at all. However, the principle of reciprocity is present in the commands to the wives and husbands and all of the formal features (direct address, exhortation, and motivation) appear in each admonition.

Several features stand out in an examination of the *Haustafel* in these three letters. First, the *Haustafel* was flexible with regard to the number of classes addressed and the order of their presentation. The fact that the same classes appear in the same order in Colossians and Ephesians is probably not an indication of an established order, but the dependence of one letter upon the oher.[12] First Peter is bound neither by the number of classes addressed nor by the sequence of their presentation.

Second, in each of the letters the admonition to slaves plays an important role. This is especially evident in Colossians where the exhortation to slaves contains fifty-six words while the corresponding admonition to masters contains only eighteen. None of the other classes addressed consists of more than thirteen words. In 1 Peter the admonition to slaves is the longest pericope in the *Haustafel* and there is no corresponding admonition to masters. Even in Ephesians where the injunctions to wives and husbands occupy the most important place in the *Haustafel*, the command to slaves is longer and more severe in tone than the one to the wives. Furthermore, it contains more than twice as many words as the corresponding exhortation to masters. As we shall observe later, this phenomenon points to a special problem concerning slaves faced by the early church.

Third, with the exception of the command to slaves, the *Haustafel* in Colossians is the briefest and has the most consistent pattern. Brevity is surely not a trustworthy criterion for dating literary material, but the combination of brevity and pattern do indicate the possibility of the presence of traditional material. Both of these features would facilitate the remembering and the transmission of the material.[13]

---

[12]The important issues of whether the same writer wrote both letters or which was the source of the other does not concern us here. The basic matter is that one is dependent upon the other.

[13]As is well known, the theory of the complex evolving from the simple does not work in the areas of sociological structure of literature. On this ground Sampley is right in cautioning against a "too facile declaration that Colossians contains the most primitive New Testament Haustafel" ("*And the Two Shall Become One Flesh*," p. 24); but he is unjustified in criticizing Carrington for using this theory. Carrington's method for arriving at the "primitive apostolic catechism" is that of removing the "Pauline notes" from the *Haustafel*. (*The Primitive Christian Catechism*, pp. 92-93.)

Fourth, the authors exercised considerable freedom in expanding various elements in the *Haustafel* form. Such expansions usually occur in the statements of exhortation or motivation and tend to have one of the following characteristics: Some contain Christological references. This is especially true of the admonitions to wives and husbands in Ephesians and to slaves in 1 Peter.[14] Others of the expansions are pragmatic in nature. For instance, in 1 Peter 3:7 the exhortation to husbands to dwell together with their wives "according to knowledge" is explained by the words "giving honor to the woman as to the weaker vessel" and this "in order that their prayers might not be hindered."[15] Still others of the expansions are based on Old Testament texts. Genesis 2:24 is quoted in Ephesians 5:31 and reference is made to the Decalogue in Ephesians 6:2, 3. Sarah's submission to Abraham is cited as a good example for Christian wives in 1 Peter 3:6.

Thus the *Haustafeln* in Colossians, Ephesians, and 1 Peter bear witness to both form and freedom in their composition. Reciprocal exhortations are present in all three of the letters and the formal features of direct address, admonition, and motivation are present in every class addressed. On the other hand, the writers were quite free to adapt and expand the *Haustafel* for their own purposes.

The Haustafel in the Pastoral Epistles. Ethical duties which are addressed to specific classes and which have to do with conduct befitting Christians in everyday life are also found in the Pastoral

---

[14]It is interesting to observe that the *Haustafeln* with Christological expansions are related to a major theological concern in the letter. In the section dealing with husbands and wives in the Ephesians *Haustafel*, the example of Christ has special ecclesiological significance. The importance of the church is one of (if not the) most important teachings of Ephesians. E. J. Goodspeed is surely right when he points out that the writer of Ephesians is not so much interested in the marriage relationship as he is in the union between Christ and the church, and that he is far more interested in marriage as a symbol than he is in right relationships in marriage. *The Meaning of Ephesians* (Chicago: The University of Chicago Press, 1933), pp. 60-62.

In the admonition to slaves in 1 Peter, Christ is set forth as the supreme example of suffering wrongfully. The significance of suffering for Christ's sake is the primary theological concern of 1 Peter. As in the case of Phil. 1:27ff, and Rom. 8:17ff., suffering for the sake of Christ is not an evil, but the mark of authentic Christian existence (1 Pet. 1:6ff., 2:16, 2:20a, 3:14ff., 4:12ff.).

[15]This is also true in Colossians 3:20 and 22. The phrase "in everything" makes clear that the injunction to children and slaves to be obedient is most inclusive. Colossians 3:23, 24 gives a practical explanation of what the "everything" includes for slaves.

Epistles. In 1 Timothy 2:8-15 men are admonished concerning the place and manner of prayer, and women are exhorted concerning their apparel and subordination to men. In 1 Timothy 6:1, 2 slaves are admonished to honor their masters and especially to render good service to believing masters. In Titus 2:1-10 aged men and women, young men and women, and slaves are instructed to fulfill certain duties and to conduct themselves in approved ways. Titus 3:1-8 is an admonition to Titus to remind the Cretan Christians "to be in subjection to rulers, to authorities, to be obedient, to be ready unto every good work. . . ." Although the passage lacks the formal features of direct address, many regard it as belonging to the *Haustafel* genre.[16] It does have the other formal features of the *Haustafel* (admonition, motivation, and the "submission" motif). Furthermore, it deals with duties and conduct related to everyday life.

Even though there are obvious parallels between the Pastoral *Haustafel* and those in Ephesians, Colossians, and 1 Peter,[17] there are also some notable differences. In the first place, the element of direct address, which is a conspicuous feature of the epistles of the Colossians-type, is entirely absent from the *Haustafel* found in the Pastorals. Not only is no specific group mentioned in Titus 3:1-8, but even in the *Haustafel* where specific groups are mentioned (2:1-10), none of the groups is addressed directly. In every case either Timothy or Titus is instructed to pass on the directions or else the third person form of the imperative is used. Secondly, not all of the classes mentioned in the Colossians-type *Haustafel* are addressed in the Pastoral *Haustafel*. Neither children nor masters are mentioned. Thirdly, in Titus 2:1-6 men and women are addressed in terms of their age (older and younger). This designation is not found in the Colossians-type. Fourthly, whereas the *Haustafel* of the Colossians-type occurs in uninterrupted units, the Pastoral *Haustafel* is separated by other passages. Lastly, the Pastoral *Haustafel* do not have as many corresponding pairs as do those in the Colossians-type. Where there are corresponding pairs, the principle of reciprocity is absent. In both 1 Timothy 2:8-15, where men and women are mentioned, and in Titus 2:1-6, where older men and women and younger men and women are

---

[16]Lillie, "The Pauline House-tables," p. 180.

[17]Hereafter called the Colossians-type *Haustafel*.

admonished, no mutual obligations of one class to the other are set forth.

From all of this it appears that even though there are some clearly recognizable patterns between the Colossians-type *Haustafel* and the codes in the Pastoral Epistles, a greater freedom in the use of the form is apparent in the Pastorals. Sampley's observation seems justifiable:

> It is not a rigid tradition that must be taken over in a fixed fashion, but may be adapted for the particular purpose of the author. For this reason, modifications or additions are frequently indicative of the author's special concerns.[18]

The Haustafeln in Early Christian Non-canonical Literature. A curious mixture of duties related to personal and ecclesiastical concerns appears in the *Haustafeln* in early Christian literature outside the New Testament. In 1 Clement 1:3, the Corinthians are praised for several commendable practices and attitudes. Among them are some which remind one of the *Haustafel* in Titus.[19] The Corinthians had submitted themselves to their rulers, honored older men, enjoined the young men to modest and fitting thoughts, and admonished the women to behave properly and to keep the "rule of obedience." In 21:6-9 the same sequence of classes is addressed in a series of hortatory injunctions and to it is added a list of instructions concerning children. 38:1, 2 contains an admonition to each man to be subject to his neighbor and this is followed by a series of reciprocal instructions to the strong and the weak, the rich and the poor, and the wise and the humble.

Two letters associated with Polycarp, the Bishop of Smyrna, contain a number of miscellaneous instructions which parallel the concerns of the New Testament *Haustafeln*. One of them is a letter written to Polycarp by Ignatius of Antioch and the other is one written by Polycarp to the Philippians. The former (in 4:1-6:1) includes instructions concerning widows, slaves, wives, husbands, bishops, presbyters, and deacons. It is interesting to observe that these instructions are addressed to Polycarp himself and the second person singular imperative form is generally used. But in 6:1 the admonition to give heed to the Bishop is in the second person plural. As Crouch points out, "This last

---

[18]Sampley, "*And the Two Shall Become One Flesh*" p. 23.

[19]Clement seems to be referring to church leaders whereas Titus (3:1) refers to rulers and authorities.

item hardly applies to Polycarp and is evidence of the traditional nature of these instructions."[20] In Polycarp's letter, *To the Philippians*, instructions are given which have to do with the duties of wives, husbands, deacons, young men, virgins, and presbyters (4:1-6:3). There is also a very brief unit of instruction concerning children (4:2). Unlike the New Testament *Haustafeln* which address such instructions to the fathers, in Polycarp's letter they are addressed to the wives.

The *Didache* also has a short list of commandments similar to the New Testament *Haustafeln*. In the "document of the Two Ways" (1:2-6:2) there is a cluster of admonitions concerning sons, daughters, masters, and slaves (4:9-11). The injunctions are primarily in the Decalogue form of "thou shalt not" but the exhortation to slaves has all of the formal characteristics of the Colossians-type *Haustafel* (direct address, admonition, and motive).

Finally, the *Epistle of Barnabas* contains a series of exhortations very much like those in the *Didache*. The second part of the "letter" repeats the teaching of the Two Ways which is found at the beginning of the *Didache*. In this section (in the form of "thou shalt" and "thou shalt not") is a list of commandments having to do with children, neighbors, slaves, and masters (19:5-7). Though the command to slaves is in the Decalogue form, it is clearly related to the materials in the *Didache*.[21]

The obvious differences in these codes from the New Testament *Haustafeln* do not obscure their equally obvious similarities. Probably the best explanation for this phenomenon is that these early Christian documents reflect a paraenetic schema which was known by the writers and which they felt at liberty to alter in accordance to the situations which they addressed.

Summary of Evidence Pointing to the Traditional Character of the Colossian Haustafel. In the light of our examination of the structure of Colossians 3:18-4:1 and our investigation of the early Christian *Haustafeln*, what conclusions may be drawn which have a bearing on the

---

[20]Crouch, *Origin and Intention*, p. 13.

[21]Didache 4:11 reads ὑμεῖς δὲ οἱ δοῦλοι ὑποταγήσεσθε τοῖς κυρίοις ὑμῶν ὡς τύπῳ θεοῦ ἐν αἰσχύνῃ καὶ φόβῳ and Barn. 19:7 reads ὑποταγήσῃ κυρίοις ὡς τύπῳ θεοῦ ἐν αἰσχύνῃ καὶ φόβῳ.

traditional character of the Colossian *Haustafel*? Let me suggest five of them.

First, it is evident that the *Haustafeln* have a special interest in certain classes of people. Admonitions to wives, husbands, children, slaves, and masters appear in nearly all of them. Furthermore, they appear in clusters and are concerned with daily social and ecclesiological life.

Second, instructions concerning wives and slaves are found in all of the lists, thus indicating a special concern for these classes.[22] It seems to me important to observe that admonitions concerning bishops, deacons, and elders are mentioned only in the documents written at the time of the turn of the first and second centuries A.D. These classes associated with the household and with ecclesiastical leadership are not unrelated. They indicate the presence of the growing problem of "freedom" and disorder which we shall discuss further on.

Third, although certain formal features are present in all of the *Haustafeln* to a greater or lesser degree, the paraenetic schema was adaptable to a variety of situations. Special theological interests were usually made known by expanding the statements of admonition or motivation with Christological assertions (such as is the case with the ecclesiological teaching in Ephesians 5:21-33 and the significance of suffering in 1 Peter 2:18-25). Reciprocity and direct address are omitted from the *Haustafeln* when church leaders are charged with passing on the instructions which deal with concrete situations in their own churches. This is most evident in the Pastoral Epistles and in Ignatius' letter to Polycarp. Direct address gives way to the "Decalogue" form in the *Haustafeln* in the *Didache* and *Barnabas*. Weidinger is probably correct in referring to a "prozess der Auflosung" of the *Haustafel* form.[23] However, even in documents where the *Haustafel* form has been altered the most, there is evidence that the writers were using preexisting materials. They keep the materials in a series. The instructions are related to "stock" classes. Sometimes instructions are included which have little or no bearing on the actual situation. The

---

[22]Slaves are not designated by δοῦλος or οἰκέτης in 1 Clement, but they are included among the "weak," the "poor," and the "humble" in 38:2.

[23]K. Weidinger, *Die Haustafeln: Ein Stück urchristlicher Paränese*, Untersuchungen zum Neuen Testament 14 (Leipzig, 1928), p. 77.

sudden admonition to "give heed to the bishop" along with the strange change from the singular to the plural in Ignatius' letter to Polycarp is perhaps the clearest example of this.

Fourth, the most highly structured forms of the *Haustafeln* are found in Colossians and Ephesians. In each of these documents the framework of the *Haustafel* unit consists of three pairs of reciprocal exhortations. In each case the first member addressed is exhorted to submission or obedience to the opposite member. The relationships are arranged in the most natural order, beginning with the closest and ending with the least close. In addition, each individual segment consists of address, instruction, and reason or motivation. Of the two letters, Colossians contains the fewest expansions. Thus the *Haustafel* in Colossians is unique in form and is the most highly structured of any of the early Christian house-tables which we have investigated. It is probably the oldest extant *Haustafel.*[24]

Fifthly and lastly, the *Haustafel* in Colossians can be omitted from its context without disrupting the flow of thought. As J. Crouch observes:

> While there is nothing contradictory between the unit and its context, it is equally true that no awkward break would be noticed if the entire section were omitted. Prayer and thanksgiving constitute the themes of exhortations in 3:16f. and 4:2, and there is no transition between vss. 17 and 18.[25]

All of these items confirm the statement we made at the beginning of this discussion on the form of the Colossian *Haustafel.* It is unlikely

---

[24]So Crouch,*Origin and Intention*, p.32, and E. Schweizer, *Der Brief an die Kolosser* (Zürick: Neukirchen, 1976), p. 159. Most scholars agree that Col. was written before Eph. Even those who do not hold to the Pauline authorship of either letter generally posit the dependence of Eph. upon Col. For a recent survey of the problem see J. B. Polhill, "The Relationship between Ephesians and Colossians," *Review and Expositor* 70 (1973): 439-50. W. Munro believes that Eph. is dependent on Col. but that the Col. *Haustafel* is dependent on the Eph. *Haustafel.* This complicated theory produces a labored treatment in which much clearer results are claimed than the evidence cited supports. "Col. iii.18-iv.1 and Eph. v. 21-vi.9," pp. 434-47.

[25]Crouch, *Origin and Intention*, p. 10. There is a possible verbal connection between 3:17 and 23 (v. 17: καὶ πᾶν ὅ τι ἐὰν ποῖητε . . . v. 23: ὅ ἐὰν ποῖητε). But 3:22-25 is more closely related to 3:22 than to 3:17. R. P. Martin rightly argues for a "logical connection between 3:18-4:1 and its immediate context (*Colossians*, pp. 117, 118). However, in terms of grammar and formal structure there is no necessary connection between 3:18-4:1 and its context.

that the exhortations in 3:18-4:1 were made on the spur of the moment. It is far more likely that we are confronted here with a paraenetic tradition which existed before Colossians was written and was known by both the writer and the recipients.

THE PROBLEM
OF THE SOURCE OF THE HAUSTAFEL

It is clear that the New Testament *Haustafeln* were not the first lists of ethical instructions for everyday life that were ever written. There were plenty of prototypes already present in New Testament times. Furthermore, there are striking similarities between the New Testament *Haustafeln* and non-Christian codes. However, there are just as many striking differences between them. At the present stage of investigation, it is just as impossible to reconstruct an original *Haustafel* as it is to reproduce an *Urkatalog* of vices and virtues. What are some of the possible sources of influence on the Christian *Haustafeln*? How much sway did these sources have on the Colossian *Haustafel*. Let us examine some of the sources and seek to draw a conclusion. Broadly speaking, there are three major sources from which the *Haustafeln* may have come.

Popular Hellenistic Philosophy

Martin Dibelius made the first detailed study of the New Testament *Haustafeln* in an excursus in his commentary *An die Kolosser, Epheser, und Philemon*.[26] His thesis was that the New Testament *Haustafeln* are Christianized versions of the ethical instructions found in popular Hellenistic philosophy. He supports his thesis by drawing attention to the fact that ἀνῆκεν in 3:18 and εὐάρεστον in 3:20 are words which express motives that were common in contemporary popular philosophy. He also notes that one would expect to find τῷ κυρίῳ rather than ἐν κυρίῳ after these words and regards the latter as a Christianized transformation of the former.[27]

---

[26]Pp. 91-92. See also Dibelius' *Geschichte der urchristlichen Literatur*, vol. 2 (Berlin and Leipzig: Walter de Gruyter & Co., 1926), pp. 67ff.

[27]In this Dibelius is followed by Lohse, *Colossians and Philemon*, p. 158, fn. 23, and H. Schlier, "καθῆκον," *TDNT* 3: 437-40.

Karl Weidinger, the student of Dibelius, carried his mentor's thesis even further in two works published in 1928.[28] He especially drew attention to a number of features in Stoic ethical lists which parallel the New Testament *Haustafeln*. From these he concluded that the *Haustafel* pattern was essentially Stoic in nature and its contents were based upon the Stoic concept of duty (καθῆκον). These Stoic duties were adaptations of the ancient Greek νόμιμα ἄγραφα and dealt primarily with the fear of the gods, honor towards parents, proper burial for the dead, and love of friends and country. Hence, the New Testament *Haustafeln* are Christian applications of the Stoic καθήκοντα.

One of the critical problems of showing a relationship between the ethics of Stoicism and those of the Christian *Haustafeln* is the fact that the ethics of early Stoicism tended to be impersonal. The treatment of moral duties was based on the cardinal virtues rather than on social relationships. How could a system which taught that social relationships were indifferent, and thus neither good nor evil, have any relationship to a household code which emphasized the importance of interpersonal relationships? Crouch, drawing upon the insights of M. Wundt and E. Schwartz, shows that it is this very problem which gave birth to the Stoic lists of duties which most closely parallel the Christian *Haustafeln*.[29] Stoic practice was not always consistent with Stoic theory. "The contradictions in Stoicism must be understood in terms of its effort to mediate between the harshness of Cynic practice and the demands of everyday life."[30] Thus Diogenes Laertius, for instance, lists among the καθήκοντα the honoring of parents, brothers, country, and friends. To neglect these things is to act contrary to duty and the dictates of reason.

καθήκοντα μὲν οὖν εἶναι ὅσα λόγος αἱρεῖ ποιεῖν, ὡς ἔχει τὸ γονεῖς τιμᾶν, ἀδελφοὺς πατρίδα, συμπεριφέρεσθαι φιλοῖς. παρὰ τὸ καθῆκον δέ, ὅσα μὴ

---

[28] *Das Problem der urchristlichen Haustafeln* and *Die Haustafeln ein Stück unchristlicher Paränese*, Untersuchungen zum Neuen Testament 14 (Leipzig: 1928).

[29] Crouch, *Origin and Intention*, pp. 47-56. "Wundt . . . traces the contradictions in the Stoic ethical system back to one basic contradiction, namely, that the Stoics began with a denial (Verneinung) of real life and then wound up by affirming it." Max Wundt, *Geschichte der griechischen Ethik*, vol. 2 (Leipzig: Englemann, 1911), p. 295. E. Schwartz, *Ethik der Griechen* (Stuttgart, 1951), p. 199 ("Hier es . . . den Rigoristen eine Seitentur geöffnet, die es ihnen möglich macht, im wirklichen Leben zu stehen").

[30] Crouch, *Origin and Intention*, p. 50.

αἰρεῖ λόγος. ὡς ἔχει τὰ τοιαῦτα, γονέων ἀμελεῖν. ἀδελφῶν ἀφροντιστεῖν. φίλοις μὴ συνδιατίθεσθαι πατρίδα ὑπερορᾶν καί τά παραπλήσια.[31]

Some scholars believe that the distinctive mark which separates the Christian *Haustafeln* from parallels in Hellenism and Judaism is the principle of reciprocity. E. F. Scott, for example, in discussing the relationship between husbands and wives in Colossians 3:18, 19, writes:

It is to be noted here, as in his treatment of other relations, he (the writer) is careful to lay stress on reciprocal duties. This was the great innovation in the law of the family. Judaism, like all the ancient religions, had assumed that all the rights were on one side and the duties on the other. Christianity insisted that wives, children, and servants had their rights as well as husbands, parents and masters.[32]

However, the following passage by Seneca (ca. 4 B.C.-65 A.D.) shows that reciprocity was not unknown in the ethical instruction of Stoicism:

Quodcumque ex duobus constat officium, tantundem ab utroque exigit. Qualis pater esse debeat, cum inspexeris, scies non minus operis illic superesse, ut dispicias, qualem esse oporteat filium; sunt aliquae partes mariti, sed non minores uxoris. In vicem ista, quantum exigunt, praestant et parem desiderant regulam, quae, ut ait Hecaton, difficilis est ... (*De Beneficiis* ii. 18. 1ff.).[33]

"Officium" in this passage refers to the duties of father and son, and husband and wife. An "officium" involving two people makes an equal demand on both. Thus, even though duties regarding everyday personal relationships are a minor element in Stoic ethical teaching, the principle of reciprocity is nevertheless present.[34]

One of the viable sources for the development of the Christian *Haustafeln*, therefore, is the ethical teaching of popular Hellenistic

---

[31]Diogenes Laertius, vii 108, quoted from Crouch, p. 53. D. Laertius lived in the early third century A.D. but his remarks are about early Stoicism.

[32]Ernest F. Scott, *The Epistles of Paul to the Colossians, to Philemon, and to the Eshesians.* The Moffatt New Testament Commentary (New York: Harper and Row, n.d.), p. 78. See C. F. D. Moule, *The Epistle of Paul the Apostle to the Colossians and to Philemon* (Cambridge: University Press, 1957), p. 127, and Hinson, "The Christian Household in Colossians," p. 496.

[33]Quoted from Crouch, *Origin and Intention,* p. 55.

[34]Crouch discusses at some length the trend toward social concern and "other-centered" ethics in Epictetus (ca. 50 A.D. to 130 A.D.), pp. 60-67.

philosophy, especially the popular moral teaching of the Stoics. Let us turn now to another possible source.

Jewish Ethical Concerns

In recent times the Jewish influence on the New Testament *Haustafeln* have been traced almost exclusively to Hellenistic Judaism. In discussing the Colossian *Haustafel*, E. Glenn Hinson affirms but does not verify that "There are parallels in the writings of Hellenistic (*but not of Palestinian*) Jews" (italics mine).[35] There are two problems with this approach. First, it assumes that there are clearly defined distinctions which can be drawn between Palestinian and Hellenistic Judaism. As E. E. Ellis has recently written:

> The sharp separation of Palestine from the Hellenistic world has now been shown to be mistaken. At the time of Christ Palestine had been a part of that world for over three centuries and had experienced not only the immigration of many Greek-speaking Gentiles but also the resettlement from the diaspora of thoroughly Hellenized Jews. Even those Jews who resisted the foreign culture were not exempt from its influence. The Dead Sea Scrolls, for example, now provide evidence that the Greek Old Testament was used in first-century Palestine even among very strict Jews. From the same period an inscription has been found in which the dedication of a Jerusalem synagogue is made in Greek, and many ossuary and sepulchral inscriptions show that Greek was widely used by the people. The grave inscriptions are especially significant, for they demonstrate that Greek was not just the language of commerce or of the upper classes but in many instances the primary or only language of ordinary Jews.[36]

Second, such a limitation imposes a one-way flow of influence from Hellenism to Judaism to the Christian communities.[37] It cuts off the possibility, indeed the probability, that much of primitive Christian ethical thought was influenced by the Old Testament and by a Judaism that had not been consciously Hellenized. On the other hand, it would be foolish not to recognize the presence of Hellenistic influence on New

---

[35]Hinson, "The Christian Household in Colossians," p. 495. Both Lohse and Crouch are of the same opinion.

[36]E. E. Ellis, "Dating the New Testament," *NTS* 26 (1980): 497.

[37]Lohse, for example, says: "In the ethics of Hellenistic popular philosophy, which was probably transmitted to the Christian communities via the Hellenistic synagogues, there was a rich collection of material from which a person could ascertain what was considered proper conduct." *Colossians*, p. 156.

Testament ethical teaching. Streams of influence flow in many directions and from several sources into the New Testament.

One of those who saw a Jewish influence on the Colossian *Haustafel* which had not been influenced by Hellenistic philosophy was Ernst Lohmeyer. In his commentary on Colossians, published in 1930, he sets forth the proposition that the Colossian *Haustafel* "came from the familiar soil of the Jewish practice of that time."[38] He draws special attention to the concept of fearing the Lord as a motive for ethical behavior. Since that idea is clearly expressed in Colossians 3:22, he believes that in it "the foundations of a specifically Pharasaic ethic" become visible.[39] He was also persuaded that the word "Lord" which occurs in 3:18, 20, 23, 24, and 4:1 refers not to Christ but to God.[40] Pressing his thesis even further, Lohmeyer noted that Judaism had a special interest in women, slaves, and children from the time of Deuteronomy to Rabbinic times. On the basis of this he postulated the necessity of the formulation of an actual code dealing with these classes. He wrote:

> Es ist deshalb auch notwendig, die leichtere Bürde ihrer Pflichten wie auf einer besonderen Tafel zu formulieren, wie es schon das Deuteronomium begonnen hat und bis in die rabbinische Zeit fortgesetzt ist. Dann ist aber auch klar, dass diese Haustafel jüdischer Tradition enstammt.[41]

To borrow a phrase from Lohmeyer, "ist aber auch klar" that his postulation of a Jewish "*Tafel*" is but a hypothetical reconstruction. But where would modern New Testament studies be without some theoretical reconstructions? Lohmeyer has performed a valuable service in showing that the three subordinate classes (wives, children, and

---

[38]Ernst Lohmeyer, *Die Briefe an die Philipper, an die Kolosser und an Philemon* (Göttingen, 1953), p. 156.

[39]Ibid., p. 158.

[40]Ibid., p. 159. Lohse rejects this interpretation and declares that the phrase "fearing the Lord" does not "refer to God as in the Old Testament and Rev. 15:4, but to Christ." (*Colossians*, p. 160.) His reasoning is not clear. He seems to imply that in the O.T. the phrase is φοβεῖσθαι τὸν θεόν (not κύριον) and lists the following LXX examples: Ex. 1:17, 21; Lev. 19:14, 32; 25:17; Ps. 54:20 (19?). But all of these passages, with the exception of the two in Exodus, define θεός as ὁ κύριος ὁ θεός ὑμῶν or else use θεός and κύριος interchangeably in the immediate context. Furthermore, the phrase "Lord Christ (3:25) is unique in the Pauline corpus. It seems likely that "Christ" is added to "the Lord" in this text to give the O.T. term Christological meaning.

[41]Ibid., p. 155.

slaves) were of special interest to Judaism. The same can be said for his emphasis on the Jewish character of the phrase "fearing the Lord." Such observations, however, do not affirm the presence of a Jewish *Haustafel.*

Professor David Daube draws attention to two other factors that suggest that the Christian *Haustafeln* may have a literary connection with originals used in Hebrew-speaking Judaism.[42] One is that a participle is used in Hebrew fashion in the admonition to servants in 1 Peter 2:18 and to wives in 1 Peter 3:1. Participles are used in a similar way in the presentation of a series of rules for the Christian life in Romans 12:9ff. How does one account for this strange use of participles? Daube traces it to a common Rabbinic mode of expression. He points out that the Hebrew participle form of legislation dominates the earlier post-biblical codifications even though that form is not once used in the Old Testament. The reason for this, he says, is that for Rabbinic Judaism the age of authoritative revelation was over and "that all further legislation bore the character of interpretation and stabilization of custom."[43] Consequently, the powerful imperative form of commandment gave way to the "participle of correct practice" in Judaism and eventually became stereotyped. It was used to express that which was expected and customary. The participial imperatives in the New Testament are semiticisms which reflect the Rabbinic participial form of social legislation.[44] With respect to the *Haustafeln* Daube says that it is important to notice that "the unattached participles are to be met with only in certain epistles of the New Testament, and even there only in a single context, in the so-called Haustafeln, dealing with the conduct of Christians in their families, their communities, and the state."[45] He concludes that both Paul and 1 Peter drew on Hebrew codes of the primitive Christian community.

---

[42]David Daube, *The New Testament and Rabbinic Judaism*, The Jordan Lectures, 1952 (London: The Athlone Press, 1956), pp. 90-105. See also "Participle and Imperative in 1 Peter," an appended note in Selwyn, *The First Epistle of St. Peter*, pp. 467-88.

[43]Daube, *The N.T. and Rabbinic Judaism*, p. 91.

[44]For opposing views see V. P. Furnish, *Theology and Ethics in Paul* (Nashville and New York: Abingdon Press, 1968), p. 39; and A. P. Salom, "The Imperatival Use of the Participle in the New Testament," *Australian Biblical Review* 11 (1963): 41ff.

[45]Daube, *The New Testament and Rabbinic Judaism*, p. 103.

The other factor to which Daube draws attention is the use of the definite article with the nominative of address (which occurs in every class addressed in the Colossians-type *Haustafel*). He believes that this may be a translation of a Hebrew vocative. The presence of both of these factors (participle and article with direct address) in the New Testament *Haustafeln* suggest to Daube a literary dependence on a Hebrew household code. It is doubtful that this is enough evidence to establish literary dependence but it does show the probable Hebrew influence on the language of the *Haustafeln*.

The Jewish wisdom literature also contains parallels to the Christian *Haustafeln*. Although Proverbs does not contain a list of duties addressed to members of the household, it does contain scattered admonitions concerning the duties of children with respect to their parents (19:26; 20:20), the responsibilities of parents to their children (13:23; 19:11; 23:13; 28:15, 17), duties toward brothers, friends, and neighbors (17:17, 27:10, 17), the attitude of a servant toward his master (27:18), and the well-known passage on the duties of a wife (31:10-31). Ecclesiasticus (7:18-36) has a long list of duties related to friend, brother, wife, servant, cattle (sic!), children, daughters, parents, priests (the *Haustafeln* in the Pastoral Epistles comes to mind), poor, mourners, and the sick. Similarly, Tobit (4:3-14) contains a list of duties concerning parents, the poor, marriage, and servants.

Several impressive parallels to the Colossian *Haustafel* occur in the writings of Philo of Alexandria (ca. 20 B.C. to 50 A.D.). Section three of *De Fuga et Interventione*, in a commentary of Genesis 16:6b-14, refers to various causes for "flight." These causes are illustrated by the relationships of wives to husbands, children to parents, and slaves to masters. In his discussion of the fifth commandment of the Decalogue, Philo refers to the old and young, rulers and subjects, those who do good works and those who benefit from them, servants and masters, and children and parents (*De Decalogo* 165ff.). The striking feature about this passage is the stress on reciprocity. The young are to honor the old and the older are to care for the younger. The receivers of benefits are to act kindly toward their benefactors and the benefactors are not to insist upon the return of their gifts. Servants are to serve with congeniality and masters are to treat their slaves with gentleness and kindness, by means of which they will put aside the inequality that exists between them.

Josephus also seems familiar with the household schema. In his apologetic work *Against Apion* (ii.190-219) he discusses the Jewish law. Although this section is not a *Haustafel* in that it does not list duties for various social groups, it does seem to reflect the household arrangement. The section is basically a discussion of Jewish law. The main headings of Josephus' summary of the Jewish law are God, temple, marriage, children, the dead, parents, friends, and aliens. In both Josephus and Philo a Stoic influence also pervades the sections dealing with household ethical duties.

It is clear that Judaism had a special concern for ethical behavior as it related to everyday life and practice. Its writings contain lists of duties addressed to the same classes mentioned in the New Testament *Haustafeln*. Some of them have materials remarkably similar in both form and content to the Colossian *Haustafel*. Although the likenesses in structure and content within the Jewish lists point to the real possibility of a common household paraenesis in Judaism, there is no evidence of the existence of a standard Jewish *Haustafel*. However, the evidence cited above clearly shows that Judaism was a major source of influence for the Christian *Haustafeln*.

Specifically Christian Circumstances[46]

Over twenty years ago K. H. Rengstorf reacted against the Dibelius-Weidinger thesis that the New Testament *Haustafeln* are but lightly Christianized versions of non-Christian paraenetic materials. On the contrary, he argues, the New Testament *Haustafeln* are distinctly Christian in origin. There are three primary reasons which he gives for this conclusion: First, he believes that the use of the New Testament *Haustafeln* by the Apostolic Fathers indicates a reverence for them as apostolic creations. He cites 1 Clement 1:3 as evidence for this. There the Corinthians are commended for admonishing wives to keep "in the rule of obedience (ἔν τε τῷ κανόνι τῆς ὑποταγῆς)." Such a "canon"

---

[46]My indebtedness to J. E. Crouch has already been noted. In this section the indebtedness becomes nearly total for neither Schroeder's unpublished dissertation (*Die Haustafeln des Neuen Testaments. Ihre Herkunft und ihre theologischer Sinn*, Hamburg, 1959) nor Rengstorf's article "Die neutestamentlichen Mahnungen an die Frau, sich dem Manne unterzuordnen," *Verbum Dei manet in Aeternum* (Festschrift O. Schmitz, Witten, 1953, pp. 131-45) were available to me.

implies apostolic authority.[47] Secondly, he argues that though six classes are addressed in the Colossian *Haustafel*, in reality the exhortations are all directed to one class: the head of the household. The head is admonished as a husband, father, and master and all of the instructions are centered around the concept of love.[48] Thirdly, Rengstorf argues for the basically Christian nature of the *Haustafel* by drawing attention to similar expressions of concern in the childhood stories of John the Baptist and Jesus. Crouch properly argues against this by pointing out that there is nothing specifically "Christian" about the family life of Jesus or John the Baptist. They both were reared in typically Jewish households.[49] In spite of the weaknesses of Rengstorf's arguments, they do point out the need to see the New Testament *Haustafeln* in a distinctively Christian setting. They share some common characteristics with non-Christian codes but they spring out of Christian needs and (as was argued earlier) point toward the existence of an earlier Christian paraenetic tradition.

Five years after Rengstorf rejected the Dibelius-Weidinger thesis, David Schroeder wrote a dissertation in which he also denied any connection between the Christian *Haustafeln* and the non-Christian household codes. He argued that the originator of the *Haustafel* was Paul the Apostle. The occasion of the *Haustafel* was a problem which arose because of Paul's declaration of the equality of all persons in Christ (Galatians 3:28; 1 Corinthians 12:13; Romans 3:22; and Colossians 3:11). The appearance of ἐν κυρίῳ in the motivation statements, rather than τῷ κυρίῳ, is evidence of Paul's own hand. As for the form of the *Haustafel* admonitions, "Paul selected the pattern of the apodictic laws of Israel."[50] In seeking to account for the Jewish tone of the *Haustafel*, Schroeder does not refer to the Jewish background of Paul as one might expect, but traces it back to Jesus. As Crouch puts it: "Schroeder comes to the somewhat amazing conclusion that they [the

---

[47]Rengstorf, *Mann und Frau im Urchristentum*, p. 28.

[48]This argument really seems to go against the evidence. It ignores the fact that the stress in the Colossians-type *Haustafel* is upon the *subordinate* member. In 1 Peter 3:7 the exhortation to husbands to love their wives is conspicuous by its absence.

[49]Crouch, *Origin and Intention*, p. 25.

[50]*Ibid.*, p. 27. Lohse objects to this by declaring that the presence of the imperative form in the Colossian *Haustafel* rules out the apodictic law hypothesis.

oldest elements of the Haustafel] were originally formulated by Jesus and were passed on by Paul through the Apostolic tradition."[51]

Like Rengstorf and Schroeder, L. Goppelt also traces the beginning of Christian social ethics to a specifically Christian beginning. Although he recognizes that the *Haustafel* materials had absorbed a Hellenistic and Jewish ethos, its essential origin is Christian because it proceeds from Jesus as the Lord and because it assimilates the Jesus tradition.[52]

In spite of the weaknesses in the arguments of Rengstorf and Schroeder, they nevertheless draw attention to a distinctly Christian situation for the use of the *Haustafel* in primitive Christianity. It is highly unlikely that a code of behavior as well established as the Colossians-type *Haustafel* just happened to come on the scene. There must have been some important reason or reasons for such a paraenetic tradition to develop in the apostolic and sub-apostolic church.

Conclusion

Our examination of popular Hellenistic philosophy, Jewish ethical concerns, and specifically Christian circumstances indicates that all three of these categories are viable sources of influence on the Christian *Haustafel*. At the same time it must be said that no single one of them can account for all of the distinctive features of the New Testament *Haustafel*. It cannot be affirmed that the *Haustafel* is a specifically pre-Christian code (Dibelius, Weidinger, and Lohmeyer). The evidence seems to suggest a Jewish *Haustafel* genre but there is no way of reconstructing an original Jewish social code. It could perhaps be said that Stoic influence seems more present in the *Haustafel* in the Pastoral

---

[51]Ibid. The so-called "Scandinavian hypothesis," which posits that the Apostolic teaching stems from Jesus, who taught his disciples to memorize his sayings so that they could be transmitted in the Rabbinic fashion, has not received wide acceptance. For this hypothesis see H. Riesenfeld, *The Gospel Tradition and its Beginnings: A Study in the Limits of Formgeschichte* (London, 1957); and B. Gerhardsson, *Memory and Manuscript: Oral Tradition and Transmission in Early Christianity* (Lund-Copenhagen, 1964). For a critique of the Riesenfeld-Gerhardsson thesis see Morton Smith, "A Comparison of Early Christian and Rabbinic Tradition," *JBL* 82 (1963): 169-76.

[52]Leonhard Goppelt, "Jesus und die 'Haustafel' Tradition," in *Orientierung an Jesus: zur Theologie der Synoptiker*, für Josef Schmid (Frieburg, Basel, Wein: Herder, 1973), pp. 93-105.

Epistles and second century non-biblical Christian codes than in those of the Colossian type. However, the phrases "fitting" and "well-pleasing" in Colossians (3:18 and 20) may indicate Stoic influence there as well.

Just as was the case with the catalogues of vices and virtues, the basic issue is not the source from which the primitive church borrowed the lists of household duties. It simply used what had become its own in the process of culturization and assimilated and revised forms and content which met its own immediate needs. Obviously both Hellenism and Judaism provided some of these elements. They also provided ethical norms so widely accepted that they could be regarded as having ultimately come from God.[53] But they did not provide an actual pre-Christian literary source for the Christian codes. Our study of the form of the Colossian *Haustafel* in the beginning of this chapter points to the probability of an established *Haustafel* tradition. Our investigation of the source of the New Testament *Haustafel* seems to confirm the Rengstorf-Schroeder-Goppelt hypothesis that the tradition itself originated in the Christian community but was influenced by Hellenistic and Jewish concerns and modes of expression.

The crucial question is: what were the circumstances in the early church that made the paraenesis set forth in the *Haustafel* necessary? To make the question even more specific: what is the purpose of the *Haustafel* in the letter to the Colossians? To that question we now turn.

THE PURPOSE OF THE COLOSSIAN HAUSTAFEL

Wittingly or unwittingly, Jack T. Sanders has drawn attention to one of the most crucial problems concerning the purpose of the Colossian *Haustafel*. With regard to the catalogues of vices and virtues, Sanders declares that one of the major reasons why the writer refers to Christian behavior is to show his readers that such conduct marks off the Christian from the non-Christian.[54] The non-Christian does the evil things listed in Colossians 3:5-9 and the Christian does the good

---

[53]Both the "unwritten laws" of Hellenism and the "Noachian Commandments" of Judaism were considered to be of divine origin by both Jews and Christians. See *The Interpreters Dictionary of the Bible*, vol. 2, "Ethics in the N.T.," by W. D. Davies.

[54]Jack T. Sanders, *Ethics in the New Testament* (Philadelphia: Fortress Press, 1975), pp. 68-81.

things listed in 3:12-17 and the Colossian *Haustafel.* The problem is that there is little in the ethical instructions in Colossians that would distinguish them "from the popular morality in both Judaism and paganism in the Roman world."[55] Therefore he concludes:

> The *Haustafel* must, therefore, be seen as completely worthless for Christian ethics. Coming early into the post-Pauline tradition, they do not even serve a useful function for the authors of Colossians and Ephesians; for the *Haustafeln* cannot truly be guides (in spite of the attempt in 3:22) for helping to bring this life into harmony with the life beyond unless the life beyond is no different from the non-Christian world—something that both authors would hotly deny.[56]

Our investigation of the sources of the *Haustafel* confirms that the New Testament *Haustafeln* do not greatly differ from the ethical instructions of Stoicism or Judaism. But does this make them useless as Sanders asserts? An examination of other alternatives concerning the purpose of the Colossians' *Haustafel* will lead to a negative answer. Let us look at three of these alternatives.

Reminder of the Traditions Received in the Baptismal Catechism

In 1928 F. S. B. Gavin sought to show Jewish antecedents to the Christian sacraments. In a chapter on baptism he compared Jewish sources describing the rite of proselyte baptism with the early Christian sources (*The New Testament,* the *Didache,* and Hippolytus' *The Apostolic Tradition*) in which the rite of Christian baptism is described. He concluded that "all the salient elements and many details of the Christian usage may be found in, or explained by, Jewish practices."[57] One of those "elements" was the instruction of the candidate in the fundamental tenets and practices of the respective faiths. In Judaism the instruction was concerned primarily with "purity" and focused attention on the numerous prescriptions in the Priestly Code. Bishop Philip Carrington, whose work on the *Primitive Christian Catechism* we have

---

[55]Ibid., p. 73.

[56]Ibid., p. 75. See above, fn. 53.

[57]F. S. B. Gavin, *The Jewish Antecedents of the Christian Sacraments* (London: S.P.C.K., New York: MacMillan, 1928), p. 56. In 1909 Rabbi G. Klein published a work which sought to prove the existence of a catechism which Jewish missionaries used with Gentile converts to Judaism. (*Der älteste Christliche Katechismus und die Jüdische Propaganda-Literatur,* Berlin) See also W. O. E. Oesterly, *The Jewish Background of the Christian Liturgy* (Oxford: The Clarendon Press, 1925).

discussed above, built upon Gavin's work.[58] He concluded that many of the traditional materials in the New Testament come from the catechism used for the instruction of new converts before their baptism. Among those materials were the catalogue of vices and virtues and the *Haustafel*. If Carrington's hypothesis is true, the following purpose for the use of the *Haustafel* in Colossians would follow: The writer warns his readers against false traditions (2:8) and admonishes them to walk in the light of the received traditions (2:6, 7). Among those received traditions are the ones received about Christ (1:15-20 and 2:9, 10) and the paraenesis taught in the baptismal catechism. Just as converts to Judaism at the time of their (proselyte) baptism had been admonished not to walk in their former pagan ways but to be holy, so had the converts to the New Israel been admonished to do the same at the time of their baptism (3:7, 12).

Of course it is not at all certain that the *Haustafel* was a part of the baptismal instruction. I am inclined to agree with Crouch that it was not.[59] But the removal of the *Haustafel* from the catechism does not rule out the existence of such a catechism. It does seem to me (as previously argued) that the catalogue of vices and virtues may very well belong to a baptismal catechism. The phrases "put to death" (3:5), "put off" (3:9), and "put on" (3:10, 12) in a pericope clearly associated with baptism (2:12-3:4) points to the existence of a baptismal catechism. Whether or not the Haustafel was a part of a baptismal catechism does not alter likelihood that it was a part of the received paraenesis which the writer of Colossians (as well as other New Testament writers) regarded as significant and thus included it in the paraenetic section of the letter. Contrary to Sanders, in such a case the *Haustafel* would not be worthless.

---

[58] Pp. 92-103.

[59] Crouch, *Origin and Intention*, pp. 15-18. Because Carrington posits different recensions of the "code of subordination" (1 Clem. 1:3) (Peter B and James differ from Eph., Col., and Peter A), Crouch rejects the entire hypothesis. He admits that Carrington's thesis makes sense if Carrington's prior assumption that husbands, fathers, and masters constitute "the elders of the community in the primitive sense of the term" holds true (p. 17). I agree with Crouch that it does not hold true. Yet on pages 79 and 99, he cites (as sources for the *Haustafel*) passages from Philo and Tobit where such an assumption is affirmed.

Instructions for Continued Life in the World
(the Problem of the Delayed *Parousia*)

Circumstances have a great deal to do with both the content and motivation of ethical teaching. Eschatological enthusiasm was high in the early days of the primitive church. The Messiah had begun his kingly reign and would bring about the ultimate overthrow of the evil powers at his *Parousia* (1 Corinthians 15:20-28). That great day was expected during the generation of those then living (1 Corinthians 15:50-58, Mark 9:1, parallels, and 13:30, parallels). Albert Schweitzer was so impressed with the absoluteness of the ethical demands of the Sermon on the Mount that he regarded them as "interim ethics" before the ultimate coming of the kingdom.[60] In at least one instance the imminent expectation of the *Parousia* produced irresponsible behavior. Second Thessalonians was written to correct that situation.

The problem of the delayed *Parousia* forced the early church to think about continued existence in an unredeemed world. The church had always had some form of ethical instruction, but the concrete situations dealing with everyday life brought about the need for special ethical instruction dealing with those situations. How should one behave in the various social roles of everyday existence? He should certainly demonstrate himself to be a creature who lived in accordance with those things which were everywhere judged to be right and just. Such behavior, though universally recognized as right, was only possible "in the Lord." The *Haustafel* served the need for this kind of instruction well. In this case, Sander's judgment that the *Haustafeln* are "completely worthless for Christian ethics" is obviously wrong.

Of course, if the *Haustafel* was developed in order to deal with the problem of the delayed *Parousia*, it would mean that the New Testament use of the *Haustafel* did not come into existence until at least the second generation of Christians. This would preclude Paul's use of the *Haustafel* and would make Colossians a post-Pauline document. Is there another possible purpose for the use of the *Haustafel* in Colos-

---

[60]Albert Schweitzer, *The Quest for the Historical Jesus*, preface by F. C. Burkitt, trans. W. Montgomery (New York: Macmillan, 1964) p. 352. C. H. Dodd counters Schweitzer's argument in *The Parables of the Kingdom*, revised ed. (New York: Charles Scribner's Sons, 1961), pp. vii, 140-42. See also Davies, *Paul and Rabbinic Judaism*, p. 169. Sanders, *Ethics in the New Testament*, pp. 1-29 contains a good discussion of the problem of ethics and eschatology.

sians that would make the Pauline authorship of Colossians a viable option? I believe that there is.

A Call to Order in an Unruly Church

One of the special features about the Colossians-type *Haustafel* is that it places major emphasis on the duties of the subordinate members of the family and particularly on the duties of slaves. Above, we drew attention to Schroeder's conviction that the occasion for the *Haustafel* was Paul's proclamation that in Christ "there is neither Jew nor Greek, there is neither slave nor free, there is neither male nor female; for you are all one in Christ Jesus (Galatians 3:28)." The gospel must have been especially good news to slaves and women.

In Judaism women, slaves, and minors were not allowed to participate fully in Jewish worship.[61] The attitude of Rabbinic Judaism toward women is still an embarrassment to modern Judaism. C. G. Montefiore and H. Loewe write:

> No amount of apologetics can get over the implications of the daily blessing, which orthodox Judaism has still lacked the courage to remove from its official prayer book. 'Blessed art Thou, O Lord, our God, who has not made me a woman.'[62]

For Judaism the sign of the "age to come" was the coming of the Spirit on all flesh. Peter's Pentecostal sermon (Acts 2) proclaimed the presence of the great Day of Salvation by quoting Joel 2:28ff. "In the last days, says God, I will pour out of my Spirit on all flesh." Specifically mentioned as the recipients of the Spirit are the young, slaves, and women. "And they shall prophecy."

For every member of the redeemed community of the Last Days to be an agent of the Spirit was very "heady" teaching. For women and slaves it was especially so. It could and did become a threat to the orderliness of early Christian life and worship. Various forms of "gnostic" ideology made the problem even more acute. The Corinthian church is the most well-known example of disorder brought about by

---

[61]Herman L. Strack and Paul Billerbeck, *Kommentar zum Neuen Testament aus Talmud und Midrash*, 6 vols. (München: C. H. Beck'sche Verlagsbuchhandlung, 1926-1961), vol. 4, part 2 (1928), p. 727.

[62]C. G. Montefiore and H. Loewe, *A Rabbinic Anthology*, selected and arranged with comments and introduction, Meridian edition (Cleveland and New York, 1963; Philade'phia: The Jewish Publication Society of America, 1963), p. 507.

pneumatic enthusiasm. It was, no doubt, not an isolated case. In 1 Corinthians 14 Paul was just as much concerned about uncontrolled prophesying in the worship service as he was about excessive and disorderly glossalalia (1 Corinthians 14:29-33a). He especially drew attention to women as the occasion for much of the confusion (14:33b-36). They are not only admonished to keep silent but to be in subjection (ὑποτάσσεσθαι is the same verb present in the *Haustafel*) "as the law says." This latter phrase probably refers either to Genesis 3:16 or to an accepted tradition concerning the position of women. In the difficult but intriguing passage in 1 Corinthians 11:2-16, the church is commended for "holding fast to the traditions" (11:2). Then women are instructed to be veiled when they pray or prophesy in accordance with a divinely-arranged structure of subordination. The emphasis is on women's place at the bottom of the structure.

Slaves are not explicitly singled out for disorderly conduct in the worship service but they do receive special attention. They were clearly a threat to the order of the Christian community. First Corinthians 7, a chapter dealing primarily with problems concerning marriage, sets forth the same principle four times, namely, that a man should remain in the calling in which he was called (verses 17, 20, 24, 26). This is not an isolated rule just for the Corinthians. Paul asserts that he ordered it in all the churches (verse 17). The rule is applied to three groups: the circumcised, the uncircumcised, and slaves. Since the first two groups include everyone, the stress is apparently upon slaves.[63] As was previously noted (page 104), slaves receive the most attention in the *Haustafel* form. Slaves, it seems, were just as susceptible to the desire to be removed from the status of inferiority as women were. After all, did not the gospel announce that there were no distinctions in Christ? It stands to reason that slaves would earnestly hope that this new relationship would be present in the church and would be especially evident in the public worship service.

From all of this it readily can be seen that women and slaves were a primary source for the potential threat of disorder in the early Chris-

---

[63]Twenty-four words are used in admonishing the circumcized and uncircumcised and forty-four for the slaves. See S. S. Bartchy, *ΜΑΛΛΟΝ ΧΡΗΣΑΙ: First-Century Slavery and 1 Corinthians 7:21*, SBL Dissertation Series 11 (Missoula, Montana: Scholars Press, 1973), pp. 58-62 for a discussion about slaves in the Corinthian congregation.

tian communities.[64] It is understandable that these classes, which had been so oppressed and restricted by the power structures of an unredeemed society, would expect release from that condition in the community of the redeemed. Total liberation from the evil powers was expected at the *Parousia*, but they wanted it then and there.

Added to this desire for equality was a corresponding desire for complete freedom in every category. It was associated with "freedom in the Spirit." Some apparently believed that the New Age had come in its fullness and based their belief on ecstatic experience. They believed that they already possessed a resurrection mode of existence (1 Corinthians 15) and were already reigning (1 Corinthians 4:8). This set them free from all human relationships (1 Corinthians 7) so that they could eat what they pleased (1 Corinthians 8-10) and do what they pleased (1 Corinthians 5:1, 2; 6:12-20). All of this obviously brought about serious disorder in the church. Of all the groups in the church who would want to believe that the *eschaton* had fully come, slaves and women would be to the fore.

The message of liberation was a central part of the gospel message from the beginning. Life in the Spirit was a part of the common experience of the earliest community. According to Acts, glossalalia and ecstasy did not begin in the churches of the Gentile mission, but in Jerusalem at the very beginning. It is likely, therefore, that the desire for freedom and equality that was a major cause of disorder in the life of the church began at an early date in the life of the church. This would allow for a pattern of instruction dealing with this problem to develop into the shape of the *Haustafel* in Colossians.

Is there any evidence within the Colossian letter that the purpose of the *Haustafel* was to maintain order in a situation where pneumatic enthusiasm and the desire for freedom threatened church unity? There are four factors which could well point in that direction. One is the notoriously difficult phrase in 2:18 which the Revised Standard Version translates "taking his stand on visions."[65] Whoever the opponents who threatened the Colossians were, they were apparently involved in

---

[64]Children obviously were not much of a revolutionary threat. They are probably present in the *Haustafel* because of the influence of Jewish tradition.

[65]For a discussion of the difficulties in this phrase see Martin, *Colossians*, pp. 92-95.

some kind of ecstatic experience which gave them occasion for pride. A second factor is the gratitude which the writer expresses for the "order" (τάξις)[66] of the church and for the firmness of its faith in Christ (2:5). The concern of the author was that his readers *walk* in the light of the received Christology (2:6). Such a walk would be demonstrated by good order (2:16-4:6). The third factor is that the affirmation of the gospel that there are no distinctions in Christ (Galatians 3:28) is also present in Colossians 3:11. Women are not mentioned in the latter, but slaves are specifically designated. This may or may not indicate that slaves were more of a threat to the orderliness of the Colossian community than women. In any event, the presence of 3:11 shows that inclusivism was a significant part of the Christology and gospel received in Colossae and the *Haustafel* would be an important tradition for dealing with the problems of disorder that such inclusivism might bring. The last factor is that the *Haustafel* is located in the midst of exhortations that have to do with matters of public worship. If the admonitions to wives and husbands, children and fathers, and slaves and masters only have to do with the general duties of everyday life, they make a strange break in the paraenetic series. If, however, the *Haustafel* is a well-known tradition used in connection with church order, the paraenetic series is consistently directed toward the same concern.

From the beginning the church has lived in the tension between form and freedom. Excessive freedom led the later writers of the New Testament and the Apostolic Fathers to place great stress on church organization and correct doctrine. Paul, who more than any other New Testament writer proclaimed that the church is the Body of Christ in which every member is endowed with the Spirit for service in Christ's stead, was also much concerned about order. Whenever tension between form and freedom ceases to exist or one prevails at the expense of the other, the church is hindered in functioning as an effective agent for Christ in an unredeemed world.

---

[66]The word may have military meaning and refer to the writer's desire for the Colossians to resist the threatening heresy or it may refer to the well-ordered condition of the church over against the unruliness exhibited in such churches as Corinth (1 Cor. 14:40). The latter is the way in which Lohse interprets it and is probably correct.

SUMMARY AND CONCLUSION

In the first section of this chapter we sought to demonstrate the traditional character of Colossians 3:18-4:1. There we observed that certain formal features are present in all of the early Christian *Hausta-feln* and that these features were susceptible to as much adaptation as the writer regarded necessary for his purpose. Within the New Testament Colossians, Ephesians, and 1 Peter (all of which have been associated with baptismal materials) have the most highly structured form. Colossians has the most formally structured features of them all. In addition, the Colossian *Haustafel* appears in a context where it could be omitted without seriously hindering the flow of thought. Indeed, if the Colossian *Haustafel* dealt only with social household duties, it would seem out of place in the context. It has an ecclesiological function in the letter and occurs in a context dealing with public worship concerns. All of this points to the strong probability that Colossians 3:18-4:1 is traditional paraenesis which was already known by the writer and his readers.

As for the source of the Colossian *Haustafel*, it seems clear that both pre-Christian Jewish and Hellenistic ideas influenced its mode of expression, but there is no evidence of literary dependence on a pre-Christian code. It seems most likely that it originated within the Christian community.

The *Haustafel* may have become a part of the baptismal instruction of new converts, but it seems highly unlikely that it originated in a primitive Christian baptismal catechism. It may have been developed to give instructions for everyday living in the light of the delayed *Parousia*. But such a purpose would date it later than the Pauline period. In my opinion, Crouch is probably right in stating that the original purpose of the *Haustafel* was to "serve as a weapon against enthusiastic and heretical threats to the stability of both the church and the social order."[67]

Although I agree with Crouch's conclusion concerning the origin and purpose of the *Haustafel*, I am forced to disagree with him and with J. Sanders on the date of the origin of the *Haustafel*.[68] In seeking

---

[67]Crouch, *Origin and Intention*, pp. 146-51.

[68]See above, fn. 56.

to refute Alfred Seeberg's hypothesis that the *Haustafel* was a part of an early Christian catechism, he asks:

> Why do no *Haustafeln* appear in the earlier Pauline epistles which contain so much alleged catechetical material? . . . could we not logically expect some evidence of the existence of a *Haustafel* in the paraenetic sections of the Thessalonian correspondence and Romans? Indeed, the absence of a *Haustafel* from 1 Corinthians, where such a form would have been extremely appropriate, is inexplicable if we must assume that Paul was already familiar with the *Haustafel* schema.[69]

In response to those questions it should be replied that although Paul does not quote the *Haustafel* tradition in 1 Corinthians, he probably did have it in mind. He reminds the Corinthians of traditions which they had received which parallel the concerns of the *Haustafel*. He refers to a tradition concerning women and order in 1 Corinthians 11:2ff. and 1 Corinthians 14:33ff. There was no need to quote what they knew. He had only to remind them of the teaching.

Though debate over the purpose of Romans still continues, the conviction that it deals with actual conditions in the Roman congregation is not persuasive. The contents of Romans deals with the gospel as it relates to the general Jewish and Gentile Christian situation in all of the churches. The paraenesis in Romans is directed toward the mutuality of acceptance and brotherly love. Even the paraenesis on the state (13:1-7) is in the context of the love commandments and contributes to the issue of mutual acceptance and love. A code of subordination dealing with unruly congregations was not appropriate for the purpose of Romans; hence, the *Haustafel* is absent.

The absence of the *Haustafel* from the Thessalonian letters poses more of a problem. It indeed would have been a useful tradition to use in those letters. However, just as is the case in 1 Corinthians, Paul does remind them of the traditions in which they had been instructed (1 Thessalonians 4:1, 2; 2 Thessalonians 2:15; 3:6ff.). Except in a broad way, he does not refer to the content of those traditions because they already were familiar with it. It was enough for him simply to remind them of those traditions. One might also add that the Thessalonian letters were written quite early in Paul's Gentile mission. At that time the *Haustafel* may not as yet have become an influential code for dealing with disorder.

---

[69]Crouch, *Origin and Intention*, p. 15.

The facts are that inordinate freedom and enthusiasm were major problems in Paul's mission and ministry. The special focus which he gave on the inclusivism of the gospel would have made the slave and women issue a very real threat to the orderliness of the church both in worship and in social issues. Paul's insistence that Jewish Christians should not expect Gentile Christians to live Jewishly gave birth to an inclusivism that specially marked his development of the gospel in Romans and Galatians. The proclamation that in Christ there are no distinctions (Galatians 3:28; 1 Corinthians 12:12, 13; and Colossians 3:11) would understandably generate a longing for full acceptance in the church by slaves and women. The Colossians-type *Haustafel* was especially appropriate for dealing with that problem. Later, when the Jew-Gentile issue faded in the life of the church, the Colossians-type *Haustafel* was not as fitting and other forms of the *Haustafel* became more useful. In other words, a post-Pauline provenance for the Colossians-type *Haustafel* is less fitting than a Pauline provenance.

The Structure
of Colossians

INTRODUCTORY MATTERS

Before the structure of the letter to the Colossians can be considered, there are two matters which need attention. One of them belongs to the discussion of paraenetic materials and is, therefore, related to the concerns of chapters 3 and 4. However, it has a bearing on the structure of Colossians and should be considered separately from the vice and virtue catalogues and the *Haustafel*. It has to do with those brief and pithy admonitions which deal with a variety of general subjects and have become known as *topoi*.[1]

The Presence of *Topoi* in Colossians

There are four types of ethical instructions in Colossians. The first kind deals with the specific problems brought about by the presence of the false "philosophy" in Colossae. Colossians 2:16-3:4 belongs to this type. The second is the traditional paraenesis associated with the

---

[1] As far as I can discover the term was used to describe short independent teachings on general subjects in the Hellenistic ethical literature. David Bradley was one of the first to use the term in connection with Pauline paraenesis. He used it to designate "short, hard-hitting teachings on specific problems" which were the "common property" of itinerant preachers and teachers. "The Topos as a Form in the Pauline Paraenesis," *JBL* 72 (1953): 238-46.

baptismal use of the vice and virtue catalogues (3:5-14). The third is the traditional paraenesis associated with the *Haustafel* (3:18-4:1). The fourth consists of short pithy exhortations concerning general church life (3:15-17 and 4:2-6). It is significant to note that the *topoi* surround the *Haustafel* and hence locate the *Haustafel* in the context of instructions dealing with general church life in worship and society.

David Bradley examined the use of the *topoi* in both Hellenistic ethical literature (Isocrates, *To Demonicus* and Marcus Aurelius, *Meditations*) and in Jewish literature of the Hellenistic period (*Sirach* and the *Testaments of the XII Patriarchs*).[2] A summary of the characteristics of a *topos*, which he observed, include the following: They are self-contained units of teaching which have a loose and sometimes arbitrary connection with their contexts. Sometimes they are strung together with a catch-word (*Stichwort*), but usually there is no connection with the adjacent *topoi*. Normally they "consist of an aggregation of proverbs or other short teachings on the same topic."[3] Sometimes, but not always, they are bound together by a recurring word. They deal with a variety of general topics related to daily life.

A number of these terse sayings surround the *Haustafel* and bear the general characteristics of *topoi*. They consist of instructions on peace (3:15), teaching one another (3:16), thanksgiving (3:17), prayer (4:2-4), and conduct toward the "outsider" (4:5, 6). All of them are related to the general subject of church life and bear the marks of "stock" or stereotype admonitions dealing with common and recurring issues. They appear to have existed before the letter was written and were useful to the writer. As we shall point out further on, these *topoi* which enclose the *Haustafel* contribute to the ordered structure of the Colossian paraenesis.

Problems Related to Structural Analysis

The second intrductory matter which requires discussion is the complicated problem of dealing with a variety of meanings of the term "structural analysis" and with the variety of approaches to the process of making a structural analysis. "Structuralism" is a popular term in the discipline of biblical studies these days. It is a term which evokes

---

[2]Ibid.

[3]Ibid., p. 243.

emotional responses ranging across a spectrum from enthusiasm to disgust. The former response is oftentimes a reaction to the myopic and speculative tendencies which sometimes show up in form criticism. The latter reaction is usually based on the confusing explanations and esoteric jargon used by some "structuralists" in explaining what it is that they are doing.

One kind of structuralism originated in linguistics (Saussure) but was made dominant in anthropology through the influence of Lévi-Strauss. It has had a considerable influence on philosophy, psychology, sociology, and literary criticism. During the last decade it has gained increasing influence in the discipline of biblical studies in North America. A basic assumption of this kind of structuralism is that human thinking is basically binary and that the function of the human brain is to mediate opposites. The antimonies of hot-cold, death-life, good-evil are, therefore, not viewed as essential differences but as relational differences. The structuralist proceeds "in such a way that the opposition, rather than being an obstacle, serves to bring about integration."[4] He or she is more interested in human systems of communication than in the meaning of that which is communicated.

A corresponding assumption of structuralism is that historical concerns have no real value in discovering meaning. The task of the structuralist is to go beyond the surface meaning of the text to the deciphering of the basic code which underlies it. Since that code is related to the binary structure of human thinking which is essentially the same in all cultures and in all periods of history, historical considerations are not really important in the discovery of meaning. Neither of these assumptions is verifiable and the latter runs counter to all that we have sought to do in our investigation of the content, source, and purpose of the traditions used by the writer of Colossians. Perhaps as this approach to the understanding of the biblical text becomes clarified and refined, it will contribute an added dimension to the discipline of biblical studies. It is not just skepticism and lack of expertise that keeps me from attempting this kind of a structural analysis. It is the awareness that the non-historical objective of structuralism almost

---

[4]R. Spivey quoting Gunter Schiwy (*Structuralism and Christianity*) in "Structuralism and Biblical Studies: The Uninvited Guest," Int. 28 (1974): 141.

completely differs from the objective of this investigation of the use of traditional materials in Colossians.

There are other kinds of structural analyses that can be more helpful for our purpose. One of them is a structural analysis of the epistolary form of Colossians which will enable us to see its shape from the perspective of its own literary genre. Another is a content or thematic analysis which will enable us to see the theological concerns of the writer and how he uses the traditional materials in developing those concerns. It is to these two tasks that we now turn.

AN EPISTOLARY ANAYLSIS OF THE LETTER TO THE COLOSSIANS

Two literary genres dominate the literature of the New Testament: gospel and epistle. Twenty of the twenty-seven New Testament documents purport to be letters and two of the seven that do not profess to be letters contain materials purporting to be letters (Acts 15:23-29; 23:26-30, and Revelation 2:1-3:22). Until recently most of the scholarly research on the formal qualities of New Testament literature concentrated on the Gospel genre. However, during the last decade the importance of the epistolary genre has been increasingly recognized. This is witnessed by the formation in 1970 of a continuing working seminar on the Form and Function of the Pauline Letter in the professional Society of Biblical Literature and a spate of articles on the New Testament letter-form in various scholarly journals.[5]

---

[5]Gordon J. Bahr, "Paul and Letter Writing in the First Century," *CBQ* 28 (1966): 465-77, and "The Subscriptions in the Pauline Letters." *JBL* 87 (1968): 27-41. William G.Doty, "The Classification of Epistolary Literature," *CBQ* 31 (1969): 183-99. Fred O. Francis, The Form and Function of the Opening and Closing Paragraphs of James and 1 John," *ZNTW* 61 (1970): 110-26. Robert W. Funk, *Language, Hermeneutics, and Word of God* (New York: Harper and Row, 1966), pp. 250-74 and "The Apostolic Parousia: Form and Significance" in *Christian History and Interpretation: Studies Presented to John Knox*, ed. William R.Farmer, C. F. D. Moule, and R. R. Niebuhr (Cambridge: University Press, 1967), pp. 249-68. Robert Jewett, "The Form and Function of the Homiletic Benediction," *ATR* 51 (1969): 18-34, and "The Epistolary Thanksgiving and the Integrity of Philippians," *NovT* 12 (1970): 40-53. Terrence Y. Mullins, "Disclosure: A Literary Form in the New Testament," *NovT* 7 (1964): 44-50; "Greeting as a New Testament Form," *JBL* 87 (1968): 418-26; "Formulas in the New Testament Epistles," *JBL* 91 (1972): 380-90; "Visit Talk in the New Testament Letters," *CBQ* 35 (1973): 350-58. Peter Thomas O'Brien, "Thanksgiving and the Gospel in Paul," *NTS* 21 (1974): 144-55, and *Introductory Thanksgivings in the Letters of Paul*,

Although significant advances have been made in the investigation of the formal dimensions of New Testament letter writing, the discipline of epistolary genre criticism has not reached the stage of refinement and sophistication attained by gospel genre criticism. Seven years ago William Doty noted that "no inclusive presentation of the epistolary literature of late Hellenism and primitive Christianity" had been made.[6] His book entitled *Letters in Primitive Christianity* attempted to fill that need. Nevertheless, he regarded his study to be merely "projecting some starting points" which were "intended to provoke further reflection and refinement."[7] Terminological difficulties still hinder epistolary research. Terms such as "form," "structure," "type," and "genre" tend to overlap and result in imprecision. Philosophical differences about the nature of language (particularly with reference to the relationship of form with content) and recent developments in linguistics, structuralism, and rhetorical criticism have added to the unsettled state of epistolary investigation. Difficulties are to be expected in any fresh approach to the literary analysis of biblical literature. The working out of the problems just mentioned and others that will come into view is bound to increase our understanding of the ancient biblical documents. Indeed, some important conclusions about the New Testament letters in general and the Pauline letters in particular can be drawn. Although the degree to which Paul's Jewish and Hellenistic background influenced the content and meaning of his letters is still very much debated, it seems clear that the form of his letters came out of the matrix of the Greco-Roman letter writing tradition. It is also clear that Paul used those traditions creatively[8] and that the Pauline

---

Supplements to Novum Testamentum 49 (Leiden: E. J. Brill, 1977). Jack T. Sanders, "The Transition from Opening Epistolary Thanksgiving to Body in the Letters of the Pauline Corpus," *JBL* 81 (1962): 348-62. Paul Schubert, "Form and Function of the Pauline Letter," *JR* 19 (1939): 365-77. John L. White, "Introductory Formulae in the Body of the Pauline Letter," *JBL* 90 (1971): pp. 91-94.

[6]William G. Doty, *Letters in Primitive Christianity* (Englewood Cliffs, N.J.: Prentice-Hall, 1972), p. ix.

[7]Ibid., p. 80.

[8]The degree of his creativity is unknown because we do not possess any church letters earlier than Paul's. Terrence Mullins, for example, has shown that the "visit talk" in Paul's letters is not as original as Funk had supposed. "Visit Talk in the Pauline Letters," pp. 350ff. Funk, "The Apostolic *Parousia*," pp. 249ff.

letter tradition in turn profoundly influenced Christian letter writing through the succeeding centuries.

Perhaps the most important result of Pauline epistolary research is the recognition that Paul's letters are not the informal, spur of the moment, somewhat chaotic dispatches that Adolf Deissmann taught us to expect.[9] Not only do they follow the basic structure of the late Hellenistic letter form, but the basic elements of the letter (including the more lengthy body of the letter) are much more formally structured than was previously seen. Although each of Paul's letters were related to some concrete historical situation, they should not be regarded as informal, impromptu writings but rather as substitutes for Paul's personal apostolic presence and his authoritative word to the churches for which he regarded himself responsible. They were letters which would be read aloud to the assembled congregations at services of worship. Such an understanding of the Pauline letters will obviously have a profound effect on their interpretation.

In making an epistolary analysis of Colossians I am keenly aware of two factors: (1) I shall be sailing (so to speak) on a largely uncharted sea. The importance of formal epistolary analysis has been recognized, but few analyses have been made of a complete Pauline letter. What little has been done has been limited to the undisputed letters of Paul (to which Colossians certainly does not belong) and, as a rule, only segments of a letter have been analyzed.[10] (2) Prejudgment is a powerful influence even in the use of a seemingly "objective" literary method. Let me illustrate this by drawing attention to some remarks of Doty about the genre of epistolary literature:

> The importance of understanding what sort of form may have been natural to Paul is manifold: (a) We are provided with a more or less standard pattern

---

[9]Adolf Deissmann, *Bible Studies*, trans. A. Grieve (Edinburgh: T.&T. Clark, 1901), pp. 3-59.

[10]An exception to this with regards to Colossians is Lohse's treatment of the thanksgiving section. *Colossians*, pp. 12-14. The rest of the commentary makes only brief remarks relative to epistolary form analysis. Recently, Franz Zeilinger made a formal thematic structural analysis of Colossians in which he comments briefly on the introduction and conclusion of the letter. *Der Erstgeborene der Schöpfung: Untersuchungen Formalstruktur und Theologie des Kolosserbriefes* (Wien: Verlag Herder, 1974), pp. 33-38, 71-72. He is concerned primarily with the content, structure, and theology of the letter. Paul Lamarche also makes a brief structural analysis of the letter in "Structure de l'épître aux Colossiens," *Biblica* 56 (1975): 453-63.

according to which Paul intended to organize his writing (sequence analysis). (b) This is of great importance with regard to those letters such as 1 and 2 Corinthians, or Philippians, which have been composed of several letters or have been rearranged in the process of being collected and copied. (c) Hence formal analysis is of importance for judging questions of authenticity: we have a sense of what *should* have been included in a genuine Pauline letter as well as noting how the pseudo-Pauline letters do or do not imitate the Pauline form.[11]

It seems to me that Doty's comment on point (a) is well-taken. The general implication of points (b) and (c) that epistolary genre criticism can assist in making judgments about the integrity and authenticity of the Pauline letters is also valid. But as the wording of these points (b and c) indicate, certain prejudgments are already present and these pre-understandings become evident in his handling of the epistolary data in the relevant epistles (see footnote 11).

In general the Pauline letter-form consists of the following structural elements: (1) salutation, (2) thanksgiving, (3) body, (4) paraenesis, and (5) closing items.[12] I shall treat each element by discussing its basic features and then analyzing the segment of Colossians that more closely relates to those features.

---

[11]William G. Doty, *Contemporary New Testament Interpretation* (Englewood Cliffs, N.J.: Prentice-Hall, 1972), p. 144. Like Doty (see Doty's chart on p. 43 in his *Letters in Primitive Christianity*), Funk and White assume that Philippians consists of fragments of more than one letter. They consequently leave chapter three out of their analysis of the letter-body. Funk, *Language, Hermeneutic, and the Word of God*, p. 272. John L. White, *The Form and Function of the Body of the Greek Letter: A Study of the Letter-Body in the Non-literary Papyri and in Paul the Apostle*, 2nd ed. corrected, Society of Biblical Literature Dissertation Series (Ann Arbor: Scholars Press, 1972), p. 75. Jewett, on the other hand, demonstrated the integrity of Philippians by an epistolary analysis of the thanksgiving section. "Epistolary Thanksgiving and the Integrity of Philippians," pp. 40-53.

With respect to the problem of authenticity, Doty assumes that Colossians and Ephesians are post-Pauline. In *Letters in Primitive Christianity*, p. 46, fn. 60, he notes that Paul habitually included statements of trust concerning his letter carriers. Since both Ephesians and Colossians have similar statements of trust, he suggests that the authors of those two letters were consciously imitating Paul.

[12]This structure is based primarily on Funk's observations, *Language, Hermeneutic, and the Word of God*, p. 270, which in turn is followed by White, *Form and Function of the Body of the Greek Letter*, p. 45, and Doty, *Contemporary New Testament Interpretation*, pp. 27-42.

The Salutation

Basic Features. It has been generally recognized that the initial salutation element contains epistolographic features that are both Jewish and Greco-Roman. The standard Greek formula "Writer to Addressee, Greetings!" is modified by characteristics common to Jewish letters. The latter tended to elaborate the writer's name with a self description and embellish the addressee with further description. M. Luther Stirewalt, Jr. suggests that:

> The naming of multiple senders and recipients is a characteristic of official correspondence especially in Jewish communities. . . . The multiple senders stood ready to witness both to the fact that a letter had been written and to the content of the message. The multiple recipients stood ready to witness both to the fact that the letter had been officially received and read, and to its content.[13]

Another Jewish feature was the tendency to give a double greeting, one of which was the greeting *shalom!*[14] Some have suggested that Paul deliberately coupled χάρις (linguistically related to the Greek greeting χάρειν) with εἰρήνη (parallel to the Jewish *shalom*). The Apocalypse of Baruch (78:2) illustrates both of these Jewish traits: "Baruch the son of Neriah to the brethren carried into captivity: Mercy and Peace!"

The Salutation in Colossians (1:1, 2). The features mentioned above are manifestly present in the opening two verses of Colossians. Paul describes himself as an "apostle of Jesus Christ through the will of God." The fact that identical descriptions are found in 2 Corinthians (widely thought to be a composite letter) and Ephesians (believed by many to be deutero-Pauline) may point to the non-Pauline authorship of Colossians. But such meager evidence is not conclusive. Surely the situations implied by both 2 Corinthians and Colossians would require a statement of Paul's apostolic right to address those communities. The addition of "Timothy the brother" in conjunction with Paul may point to the official character of the letter in accordance with Stirewalt's suggestion noted above. Whether or not Timothy had any personal

---

[13]M. L. Stirewalt, "Paul's Evaluation of Letter Writing" in *Search the Scriptures*, Festschrift for R. T. Stamm, ed. J. M. Meyers and others (Leiden: E.J. Brill, 1969) pp. 179-96.

[14]It is interesting to observe that two of the letters in the N.T. which are professedly written by Jews follow the Greek pattern in the greeting (Acts 15:23 and James 1:1).

connection with the Colossian church cannot be known for certain. In any event he was a well-known and trusted Christian leader who could testify to the validity of the Gospel which Paul preached (note Colossians 1:5 and 23) and of the traditions which the latter cites in his letter. The description of the Colossians as "saints and faithful brethren in Christ" is not so much a description of their religious condition as it is the use of Old Testament designations for the people of God placed in the new eschatological context ("in Christ"). Here as in 1 Corinthians the description of the recipients has more to do with status than experience. Such a description also fulfills the Greek epistolary function of expressing *philophronesis* (the friendly relationship).

The Thanksgiving

Basic Features. The most thoroughly examined element of the Pauline letter-form is the thanksgiving section. This is due largely to Paul Schubert's very influential monograph on *The Form and Function of the Pauline Thanksgivings.*[15] Schubert noted that two forms of what he called the εὐχαριστία (thanksgiving) period regularly followed the salutation in the Pauline letters. The primary form begins with the phrase εὐχαριστῶ τῷ θεῷ followed by from one to three participial phrases, which in turn were followed by a clause subordinate to the participles. The secondary form also begins with the εὐχαριστῶ phrase but is followed by a ὅτι clause and another clause subordinate to the ὅτι clause and introduced by ὥστε. Sometimes the εὐχαριστῶ phrase is replaced by εὐλογητὸς ὁ θεός.[16] Schubert demonstrated that the thanksgiving periods reflect the Hellenistic epistolary style. The writer thanks the gods and then gives reasons for the thanksgiving (usually because the gods have delivered the writer or the recipients from some calamity).[17] The Pauline thanksgiving follows the Hellenistic structure but usually modifies the reason for the thanksgiving. The reason is

---

[15] *Beihefte zur Zeitschriit für die neutestamentliche Wissenschaft* 20 (1939). In the field of epistolary research no work is referred to more than this one. P. T. O'Brien, *Introductory Thanksgivings in the Letters of Paul* (Leiden: E. J. Brill, 1977) seeks to add to Schubert's research concerning the function of the Pauline thanksgivings by noting that besides the epistolary function of indicating the main themes of the letter, the Pauline thanksgivings also have pastoral, didactic, and paraenetic functions.

[16] Ibid., pp. 35ff.

[17] Ibid., pp. 17, 24-26.

nearly always because of the faithfulness or good state of the congregation being addressed.[18]

While Schubert has shown that the thanksgiving periods reflect Hellenistic epistolary style, James M. Robinson has demonstrated that they also mirror primitive Christian liturgical style and are related to the Jewish *hodayoth* (thanksgivings) and *berachoth* (blessings) formulae.[19] Béda Rigaux thinks that the Pauline thanksgivings are a carry-over from Paul's preaching practices. This may explain why they not only fulfill the function of the thanksgiving in the epistolary sense but also tend to announce the basic themes of the letter.[20] In any event, the significant contribution of Robinson is that it places the Pauline letter in a liturgical situation. This has important hermeneutical implications. It shows that the Pauline letters are not just the conveyors of information, warnings, admonitions, and requests. They are religious documents dealing with the warp and woof of the nature and mission of the church.

Jack T. Sanders has furthered Schubert's work by dealing with the closing of the thanksgiving period. Schubert was aware that he had not clearly worked out the ending of the thanksgiving.[21] Since Sanders' observations are related to an especially difficult problem in making an epistolary analysis of Colossians, I shall fully quote a summarizing paragraph (including a footnote) from his article.

---

[18]In 2 Corinthians 1:3ff. the reason is parallel to the general Hellenistic practice of thanking God for deliverance from calamity.

[19]James M. Robinson, "The Historicality of Biblical Language," in *The Old Testament and Christian Faith*, ed. B. W. Anderson (New York: Harper & Row, 1963), pp. 132, 146, 149 (fn. 29). A more exhaustive treatment is found in "Die Hodajot-Formel in Gebet und Hymnus des Frühchristentums," in *Apophoreta*, Festschrift für Ernst Haenchen, ed. W. Eltester (Berlin: Alfred Topelmann, 1964), pp. 194-235. Fred O. Francis also notes that the opening paragraphs of the N.T. letters announce the themes of the letters. "Form and Function of Opening and Closing Paragraphs," pp. 110-26.

[20]Béda Rigaux, *Letters of St. Paul*, Contemporary Studies, trans. Stephen Yonick (New York: Herder & Herder, 1968), p. 122.

[21]He wrote: "In some cases, however, it is not easy to say where the thanksgivings terminate. In some cases one becomes aware that the thanksgiving has come to a close when one suddenly finds himself 'in mediis rebus of the letter.'" *Form and Function of the Pauline Thanksgivings*, Beihefte zur Zeitschrift für neutestamentliche Wissenschaft 20 (Berlin: Topelmann, 1939), p. 4.

Thus the end of most of the εὐχαριστῶ periods has been formally defined. This has been done in two ways: first, by showing that a formula of injunction regularly follows the opening epistolary thanksgivings (εὐχαριστῶ period) and introduces the body of the letter; and second, by pointing to the closing forms of the periods themselves, which forms replace the traditional *beracha* at the close of the prayer as the thanksgiving replaces it at the opening. These forms, either liturgical units or forms related to liturgical units[18] have been the doxology (1 Tim. 1:17; Phil. 1:11; Eph. 1:14; 1 Pet. 1:7), a surrogate for the *beracha* (1 Cor. 1:9; 2 Thess. 3:3), and another form showing a somewhat looser relationship to the *beracha* (1 Thess. 3:11f.; 2 Thess. 2:16). As was also seen, 2 Thess. 1:12 and Philm. 7 give other evidence of the necessity to employ in some way a liturgical unit at the close of the epistolary thanksgiving—the one by recalling the greeting, the other by recalling the thanksgiving.

[Footnote 18] That a liturgical ending is not more prominent at the end of the prayers (although Paul occasionally uses a doxology to close a unit within a letter; cf. Rom. 11:36; Gal. 1:5) may be explained by the fact that the prayer itself serves as the introduction, the beginning of the letter. Thus the closing characteristics of the prayer tend to be diminished so that the prayer may move easily into the body of the letter.[22]

To summarize: Sanders affirms that the end of the epistolary thanksgiving is marked by (1) a formula of injunction that immediately succeeds the opening thanksgiving period and (2) the presence of liturgical materials. Sometimes the prayer element of the thanksgiving serves as the introduction to the body of the letter.

The basic features of a Pauline epistolary thanksgiving, then, are the εὐχαριστῶ formula or its surrogate, intercession, and a liturgical conclusion. It shows that the letter belongs to the worshiping life of the church and serves to "telegraph" the main themes of the letter.

The Thanksgiving in Colossians (1:3-23). All three of the basic features of the Pauline epistolary thanksgiving are present in Colossians: the statement (1:3-8), the intercession (1:9-11), and the liturgical closing (1:12-23).

The εὐχαριστῶ Statement (1:3-8). The structure of the εὐχαριστῶ statement is as follows:

εὐχαριστοῦμεν τῷ θεῷ. . .	3a
. . . προσευχόμενοι	3b
ἀκούσαντες τὴν πίστιν* . . . καὶ τὴν ἀγάπην*	4

---

[22]J. T. Sanders, "The Transition from Opening Epistolary Thanksgiving to Body in the Letters of the Pauline Corpus," *JBL* 8 (1962): 361.

$$
\begin{array}{ll}
\text{διὰ τὴν ἐλπίδα*} \ldots & \text{5a} \\
\text{ἥν προηκούσατε} \ldots & \text{5b} \\
\text{καθὼς καὶ ἐν παντὶ τῷ κόσμῳ} \ldots & \text{6b} \\
\text{καθὼς καὶ ἐν ὑμῖν.} \ldots & \text{6c} \\
\text{καθὼς ἐμάθετε ἀπὸ 'Επαφρᾶ} & \text{7a}[23]
\end{array}
$$

In the main, the εὐχαριστῶ statement (opening of the thanksgiving) agrees with the primary form noted by Schubert. The verb (εὐχαριστῶ) is in the plural rather than the singular because of the multiple-writer phrase in the salutation. There are two participial phrases (3b, 4). The subordinate clause is in the form of a prepositional phrase rather than the full verb clause noted by Schubert.

Two other formal features stand out in the εὐχαριστῶ statement. The first is the presence of the well-known triad of faith, hope, and love. It is difficult to know whether this formulation was the creation of Paul or was a fixed type of phraseology already known to him. The triad occurs in 1 Corinthians 13:13 in a passage that seems to have been composed prior to 1 Corinthians and used by him because of its appropriateness to the context dealing with spiritual gifts. Lohse notes that

> 1 Thessalonians 5:8 joins the triad with a quote from Isaiah 59:17, "put on the breastplate of faith and love, and for a helmet the hope of salvation."... The scriptural passage has only two objects, breastplate and helmet; if the three concepts of faith, hope, and love are nevertheless brought into connection with them, obviously this triad was already a fixed expression.[24]

The second formal feature is the presence of the triple καθώς clauses. These clauses stress that the Colossians as well as "all the world" (6b) had heard the gospel. The gospel which is called "the word of truth" (5b) is both dynamic (καρποφορούμενον καὶ αὐξανόμενον) and the source of the knowledge of the hope that was laid up for them in the heavens (5a). The εὐχαριστῶ statement, then, not only gives the reason for the thanksgiving to God but also serves to announce "the epistolary situation" as Schubert called it. The basis of the hope and love of the Colossians is the hope already laid up for them in the heavens. That hope is the heart of the gospel. The letter will stress

---

[23]Lohse makes a similar but not identical structural analysis. *Colossians*, p. 14. Asterisks draw attention to the triad of faith, hope, and love.

[24]Ibid., p. 16.

the completeness and finality of Christ's work (1:15-20; 2:9-15) as the guarantee of that hope. By his death he has already triumphed over the "rulers" and the "powers" (1:20; 2:13-15) so that the Colossians do not need to venerate (or placate) them (2:18). The decisiveness and totality of Christ's reconciling work is declared in the gospel and disclosed in the traditions which they had been taught. It is this truth which is power-laden and in which they must walk (2:6, 7). They must not conduct themselves in accordance with the traditions which are according to men and the elemental spirits (2:6-8b) but those which are according to Christ (2:8; 3:1-4:6).

The Intercession (1:9-11). In the Greco-Roman letter the thanksgiving was usually for deliverance from some kind of disaster and the prayer was often some kind of health-wish for the recipient. The opening of Colossians, like many of the Pauline thanksgiving periods, transforms the Greco-Roman form and gives thanks for the good condition of the church and prays for the continuance of that condition.

The following is an analysis of the structure of the intercession segment:

9a gives the reason for the intercession.
  Διά τοῦτο . . . οὐ παυόμεθα ὑπὲρ ὑμῶν
  προσευχόμενοι

9b gives the contents of the intercession.
  ἵνα πληρωθῆτε τὴν ἐπίγνωσιν τοῦ θελήματος

10, 11 give the reason for the contents of the prayer.
  περιπατῆσαι ἀξίως τοῦ κυρίου . . .
      εἰς πᾶσαν ἀρεσκείαν
      ἐν παντὶ ἔργῳ ἀγαθῷ
    καρποφοροῦντες . . . τῇ ἐπιγνώσει τοῦ θεοῦ
    ἐν πάσῃ δυνάμει δυναμούμενοι
      κατὰ τὸ κράτος τῆς δόξης αὐτοῦ
      εἰς πᾶσαν ὑπομονὴν . . .
      μετὰ χαρᾶς

There are three formal features which stand out in the intercession:

First, the reason for the intercession is identical with the reason for the thanksgiving. The διὰ τὴν ἐλπίδα of 5a is recapitulated in the διὰ τοῦτο of 9a.

Second, several words and phrases in the thanksgiving statements are repeated in the intercession.

Intercession (1:9-11)	Thanksgiving (1:3-8)
ἀφ᾽ ἧς ἡμέρας (9a)	ἀφ᾽ ἧς ἡμέρας (6b)
ἠκούσαμεν (9a)	ἀκούσαντες (4)
ἐπίγνωσιν (9b) ἐπιγνώσει (10)	ἐπέγνωτε (6c)
καρποφοροῦντες καὶ	καρποφορούμενον καὶ
αὐξανόμενοι (10)	αὐξανόμενον (6b)

Third, there is an emphasis on "all" (πᾶς) in the intercession.

ἐν πάσῃ σοφιᾳ καὶ συνέσει   9b
    εἰς πᾶσαν ἀρεσκείαν   10a
ἐν παντὶ ἔργῳ ἀγαθῷ   10b
ἐν πάσῃ δυνάμει   11a
    εἰς πᾶσαν ὑπομονὴν καὶ μακροθυμίαν   11b

Another factor to observe is that the intercession (as well as the thanksgiving statement) "telegraphs" the main themes of the epistle. The content of the prayer is that the Colossians might be filled with the knowledge of God's will in all spiritual wisdom and understanding (9b). The reason for that content is that they might walk worthily of the Lord (10, 11). The two major themes of Colossians are a concern for an understanding of that which God has done in Christ (as set forth in the gospel and the received traditions) and a lifestyle befitting the people of God. Christology and paraenesis are the two fundamental matters around which the entire letter is centered.

The Liturgical Closing (1:12-23). The most difficult part of making an analysis of the thanksgiving section of the Colossian letter is discerning its closing. The Revised Standard Version concludes it with verse 14. The American Standard Version concludes it with verse 23. Franz Zeilinger, who is more concerned with the thematic structure of Colossians than with its epistolary structure, ends the thanksgiving section at verse 11.[25] Peter O'Brien, contrary to the position argued on pages 13-23 above, argues the the participle εὐχαριστοῦντες in verse 12 belongs with the three participles καρποφοροῦντες, αὐξανόμενοι, and δυναμούμενοι in verses 10 and 11 and defines "more precisely what it

---

[25] *Der Erstgeborne der Schöpfung*, pp. 34-37.

means 'to walk worthily of the Lord.' "[26] He consequently ends the thanksgiving section at verse 14 and admits that "It does not have a well-rounded and clear-cut climax, but passes imperceptibly from the form of a prayer to that of a creed or hymn."[27] Although he recognizes that an impressive number of liturgical phrases are present in verses 12-14, he formally disassociates this pericope from 1:15-20 which is also highly liturgical in style and form. He makes no attempt to explain how the latter relates to the preceding or succeeding context.

As was mentioned above, James M. Robinson sought to demonstrate the liturgical background of the epistolary thanksgiving by tracing the antecedent of the εὐχαριστῶ and εὐλογητός phrases in the New Testament thanksgiving periods to the Jewish prayer forms known as the *hodayoth* and the *berachoth*. He noted that the introduction of Christian content into Jewish blessings became a problem for Judaism. Consequently, " 'Normative' Judaism tended increasingly to prefer Berachoth to Hodayoth" and "Primitive Christianity increasingly preferred Hodayoth."[28]

Since it was the Jewish custom to begin and end a prayer with a *beracha*, it is to be expected that a *beracha* or some liturgical equivalent would close the epistolary thanksgivings. Jack T. Sanders built upon this expectation and observed that the thanksgiving periods in the New Testament letters end with doxologies or some other substitute for the *beracha*.[29] In addition he noted that immediately preceding the body-opening formula of a letter a prominent "eschatological climax" is present in several Pauline letters.[30]

There are, then, the following characteristics of the epistolary thanksgiving closing: (1) a doxology or some substitute liturgical form and (2) a prominent eschatological climax. The latter is not present in all of the Pauline letters but it is present in Colossians. One might say that both features are extraordinarily present because of the unusual length of the thanksgiving closing.

---

[26]P. T. O'Brien, *Introductory Thanksgiving in the Letters of Paul*, Supplements to Novum Testamentum, vol. 49 (Leiden: E. J. Brill, 1977), p. 73.

[27]Ibid., p. 75.

[28]Robinson, "The Historicality of Biblical Language," p. 132.

[29]Sanders, "Transition from Thanksgiving to Body," p. 357ff.

[30]Ibid., p. 355.

The Liturgical Character. Several scholars have noticed that Colossians 1:12-14 does not belong with the intercession segment (9-11). R. P. Martin asserts that "we should regard verse 12 as beginning a new section, with the Greek participle (rendered *giving thanks*) having the force of an imperative mood."[31] On pages 12-19 above I argued for the traditional character of these verses. The opening εὐχαριστοῦντες points to the confessional character of the unit, the change of pronouns and the style and language strongly suggest that the writer was using an outside source, and the manner in which the concepts are related to the exodus motif and the sacrament of baptism are all indicators of the probable liturgical background of the passage. This conclusion receives further support from the literary form of the pericope. The phrase εὐχαριστοῦντες τῷ (verse 12) . . . ὅς (verse 13) is very closely related to the *beracha* which ends the Jewish prayer. Εὐλογητὸς ὁ θεός, ὅς is a Greek translation of the Old Testament and Jewish *barukh YHWH 'asher* (blessed is Yahweh, who . . .). In Colossians the εὐλογητὸς (*beracha*) is replaced by εὐχαριστοῦντες (*hodaya*) in accordance with the primitive Christian preference noted above. The rest of the phrase follows the *beracha* form. Thus the liturgical *beracha* formula which ends Jewish prayers also follows the intercession in Colossians.

We have already observed the hymnic character of Colossians 1:15-20. Its hymnic nature and liturgical setting has long been recognized. Questions about the source of the hymn continue to linger but the fact that it belongs in the milieu of the public worship of the primitive church is rarely doubted. The entire passage from verses 12-20 abounds with liturgical phraseology.

The Eschatological Character. In many of the Pauline letters the thanksgiving is marked by striking eschatological language. Colossians is no exception. Here the emphasis is on the "already" aspect of eschatology in the liturgical materials and upon the "not yet" aspect in the application of the liturgical materials. In the *beracha* formula of 1:12-14 the thanksgiving (or eulogy) is given to the God who has already effected salvation and redemption in Christ. In the Christ-hymn the central stress is upon protology and Christ is celebrated as the Creator and Sustainer of all things. This protological emphasis

---

[31]R. P. Martin, *Colossians*, p. 53.

serves as the springboard for an eschatological climax. The Creator (protology) of all things is also the "firstborn from the dead" and the Reconciler of all things (eschatology). If Eduard Schweizer is right that the words "making peace by the blood of his cross" and "through him whether things upon the earth or in heaven" are redactions to the hymn,[32] then obviously the writer chose to emphasize the "already" aspect of Christ's eschatological work. That becomes unmistakably clear in the application of the hymn to the readers. "And *you* . . . he has *now* reconciled in the body of his flesh through death to present you holy . . . before him, if you remain in the faith . . . not moved from the hope of the gospel which you heard. . ." (1:21-23).[33]

If liturgical and eschatological features are marks of the thanksgiving closing, Colossians 1:12-23 readily fulfills those qualifications.

Summary. The epistolary thanksgiving in Colossians consists of three parts. The first is the εὐχαριστῶ statement (1:3-8), which is structurally patterned after the Hellenistic epistolary form and is kin to the Jewish *hodayoth*. It discloses the main theme of the letter. The second is the intercession segment (1:9-11), which is structurally related to the Greek epistolary form and lexically related to the εὐχαριστῶ statement. It functions to "telegraph" the main themes of the letter. In content it is a prayer for the Colossians to be filled with a knowledge of God's will so that they might walk worthily of the Lord. The confessional and paraenetic traditions which underlie the body of the letter are especially fitting for the fulfillment of the goal of this prayer. The third part is the thanksgiving closing (1:12-23). This is the lengthiest segment of the period and is liturgically related to the closing *beracha* of the public Jewish prayers. It consists of traditional confessional and hymnic materials and is marked by an eschatological emphasis that is applied to the readers. The unusual length of the closing is due to the traditional materials used and to the historical situation of the letter.

The Body of the Letter

John Lee White writes:

> I am of the opinion . . . that we have not adequately delineated the body of the Pauline letters. Though we have established some criteria for the formal

---

[32]E. Schweizer, "The Church as the Missionary Body of Christ," pp. 6-7.

[33]It is significant to observe that in these verses we have the third incidence of the thanksgiving period "headlining" the main themes of the letter.

opening, and Funk has made a rather thorough analysis of the body-closing, we still do not know how the theological argument (the "body-middle") is formally conceived.[34] The body of the letter is less sterotyped than either the opening or closing statements, since it is the message part of the letter. The less homogeneous nature of the body has been, therefore, one of the greatest hindrances to formal analysis.[35]

White made a comparison of the body of the private Greek letters with that of the Pauline letters and noted that both have three distinct sections: the "body-opening," the "body-middle," and the "body-closing." In both groups of letters the transition point at which each of the three sections begins is marked by a stereotyped "formulaic or quasi-formulaic construction." Furthermore, the function of the letter-body in both the Pauline letters and the papyri is basically the same. It is the "message" part of the letter, "containing the primary information which the writer wishes to convey."[36] The main difference between the Pauline letters and the papyri is length. Each of the sections in the Pauline letters is much longer than those in the papyri.[37]

We shall proceed by examining each of the three sections of the body. In each section I shall list the basic features and analyze the body of Colossians in the light of those features.

The Body Opening

Basic Features. Jack T. Sanders's article on "The Transition from Open Epistolary Thanksgiving to Body in the Letters of the Pauline Corpus" analyzes a formal phrase that introduces the body of the letter. The function of that formula was either to counsel or to inform the readers.[38] White sought to correct Sanders by noting that Sanders "takes what are two discrete formulae in the common letter tradition (the 'request' formula and the 'disclosure' formula) and collapsed them into one form." Besides these two formulae White attempts to identify four additional ones which may introduce the body of the Pauline letter. They are as follows:

---

[34]White, *The Form and Function of the Body of the Greek Letter: A Study of the Letter-Body in the Non-literary Papyri and in Paul the Apostle*, p. 45.

[35]J. L. White, "The Introductory Formulae in the Body of the Pauline Letter," *JBL* 90 (1971): 91-97.

[36]Ibid., pp. 93, 94.

[37]Ibid.

[38]Sanders, "Transition from Thanksgiving to Body," pp. 348-57.

a. The *Disclosure Formula* which contains a verb of desiring (usually θέλω in the first person indicative), a verb of knowing in the infinitive form, a vocative of address, and the matter disclosed (usually introduced by ὅτι).

b. The *Request Formula* which contains two major elements: a background section and a request section. The background period may precede or succeed the request period. When it precedes it, ἐπεί or ἐπειδή usually introduces it. When it succeeds, a ἵνα clause is normally used. The request section contains a verb of request (παρακαλῶ), the vocative, and the content of the request which may be introduced by a variety of means.

c. The *Joy Expression* which is usually related to the arrival of news and expresses relief over the addressee's welfare and the significance of the letter for the sender.

d. The *Astonishment Expression* marked by θαυμάζω and the object of astonishment introduced by ὅτι.

e. The *Statement of Compliance* which either reminds the recipient of instructions previously given or informs them that they have complied with those instructions. The formal features are an introductory adverb (ὡς, καθώς, or καθότι), a verb of instruction, and the contents of the instruction (usually introduced by περί).

f. The *Formulaic Use of the Verb of Hearing or Learning* usually marked by (1) an adverb denoting degree, (2) either the verb λυπέω ("I grieve") or ἀγωνίζομαι ("I agonize"), (3) either ἀκούω ("I hear") or ἐπιγινώσκω ("I learn") in the aorist tense, and (4) the contents of the report stated in a variety of ways.[39]

Using only the undisputed letters of Paul (Romans, 1 and 2 Corinthians, Galatians, Philemon, Philippians, and 1 Thessalonians) and limiting the statistics to the body-opening, the *Disclosure Formula* is to be found in five letters (Galatians 1:11; Romans 1:13; 1 Thessalonians 2:1; Philippians 1:12; 2 Corinthians 1:8), the *Request Formula* in two (Philemon 8ff.; 1 Corinthians 1:10), the *Joy Expression* in two (Philemon 7; Philippians 4:10), the *Astonishment Expression* in one (Galatians 1:6), and the *Hearing Formula* in one (Galatians 1:13ff.).

The formulae are not limited to the body-opening and often serve as transitional statements in other parts of the letter-body. More than

---

[39]White, "The Introductory Formulae in the Body of the Pauline Letter," pp. 93–97.

one introductory formula may be used in both the Hellenistic and the Pauline letters.[40] There are four of them in Galatians. The *Disclosure Formula* is the one most frequently used and is also the most stereotyped.[41] However, none of the formulae is so exactly set that some alteration is not possible. The combining of elements from different formulae may occur.

The Body-Opening in Colossians (1:24-2:5). From the above it can be seen that a variety of formulae and themes may make up the body-opening of a letter. One of the features that stands out immediately in Colossians is the theme of Paul's apostolic call and ministry. This is linked to his expression of deep concern for the Colossians and an affirmation that he is with them "in spirit." Along with this theme of apostolic authority and presence there is the existence of a number of introductory formulae.

Since our discussion above primarily deals with the presence of introductory formulae in the letter-body opening, let us examine Colossians in the light of those formulae first.

The lengthy closing of the thanksgiving period makes it difficult to discern where the body begins. However, if our analysis of the thanksgiving period is valid, the body begins in 1:24. The very next element in the letter-form after the thanksgiving is a *Joy Expression*. In this instance the joy is related both to the addressees and to the writer. Paul rejoices that his sufferings are for the sake of the Colossians. It could also be pointed out that a *Joy Expression* concludes the section which I have designated as the body-opening (χαίρων καί βλέπων ὑμῶν . . . in 2:5). In the *Joy Expressions* one of the functions of the epistolary genre becomes manifest. A basic purpose of the letter is to demonstrate a friendly relationship (*philophronesis*). An appropriate way to show that relationship is to express joy over the good condition of the readers. An appropriate place to express such joy is in the body-opening.[42]

---

[40]Ibid., p. 96.

[41]See T. Y. Mullins, "Disclosure: A Literary Form in the New Testament," *NovT* 7 (1964): 44-50.

[42]This insight should help us temper our evaluation of the historical situation of the Colossian church. The expression of joy was sincere to be sure. But it was also the fitting thing to do and should not therefore be interpreted as indicating that the faith and steadfastness of the Colossians was extraordinary.

The next formulaic element that is most evident in the Colossians body-opening is the *Disclosure Formula:*

Θέλω γὰρ ὕμᾶς εἰδέναι ἡλίκον ἀγῶνα
ἔχω ὑπὲρ ὑμῶν καὶ τῶν ἐν
Λαοδικείᾳ (2:1)

The formula includes the verb of desiring (θέλω) and the aorist infinitive of knowing (εἰδέναι). It has no vocative of address or ὅτι conjunction to introduce the objective clause. It does have the required objective clause, however, and the ὅτι is not present because the clause begins with an adjective of magnitude (ἡλίκον).

Let us now turn to the theme of the apostolic authority and presence in the body-opening. Heikki Koskenniemi demonstrated that *philophronesis, parousia,* and *homilia* are basic themes in the Greek letter and were so from the beginning.[43] Since a letter is really a substitute for the personal presence of the writer, it is not uncommon to find an expression of desire to be present with the recipient or a statement of plans to visit the recipient. As Terrence Mullins puts it: "visit talk" is "a common epistolary theme."[44] The motif "absent in body, but present through letter" is an obvious spin-off of the desire of the writer to be in the presence (*parousia*) of the addressee.

Robert W. Funk, while admitting that it is a natural inclination in letter writing for a writer to express his desire to be present with or to visit his readers, also sees that such expressions have important theological significance in the Pauline letters. Paul so often expresses his intention to send a personal emissary or to pay the congregation a personal visit and does so in a more or less distinctive part of the letter that Funk attempted to establish such expressions as a formal structural element in the Pauline letters. He calls such elements "apostolic *parousia*"[45] and seeks to demonstrate their formal structure by an analysis of Romans 15:14-33. He affirms that there are five distinct items with twelve subdivisions in the "apostolic *parousia*." Terrance Mullins observes that only one of them persists in all of the apostolic

---

[43]Heikki Koskenniemi, *Studien zur Idee und Phraseologie des griechischen Briefs bis 400n. Chr.,* Annales Academiae Scientiarum Fennicae (Helsinki, 1956).

[44]Mullins,"VisitTalk," pp.350-58, especially 352-55.

[45]Funk, "The Apostolic Parousia," pp. 249-68, and *Language, Hermeneutic, and Word of God,* pp. 250-74.

parousia passages and asserts (correctly, I think) that the "apostolic *parousia*" is not an epistolary form, but an epistolary theme.[46] Be that as it may, the value of Funk's work is that what functions in the Greek letters as a means of maintaining *philophronesis* (friendly relationship) has a quite different primary function in the Pauline letters.

What is the function of the "apostolic *parousia*"? It is to make present the apostolic authority.

> Paul must have thought of his presence as the bearer of charismatic, one might even say eschatological, power. One is reminded of the power of the apostolic presence in Acts 5:1-11 and of the threatening character of the promise to come in the letters to the seven churches (Revelation 2:5b, 16, 25; 3:3b, 11).[47]

Paul regarded his apostolic presence under three related aspects: the letter, the personal emissary, and his own personal presence. All three aspects were bearers of the apostolic authority. He prefers the latter (personal presence) but regards the other two as surrogates for his presence. Tychicus and Onesimus function as such surrogates in 4:7-9.

The usual structure of the Pauline letter is salutation, thanksgiving, body, paraenesis, and closing element. The usual position of the "apostolic *parousia*" is just after the body-closing and before the paraenesis.[48] Among the seven undisputed Pauline letters, Romans and Philippians are exceptions to this order. In Romans, passages related to the "apostolic *parousia*" are found at both the beginning (1:5-15) and near the end of the letter (15:15-29). The same is true in Colossians. Why is the "apostolic *parousia*" located at the beginnings and near the endings of these two letters? The answer, no doubt, is related to the fact that neither of these churches were founded by the writer. In the Colossian situation, where the writer must warn the church of erroneous teaching and affirm the truth, it was essential that he establish his authority to do so. In the body-opening Paul's apostolic authority is affirmed in 1:22-29 and his apostolic presence is declared in 2:5 in "presence/absence" language.[49]

---

[46]Mullins, "Visit Talk," pp. 351, 352.

[47]Funk, "The Apostolic *Parousia*," p. 265.

[48]Ibid., p. 263, fn. 1, and p. 268.

[49]The presence/absence motif occurs in various forms in 1 Thess. 2:27; 1 Cor. 5:3; 2 Cor. 10:1ff., 10:10ff., 13:2, 10; Phil. 1:27, 2:12 as well as in Col. 2:5. The significance of

The letter body-opening of Colossians, then, is 1:24-2:5. It immediately succeeds the thanksgiving period, contains introductory formulae, and expresses a common epistolary theme (friendly relationship). The theme usually consists of "visit talk" or a "travelogue" (as Funk and others often call it). It can also be expressed in "presence/absence" language. Both of these features are present in the Colossian body-opening. In the Hellenistic letters the theme ordinarily serves to maintain the friendly relationship (*philophronesis*) existing between the writer and the addressee. In the Pauline letters it also functions to establish or assert apostolic authority. Normally the "visit talk" theme fittingly occurs at the close of the letter in both the Hellenistic and Pauline letters. In Colossians it occurs at the beginning of the letter as well as at the close. The historical circumstances of the letter make these positions appropriate and almost necessary.

The Body Middle

Basic Features. Whereas the presence of transitional devices and conventional themes as well as the function of the body-opening and body-closing makes them relatively easy to analyze, the analysis of the body-middle is difficult. The bodies of Greco-Roman letters were usually so short and the body-openings so frequently dove-tailed into the body-closings that an analysis of the formal features of a body-middle is practically impossible. The absence of formal conventions in the body-middle made it possible for the writers of the New Testament letters to express themselves in their own creative ways. This is not to say that there are no formal elements (transitional devices, traditional materials, and rhetorical styles) in the body-middles of New Testament letters. These elements are clearly present in more elaborate ways than was once perceived, but they are adapted and transformed by the writers to fit their historical situations.

After making an extensive examination of the body-middle in Philemon, Galatians, Romans, 1 Thessalonians, Philippians, and 1 and 2 Corinthians, John Lee White made the following observations:

> The body-middle of the private Greek letter tends both to be more loosely structured, and more inconsistent in the use of discrete formulae to indicate transitions, than either the body-opening or body-closing sections. Paul, on

---

Paul's presence as the bearer of apostolic authority is especially pronounced in the Corinthian correspondence but is implied in all of the passages cited.

the other hand, constructs the body-middle carefully and employs discrete formulae at each of the major points of transition.

Paul constructs the body-middle, for example, as a two-membered entity (in every letter but Philemon). The first of these two parts is always a tightly organized theological argument; the second part, immediately following, is less tightly constructed, and this is the place where the principles espoused in the preceding are concretized. The message introduced in the body-opening, consequently, is developed according to its theoretical and practical aspects, respectively.

And, Paul is more perspicuous in his use of formulae in the body-middle, perhaps, than in either the body-opening or body-closing. He creates transitional constructions which are expressive of, and interwoven integrally into, the theological argument.[50]

The Body-Middle in Colossians (2:6-4:1). The basic function of the body-middle is to carry forward the matters introduced in the body-opening. Paul's concern that the Colossian church (and all of the churches of the upper Lycus valley) walk in the light of the received traditions is carried forward with two "responsibility" statements in 2:6-8 (walk in the light of the Christological traditions [2:6, 7] and "see to it that no one makes prey of you" [2:8]). These statements are followed in 2:9, 10 by a reference to the Christ-hymn (1:15-20)

White's observation that the Pauline body-middle contains two discrete parts holds true for the Colossian letter. The "tightly organized theological argument" (part 1) is carried out in 2:9-15. The practical application of the theological argument (part 2) is developed in 2:16-3:4 and further developed by the use of traditional *paraenesis* in 3:4-4:1 (the vice and virtue catalogues and the *Haustafel*).

Colossians 2:9-15 comprises the theological argument. It is based upon a reference to the liturgical tradition set forth in the Christ-hymn (1:15-20). The last two verses of the hymn (1:19, 20) assert that all the fullness dwells in Christ and that he reconciled all things by making peace through the blood of his cross. Precisely the same affirmations form the focal points of the theological argument in 2:9-15. In Christ dwells all the fullness (2:9). The death of Christ on the cross was the means by which he triumphed over sin and the principalities and powers (2:14, 15). The believers participate in the consequences of that triumph by means of solidarity "in Christ" which is experienced through baptism.

---

[50]White, *The Form and Function of the Body of the Greek Letter*, pp. 96, 97.

Colossians 2:16-3:4 comprises the situational application of the theological argument. It falls into two major sections: 2:16-19 and 2:20-3:4. The structure of 2:16-19 is as follows:

οὖν
μή τις ὑμᾶς κρινέτω
    ἐν βρώσει καὶ ἐν πόσει. . .
        ἅ ἐστιν σκιὰ . . .
μηδεὶς ὑμᾶς καταβραβευέτω θέλων
    ἐν ταπεινοφροσύνῃ καὶ . . .
        ἅ ἑόρακεν . . .

The theological argument is applied to the Colossians by means of the connecting link οὖν (therefore) and consists of two imperative prohibitions, μή τις ὑμᾶς κρινέτω (let no one judge you) and μηδεὶς ὑμᾶς καταβραβευέτω (let no one disqualify you). The prohibitions are related to specific spheres of concern connected with the historical situation.

The second section of the situational application of the theological argument (2:20-3:4) consists of two first-class conditional sentences which are related to the baptismal motif introduced in 2:12. They have to do with having died with Christ (2:20-23) and having been raised with him (3:1-4). The first conditional sentence shows the incongruity of having died with Christ and living in the world under the power of the "elemental spirits." Such an existence is described as submitting to regulations concerning "things (ἅ, ἅτινα)" which "perish as they are used," are "according to human precepts and doctrines" and have "an appearance of wisdom." These regulations, set forth in apodictic commands ("do not handle, do not taste, do not touch"), appear to be a quotation of the opponents' teaching and related to the historical situation.

The second conditional sentence (3:1) is a command to live in the light of the reality of having been raised with Christ. The command is to seek the "things that are above." Colossians 3:2 reaffirms that command and 3:3, 4 is a summary of the theological argument set forth in an eschatological "already but not yet" frame of reference.

For you have died and your life is hid with Christ in God. When Christ who is our life appears, then you also will appear with him in glory (RSV).

Let us conclude our discussion of the Colossian body-middle by noting two other matters. The first one has to do with factors which agree with John Lee White's observation that the Pauline body-middles are more carefully constructed than the body-middles of the private Greek letters. This is borne out by the consistent use of a single transitional device and the use of repetitious phrases. The transitional formula is οὖν with the imperative. It occurs in 2:6, 16, and 3:1. The repetitious phrases are the use of ἐν with a pronoun referring to Christ in the theological argument section (ἐν αὐτῷ, 2:9, 10, 15; ἐν ᾧ, 2:11, 12) and σύν with a reference to Christ in the application of the theological argument section (σύν Χριστῷ, 2:20; 3:3, 4; συνηγέρθητε τῷ Χριστῷ, 3:1).

The second matter to be observed is the location of the traditional paraenesis in the Colossian letter. It has been noted above that paraenesis is a discrete part of the Pauline epistolary form and normally follows the body-closing.[51] In Colossians, however, it is a part of the body-middle. Is there an explanation for this phenomenon? An affirmative answer readily can be given. The entire body-middle is marked by imperatives. The theological argument section is introduced by an imperative (2:6-15) and the application of the theological argument consists almost entirely of imperatives. The paraenetic section is a natural part of the body-middle. Furthermore, the paraenetic section is largely made up of traditional material (3:5-4:6). Since the body-middle is essentially a warning against false teachings and traditions and an admonition to walk in the light of the received traditions, the use of large amounts of traditional paraenesis is most appropriate.

The body-middle thus consists of 2:6-4:1. It is marked by repetitious transitional devices and phrases and consists of a precise theological argument (2:9-15) and an application of that argument (2:16-3:4) which is, in turn, supported by the presence of traditional paraenesis (3:5-4:1).

The Body-Closing
Basic Features. On the basis of a style and sequence analysis of the seven undisputed letters of Paul, Robert Funk concludes that the body-closing usually consists of two themes: an eschatological conclusion which corresponds to the eschatological climax rounding off the

---

[51]Ibid., p. 45; Doty, *Letters in Primitive Christianity*, p. 27; Funk, *Language, Hermeneutic, and Word of God*, p. 261; Dibelius, *A Fresh Approach to the New Testament and Early Christian Literature*, pp. 143, 144.

hodaya or *beracha* (Sanders) and a travelogue which functions to stress the importance of the apostolic presence.[52]

John L. White carried the formal analysis of the body-closing further. Using the same undisputed letters of Paul, he compared specific formulaic types in the Pauline body-closings with similar formulae in the private Greek letters.[53] He isolated three discrete formulae in the Pauline body-closings which, though not identical in form with the private letters, carry forth the same essential functions. They are (1) the *Motivation for Writing* formula, (2) the *Confidence* formula, and (3) the "Apostolic *Parousia*" formula.[54] It seems to me that White goes too far in classifying these as clear-cut formulae, but he has succeeded in demonstrating the presence of regularly recurring themes.[55]

In general the Pauline body-closings function to (1) repeat the occasion for writing, (2) to express confidence that the readers will fulfill his desires for them (or warn them against the consequences of not fulfilling them), and (3) to express his desire or promise to visit them. If the apostle is unable to visit in person, the latter function is expressed by a statement concerning the sending of an emissary who will, in effect, be a substitute for the apostolic presence. White's "formulae" are really themes which fulfill these functions. Paul does not bind himself to strict body-closing formulae but he does, wittingly or unconsciously, conclude the bodies of his letters with functional statements represented by these formulae. In addition, the body-closings in the Pauline letters usually contain eschatological statements.

The Body-Closing in Colossians (4:2-9). The entire body of the Colossian letter is so thoroughly permeated with paraenetic expressions that the precise beginning of the body-closing is problematic.

---

[52]Funk, *Language, Hermeneutics, and Word of God*, pp. 264, 265 and "The Apostolic *Parousia:* Form and Significance," pp. 249-68.

[53]White, *Form and Function of the Body of the Greek Letter*, pp. 25-31.

[54]Ibid., pp. 61, 85, 97-99.

[55]White is correct in seeing the presence of formulae in the *Motivation for Writing* and *Confidence* expressions in Philemon, Galatians, and Romans. However, in the other four undisputed letters these formulae disappear and become themes. I have already expressed agreement with T. Y. Mullins that the "Apostolic *Parousia*" is a theme and not a form. See above, at fn. 46.

Every major transition in the body-opening and body-middle takes the form of an imperative construction. It would not be surprising if the body-closing should have a similar construction.

There are no stereotyped formulae for the *Motive for Writing* or *Confidence* statements as White would lead us to expect. Indeed, such formulae are present in only three of the seven undisputed letters of Paul (Romans, Galatians, and Philemon), so that their absence is more general than their presence. The main question is: do the functions implied by White's formulae exist in 4:4-9? Let us try to answer this question by examining the pericope in the light of the threefold function of the Pauline body-closing mentioned above.

First, the body-closing functions to repeat the occasion for writing the letter. From all that we have said in this epistolary analysis it is clear that the thematic refrain of the letter is Paul's concern as an apostle that the Colossians walk in the light of the received Christological and paraenetic traditions so that they would not be led astray by proponents of fallen human and wordly traditions. This refrain is present again in the series of imperatives in 4:2-6. "Continue steadfastly in prayer" (4:2), "Walk in wisdom toward outsiders" (4:5), "Redeem the time [participial imperative]" (4:5), and "Let your speech be always in grace" (4:6) are typical *topoi* which usually occur at the end of a letter. They are brought together in such a way to reemphasize the basic concerns of the apostle for his readers. The recurring motif of thanksgiving (1:12; 2:7; 3:15, 17) is present again in 4:2. Concern for proper understanding of the significance of Christ (1:15-20; 2:6, 7; 2:9-15) manifests itself again in Paul's request for prayer that he might make the "mystery of Christ" as clear as he should (4:3, 4). A manner of life based on understanding (2:6, 7), which is defensible before critics (2:8, 16-23), and which winsomely demonstrates to outsiders the new (eschatological) relationship with God (3:5-4:1) is recapitulated in the apodictic commands in 4:5, 6.

Second, the body-closing functions to express the writer's confidence that the readers will fulfill his requests or to call them to responsible action. One might reason that a clear-cut confidence statement is absent in Colossians because Paul did not know his readers personally, nor they him. He may have been uncertain about their attitude toward his apostolic authority. On the contrary, the very fact that Paul solicits their prayers for his ministry, and precisely over the issue of a proper proclamation of the significance of Christ, indicates that he did have confidence in them and that they would heed the injunctions that he made in the letter. The church worship setting of the traditional *topoi* in 3:16, 17 and 4:2-7 coupled with Paul's request for public prayer for his ministry shows the apostle's firm confidence in the Colossians.

Third, the body-closing functions to express the writer's desire to be present with his readers in person or through an emissary. In the Pauline letters this expression is not primarily for the personal satisfaction of the apostle but for the benefit of the community. The apostolic presence is like an eschatological power which brings blessing or judgment. So important is it, that in those instances where Paul cannot personally visit his readers, he expresses his intention to send a surrogate for his presence in the person of a trusted and well-known colleague. The "Apostolic *Parousia*" is nearly always the last item in the body-closing.

In Funk's frequently mentioned article on "The Apostolic *Parousia*," he describes a basic form that Paul regularly uses when he plans to send an apostolic emissary. It consists of three parts: (1) an introductory formula consisting of ἔπεμψα (I sent), ὑμῖν (to you), and the name of the one sent, (2) a credentials clause describing the emissary, and (3) a purpose clause in the form of a ἵνα statement or infinitival phrase.[56] All three of these formulae are present in 4:7-9.

(1) Introductory formula: Τύχικος . . . ὅν ἔπεμψα πρὸς ὑμᾶς (Tychicus whom I sent to you)

(2) Credentials clause: ὁ ἀγαπητὸς ἀδελφὸς καὶ πιστὸς διάκονος καὶ σύνδουλος ἐν κυρίῳ (the beloved brother and faithful minister and fellow servant in the Lord)

---

[56]Funk, "Apostolic *Parousia,*" pp. 252, 255-258. He shows the presence of the form in 1 Cor. 4:17; 1 Thess. 3:2-5; Phil. 2:19-23, 25-30; 2 Cor. 9:3-5; 1 Cor. 16:1-3.

(3)   Purpose clause: εἰς αὐτὸ τοῦτο, ἵνα γνῶτε τὰ περὶ ἡμῶν καὶ παρακαλέσῃ τὰς καρδίας ὑμῶν (for this very purpose, that you may know the things concerning us and that he may comfort your hearts)

Verse 9 adds the name of Onesimus and includes all of the parts of the emissary form again. Colossians 4:7-9, then, functions as the "Apostolic *Parousia*" and is the last item in the body-closing. In response to the question concerning whether 4:2-9 fulfills the three functions of the body-closing, the answer is yes.

One more item remains to be investigated. It was mentioned above that the Pauline body-closings usually contain eschatological language. Is this true of Colossians? This is a most difficult question because the phrase "eschatological language" usually means whatever its user wants it to mean.[57] It is sometimes restricted too severely and made to refer only to apocalyptic or futuristic end-time concepts. It is sometimes used too broadly to refer to existential encounters or experiencing the nearness of God. It is generally agreed that the gospel announces the presence of an eschatologically new age and that the earliest Christians were convinced that they were living in that age. Eschatological language, then, deals both with the end of time and with the newly realized age. It is this phenomenon which gives it a multi-dimensional complexity.

Since the body-closing usually contains eschatological language, statements in the body-closing which may or may not have an eschatological connotation should probably be regarded as eschatological. Ralph Martin asks the question about the meaning of the phrase "being watchful in it (prayer) with thanksgiving" (4:2):

> Is Paul simply remarking on the believer's general stance: be watchful to continue the practice of prayer at all times (so Lohse)? Or, is he reminding the Colossians of the need to overcome the tendency to drowsiness when the mind at prayer concentrates in a spiritual exercise? Or, can it be that his thought takes in an eschatological dimension (see the uses of the verb γρηγορεῖν in relation to the *parousia*, given in Oepke, *TDNT* ii, p. 338) as he

---

[57]W. Doty, "Identifying Eschatological Language," *Continuum* 7 (1970): 544-61.

bids his readers to be on the alert in expectation of the coming Lord (so Conzelmann)?[58]

Martin is inclined toward the last view. His opinion is supported on formal grounds by the presence of the phrase in the body-closing. Paul's request for prayer for an "open door" to speak "the mystery of Christ" also has the tone of eschatological urgency, as does the *topos* on redeeming the time (4:5b).

To summarize, Colossians 4:2-9 contains the basic features of a Pauline body-closing. It restates Paul's basic concern for the Colossians. It shows his confidence in them by requesting their prayers for his ministry. It guarantees the authority of his word to them through the sending of a trusted apostolic emissary. It contains probable eschatological language.

The Letter-Closing

The letter-closing can be treated briefly because it is easily identified by the presence of standard items and because of the brevity of the Colossian letter-closing.

Basic Features. The private Greco-Roman letters uniformly closed with a health wish and a word of farewell (ἔρρωσε).[59] The latter is never found in the letters of the Pauline corpus and the former is regularly replaced with a benediction.

The most common features of the Pauline letter-closing are the presence of one or more benedictions (found in all of the letters[60]), a list of greetings both from Paul and others who were with him (found in six of the letters[61]), and a reference to Paul's writing in his own hand (found in five of the letters[62]). Two other items worthy of mention are

---

[58]Martin, *Colossians*, p. 125.

[59]Doty, *Letters in Primitive Christianity*, pp. 11-15, 39.

[60]Including the Pastorals.

[61]Romans 16:3-16, 21-23; 1 Cor. 16:19, 20; 2 Cor. 13:13; Phil. 4:21, 22; Philem. 23, 24; Col. 4:10-17.

[62]First Corinthians 16:21: Gal. 6:11; 2 Thess. 3:17; Philem. 19; Col. 4:18a (Rom. 16:22 contains a word of greeting from "Tertius, the one who wrote the letter"). See Gordon J. Bahr, "Paul and Letter Writing in the First Century," pp. 465-77, who discusses the possible uses of secretaries and the means of transcription in ancient letters.

the presence of doxologies[63] and instructions to greet one another with a holy kiss.[64]

The Letter-Closing in Colossians (4:10-18). Three of the above features are present in the Colossian letter-closing. Colossians 4:10, 11 includes greetings from three Jewish Christians (Aristarchus, Mark, and Jesus called Justus). Colossians 4:12-14 contains greetings from Epaphras, Luke, and Demas. Colossians 4:15-18a consists of Paul's greetings to the Laodiceans and the Colossians.

A reference to Paul's own handwriting appears in 4:18a. Such statements are present only in those letters where Paul's apostolic authority is of very great importance (see references in footnote 64). Such a reference is almost predictable in a letter where the "Apostolic *Parousia*" function occurs in two different forms, one at the beginning of the letter-body, and the other at the close (2:5 and 4:7-9). It seems to me that the "signature" statement points to the probable authenticity of Colossians. With the exception of 2 Thessalonians, such statements occur only in the undisputed letters. It seems quite unlikely that the "Apostolic *Parousia*" sub-themes (presence/absence and the apostolic emissary form) would be so well-known that a later disciple of Paul would be influenced to augment it with a "signature" statement.

The short benediction "grace be with you" concludes the letter.

Conclusion

We have now reached the end of our epistolary analysis of Colossians. Let me conclude by summarizing the epistolary analysis in outline form and making some short comments on the usefulness of epistolary analysis for arriving at decisions about the authenticity, integrity, and purpose of the letter to the Colossians.

Outline Analysis

I. Salutation 1:1, 2
II. Thanksgiving 1:3-23
   A. Εὐχαριστῶ period 1:3-8

---

[63]Rom. 16:25-27 (which many think to be non-Pauline); Phil. 4:20; 1 Thess. 5:23, 24. See Robert Jewett, "The Form and Function of the Homiletic Benediction," pp. 18-34.

[64]Romans 16:16; 1 Cor.16:20b; 2 Cor.13:12; 1 Thess 5:26; and 1 Pet. 5:14.

B. Intercession 1:9-11
C. Closing (marked by liturgical materials and eschatological themes) 1:12-23

III. Letter-Body 1:24-4:1
A. Body-Opening 1:24-2:5
B. Body-Middle 2:6-4:1
C. Body-Closing 4:2-9

IV. Letter-Closing 4:10-18
A. Greetings 4:10-17
B. "Signature" statement 4:18a
C. Benediction 4:18b

The Usefulness of Epistolary Analysis. What can one say about the usefulness of epistolary analysis for investigating the issues of authorship and integrity of the New Testament letters? I find myself in agreement with Funk, Doty, and others that it can be of real help.[65] At the same time I find myself quite unpersuaded by some of their conclusions. They decide, for example, that Philippians contains fragments of more than one letter and that Paul did not write Colossians. This is certainly not the place to discuss the integrity of Philippians, but an epistolary analysis of that letter which takes into account thematic structure and sequence factors as well as an investigation of the Thanksgiving section[66] points to its integrity. As for the authorship of Colossians, it is as much a methodological error to assume its non-Pauline authorship as it is to assume its Pauline authorship and allow that assumption to color remarks about its epistolary features. The epistolary analysis of Colossians made above shows that the epistolary features of this letter fall well within the spectrum of that which may be expected in an authentic Pauline letter. The major problems about the authorship of Colossians are related to theological, lexical, and stylistic matters which are quite aside from its epistolary form. Many of these issues are directly related to the sections of the letter where traditional materials are present. The persuasion that the non-Pauline authorship of Colossians is an "assured result" of literary criticism is

---

[65]Funk, *Language, Hermeneutic, and Word of God*, pp. 270-74; Doty, *Contemporary New Testament Interpretation*, pp. 144-45.

[66]Jewett, "The Epistolary Thanksgiving and the Integrity of Philippians," pp. 40-53.

premature and warranted neither by the use of the traditional materials nor by the use of the traditional epistolary form.

An epistolary analysis is of substantial help in arriving at conclusions concerning the authorship and integrity of a New Testament letter when it is used in conjunction with other approaches. Its usefulness for isolating the major themes of a letter also make it a valuable aid in determining the purpose of a letter as well as the writer's letter-writing habits and practices.

We have shown that Colossians not only bears the major distinctive marks of the Greek epistolary genre, but that it also conforms to a remarkable degree to the kinds of features that characterize the undisputed letters of Paul. It now remains for us to make a thematic structural analysis of Colossians which will indicate the writer's basic situational and theological concerns and show how he used the traditional materials which we have previously investigated.

A THEMATIC ANALYSIS OF THE LETTER TO THE COLOSSIANS

In light of the problems related to structural analysis which we mentioned above, it would be advisable for me to describe what I mean by a thematic structural analysis. There are two basic objectives for such an analysis. The first one is to define the limits of the major themes of a literary composition. An epistolary analysis is helpful for this task but inadequate. The second objective of a thematic analysis is to discern the basic concern of the major themes and to identify the subthemes by which the main themes are developed. Such an analysis will, of course, keep in mind the various functions of the epistolary units, but will focus primarily on an analysis of the contents of the letter in such a way that it will expose the development of its main themes and hence throw light on its main purpose. An ancillary task, which is especially significant for our investigation of the use of traditional materials in Colossians, is to locate those materials in the composition of the letter and see how they are used in the development of the major themes and subthemes.

The major themes of the letter to the Colossians are developed in 1:1-23; 1:24-4:6; and 4:7-18. These sections, in the main, comprise the letter-opening, letter-body, and letter-closing of an epistolary analysis, but they also constitute the introduction, the main argument, and the conclusion of a thematic analysis. Let us attempt to identify the basic themes and primary concerns of each of these units and observe how the traditional materials are used in them. I shall try to avoid using any historical or theological presuppositions and be as objective and brief as possible.

The Introduction (1:1-23).

Basic Theme. Certain words and concepts stand out in the introduction to Colossians by virtue of repetition or location in the context. These words and notions will help us identify the main theme and concern of the unit. The words are λόγος (1:5), εὐαγγέλιον (1:5, 23), κηρύσσω (1:23); ἀκούω (1:5, 6, 23), μανθάνω (1:7), ἐπίγνωσις (1:6 [verb form], 1:9, 10); and καρποφορέω and αὐξάνω (1:6, 10). These words point to a sequential unit which gives shape to the main theme of the introduction; gospel—response—growth. The gospel is called "the word of truth" (1:5) and contains the proclamation of the "hope laid up in heaven" (1:5, 23). Response to the gospel produces understanding and growth (1:6, 9-11), and it is essential that one keep on hearing and responding to the gospel (1:23). Perhaps the main theme or topic of the introduction section could be summed up with the phrase "the necessity of continued response to the Gospel."

Development of the Theme. The theme is developed in the epistolary Thanksgiving period. The writer thanks God that his readers had responded to the gospel which they had heard from and been instructed in by Epaphras (1:3-8). He prays that they might grow in their understanding of the gospel and in the spiritual and moral fruits that response to the gospel brings (1:9-22). The unit concludes with a statement of the necessity of continued response to the gospel and of Paul's special commission to minister it (1:23). It is worthy of note to observe that the introduction unit begins and ends with a declaration of Paul's apostleship (1:1) and his sense of special responsibility to minister the gospel (1:23).[67]

The Use of Traditional Materials. One of the difficult tasks in making an epistolary analysis of Colossians is to identify the Thanksgiving-closing. Because of the liturgical and eschatological characteristics of 1:12-23 it seems likely that these verses form the

---

[67]Note the use of the emphatic pronoun in verse 23.

closing. If the investigation we made in chapter 2 is valid, then it is clear that the bulk of this passage (verses 12-20) consists of confessional and hymnic traditional materials and the last three verses (1:21-23) are an application of these materials to the readers.

An examination of the contents of the liturgical section shows that it celebrates the central message of the gospel. God has qualified the celebrants to be His Own unique people and has delivered them from the dominion of darkness to the kingdom of His beloved Son (1:12-14). The Son is both the Creator and Redeemer of the cosmos and has brought both peace and reconciliation by his death (1:15-20). This reconciling work of the Son is applied to the readers and is conditioned upon persistence in the hope proclaimed in the gospel (1:21-23). In Pauline terms the gospel is the proclamation of the salvific work of God accomplished through His Son (Romans 1:1-4, 16, 17). This is clearly the declaration of the liturgical materials cited in 1:12-20.

The traditional materials in 1:12-20 were already known by the readers and may have been taught to them by Epaphras (1:7). As we mentioned earlier,[68] 1:12-24 seems to have been drawn from confessional materials related to baptism and was coupled with the Christ-hymn which was sung in the worshiping community. Whatever their former origin or function may have been, the traditional materials in 1:12-20 would have been recognized as that which had been taught previously and they serve as a summary of the gospel concerning Christ which had been proclaimed to them and which they had received.

The Main Argument (1:24-4:6)

Basic Theme. The basic theme of the main argument is located in 2:6-15. It is preceded by a section establishing the apostolic right of the writer to instruct and admonish his readers (1:24-2:5) and is succeeded by paraenesis related to the main theme (2:16-4:6). The main theme has both a positive and a negative formulation. Positively, it is an admonition to walk in the light of the Christology in which they had been instructed (2:6, 7). Negatively, it is a warning not to be carried away by the "philosophy" and "vain deceit" which was "according to the traditions of men" and the "στοιχεῖα of the world" and not "according to Christ" (2:8, 9).

---

[68]See above, chapter 2, "The Traditional Character of Colossians 1:12-14."

The Development of the Main Theme. The main theme is preceded by and introduced by an authority statement which affirms the apostle's responsibility for the church in general (1:24, 25) and the churches of the upper Lycus valley in particular (2:1). As an apostle, Paul spoke and acted in the stead of Christ. He regarded his own sufferings as in some way "filling up that which is lacking in the afflictions of Christ" on behalf of the church. He regarded his own ministry for the church as a stewardship given to him by God "to fulfill the word of God" (1:26), which is associated with the gospel in 1:5 and with the "mystery" hidden before the ages but not made known in 1:26. The content of the "mystery" is that Christ is the "hope of glory" (see also the concept "hope" in 1:5 and 23) for "every man"[69] and that includes Gentiles (1:17, 28). It is this conviction that he is ministering in the stead of Christ on behalf of the church to make the "mystery" known that caused the apostle to strive with all his God-given energy in this special ministry (1:29). He was particularly concerned that the Colossians, Laodiceans, and others who had not seen him personally would understand and experience the consequences of this "mystery" (or gospel) which is about Christ (2:2, 3). The writer was so concerned that the apostolic ministry be fulfilled in the churches in the region of Colossae that he declared that even though he was not with them "in the flesh," his (apostolic) presence was with them "in spirit" and that he was apprehensive about someone deluding them through fancy speech (2:4, 5). To summarize: the basic theme of the "main argument" section is preceded by a statement affirming the apostolic authority and concern which, in a sense, validated the writer's right to admonish and warn his readers about walking in the light of the received teaching about Christ.

Verses 9-15 of chapter 2 provide a summary of the Christological teaching to which the writer referred. The summary declares the participation of the readers in the reconciling work of Christ based on their experience of baptism. This in turn is followed by a paraenetic section which indicates what walking in the light of the received Christological tradition implies. The paraenesis is connected with the proclamation of participation in the triumph of Christ with the repeated use of the word οὖν (2:16; 3:1; 3:5; 3:12). The paraenesis in 2:16-3:4 is situational and

---

[69]Note the threefold πάντα ἄνθρωπον in 1:28.

deals explicitly with admonitions related to the threat of the "philosophy." The admonitions are associated with the baptismal ideas of dying together and being raised together with Christ (2:20 and 3:1). The paraenesis in 3:5-4:6 is standard paraenesis which is applicable to the whole church in general.

The Use of Traditional Materials. With the exception of the statement concerning apostolic authority and concern (1:24-2:5) and the admonition to walk in the light of the received Christology (2:6-8), most of the "main argument" section (or letter-body in an epistolary analysis) consists of the use of traditional materials. Colossians 2:9, 10 is a summary statement of one of the foci in the Christ-hymn (see 1:18). Colossians 2:11-13 is a lyrical section composed of baptismal motifs and language which declares participation in the death and resurrection of Christ. Colossians 2:14 and 15 is the quotation of a previously existing hymn which celebrates the significance of the death of Christ and which has a clear association with verses 1:16 and 20 of the Christ-hymn and with verses 1:21 and 22 in the application of the Christ-hymn to the readers.

Colossians 2:16-3:4 is the only passage in the "main argument" which does not allude to or cite traditional materials. It is permeated with baptismal language but the basic concern of the pericope is related to the actual situation in Colossae and Laodicea. However, from 3:5 to 4:6 we encounter an uninterrupted flow of traditional paraenetic materials. They all have to do with the manner of life expected from those who have been baptized. They deal with moral concerns (the catalogues), ecclesiological order (the *Haustafel*), and church and social matters (the *topoi*). In the light of the received Christology (1:15-20; 2:9-15), the readers ought not to be tricked into the practices advocated by the "philosophy" (2:16-3:4) but should walk in the light of the received paraenesis (3:5-4:6).

The Concluding Section (4:7-18)

Basic Theme. The conclusion of the letter consists of final greetings and a benediction. Is there anything in this standard letter-closing that can be identified as a basic theme or main concern? The following observations point to the basic theme of the importance of carrying out the admonitions and instructions of the letter.

First, the section begins with an "authority" statement which affirms the apostolic presence and concern. In 4:7-9 Tychicus is identified as the apostolic emissary. He will not only inform the readers of Paul's situation but will carry out Paul's ministry to them. Paul was in prison (4:3, 18) and was participating in the "messianic affliction" (1:24). His stated desire for the readers was that he might comfort their hearts (2:2). Tychicus was sent by Paul "for this very purpose" that "he might comfort your hearts."

Second, the greetings sent to the Colossians by the companions of Paul are from people who had a significant bearing on the importance of the letter. The first three (Aristarchus, Mark, and Jesus called Justus) are specifically designated as the only Jewish Christians among Paul's fellow-workers (4:10, 11). As I shall seek to show in the next chapter, greetings from Jewish Christians would have special significance for the Colossian situation. Epaphras was probably the founder of the churches in the upper Lycus valley and was the one who taught them "the word of truth, the gospel" (1:5-7). It is probable that the readers first learned the traditions cited in letter through the ministry of Epaphras. Luke and Demas were well-known "fellow-workers"[70] of Paul in the Gentile mission. Paul is described in the letter as being keenly aware of his divine appointment as the apostle to the Gentiles and of the special significance of the "mystery" he preached for the Gentiles (1:27, 28). Although there is some doubt about the text of 4:15,[71] it seems likely that Nympha was a respected woman in whose house the Laodicean church met. If this is so, the senders and receivers of greetings include a woman and a slave (Onesimus, 4:9). Onesimus is described as a "faithful and beloved brother" who is a member of the community. The letter to Philemon, which is so closely associated with Colossians, bears witness to the importance of Onesimus to Paul. Nympha and Onesimus bear witness to the inclusiveness of the gospel (1:28; 3:11) and are representatives of the social classes addressed in the *Haustafel*.

Third, the letter had importance for other churches in the Lycus valley and Paul instructs the readers to make sure that the Laodiceans

---

[70]See Philem. 24 and 2 Tim. 4:10, 11 for other N.T. references to Luke and Demas. See also E. E. Ellis for the significance of the term "fellow-workers." "Paul and His Co-Workers," *NTS* 17 (1970-1971): 437-52.

[71]Byzantine and Western texts have the masculine αὐτοῦ instead of the fem. αὐτῆς.

read it also (4:16). All three of these observations show that the writer wanted his readers to understand the importance of his letter.

Summary. An outline of the thematic analysis follows:

I. The Introduction Section (1:1-23)
- A. Basic Theme: The necessity of continued response to the received gospel.
- B. Development of the Theme
  1. Thanksgiving for the readers' response to the gospel which had been taught by Epaphras (1:3-8).
  2. Prayer for growth in understanding the gospel and in the fruit it produces (1:9-22).
  3. Statement of the necessity of continued response to the gospel (1:23).
- C. The Traditional Materials Used: Baptismal and hymnic material which summarize the central proclamation of the gospel (1:12-20).

II. The Main Argument (1:24-4:6)
- A. Basic Theme: Walk in the light of the received Christology and do not be tricked by the "philosophy."
- B. Development of the Theme
  1. Statement of Apostolic authority and concern (1:24-2:5).
  2. Admonition to walk in the light of the received Christology (2:6-15).
  3. Admonitions indicating what such a walk means (2:16-4:6).
- C. The Traditional Materials Used
  1. Reference to the "fulness" teaching in the Christ-hymn (2:9, 10).
  2. Liturgical section made up of baptismal motifs and language (2:11-13.
  3. Hymn celebrating the significance of the cross (2:14, 15).
  4. The vice and virtue catalogues (3:5-15).
  5. The *Haustafel* (3:18-4:1).
  6. *Topoi* (3:16, 17 and 4:2-6).

III. The Concluding Section (4:7-18)
- A. Basic Theme: The Importance of the Letter.
- B. Development of the Theme
  1. The Apostolic Emissary (4:7-9).
  2. Greetings from significant people (4:10-14).

3. Instructions to share the letter (4:15-17).
4. The Apostolic signature and benediction (4:18).

The following table shows the location and extent of the traditional materials in Colossians:

Non-traditional materials	Traditional materials
1:1-11	
	1:12-23
1:24-2:5	
	2:9-15
2:16-3:4	
	3:5-4:6
4:7-18	

CONCLUSION

Two brief but very important observations can be made from these epistolary and thematic structural analyses. The first one is that the epistolary features of Colossians fall well within the spectrum of those which are present in most of the undisputed Pauline letters. This in no way "proves" that Paul was the author. Just as importantly, the data cannot be used to prove that he did not write it. Whoever wrote it included all of the basic features of a Pauline letter but did it in such a way as to avoid a slavish imitation of the Pauline letter-form. An epistolary analysis gives no clear reason for rejecting the authenticity of the letter.

The second observation is that a thematic analysis of the letter focuses attention on its fundamental purpose. An identification of the main themes and an observation of how they are developed, makes it clear that the writer's basic purpose was to admonish the readers to walk in the light of the gospel which they had received. The central contents of that gospel had to do with Christ and the triumph of his cross. The readers must not be tricked into a manner of life inconsistent with that received teaching. The warnings against the "philosophy" are not so much directed against an erroneous Christology which it taught (although such an erroneous Christology is implied), but they are directed toward a manner of life inconsistent with the received Christology.

An additional observation can be made which is vital to our investigation. It shows that the themes of the letter are developed by the use of an unusually large amount of Christological and paraenetic traditional material. The Greek text of Colossians published by the United Bible Societies contains 199 lines of text. Of those 199 lines, eighty-eight of them are citations of or direct allusions to traditional materials. Nearly fifty percent of the introduction section consists of traditional materials (twenty-three of forty-seven lines). Over fifty-two percent of the main argument section consists of traditional materials (sixty-five of 124 lines). This does not include epistolary formulae or "stock" theological terms and phrases. In the light of the main purpose of the letter, it is not at all surprising to find such an unusual amount of traditional materials.

It remains to be asked whether the purpose of Colossians, the traditions used, and the theological perspectives from which the main themes are developed are consistent with the letter's claim to be the product of Paul. Do these items point to a post-Pauline provenance or can they best be understood in the light of the special concerns and historical circumstances of Paul himself? The answers to these questions will be the objective of the next and final chapter of our investigation.

6

The Authorship and Purpose of Colossians

PRELIMINARY OBSERVATIONS

We are now ready to consider the implications of our investigation for determining the authorship and purpose of Colossians. What inferences can be drawn about these matters from our examination of the presence and use of probable hymnic, confessional, and paraenetic materials in the letter?

The most obvious implication is that a lexical and stylistic analysis of Colossians is of very little value in establishing authorship. Since approximately fifty percent of the letter-opening and letter-body consists of traditional materials and the short letter-closing is made up of standard epistolary features, very little text is left for an analysis of the writer's own manner of expression. Furthermore, the remaining text is permeated by standard epistolary formulae and customary theological expressions. Of equal importance is the fact that the presence of the large amount of traditional material is in full accord with the purpose of the letter. Since the central admonition of the letter is the call to a walk that is in accord with the received Christology, the presence of Christological and paraenetic traditions is to be expected. This is to say that the *primary* purpose of the traditional materials is not to impress the readers with the apostolicity of the document (though that purpose is achieved), but to remind them of what they had been taught about

Christ and the gospel and to indicate the implications of those teachings for their historical situation. There is nothing artificial about the presence of the traditions. They belong to the flow of the argument and the intent of the letter. Lexical and stylistic analysis helps in identifying the presence of the traditions but offers very little help in identifying the author.

The inadequate amount of "nontraditional" text is not the only problem in making a linguistic and stylistic analysis relating to authorship. The handwritten "signature statement" in 4:18 would lead one to conclude that the author (whether Paul or someone else) wanted his readers to know that the letter itself was not in the handwriting of the Apostle. We do not know whether the amanuensis was just a copyist or whether he exercised some freedom in the composition of the letter. An investigation of the letter-writing practices of the first century leads to the conclusion that a trusted secretary could have considerable freedom in the wording of a letter.[1] This led Gordon Bahr to conclude:

> In view of the influence which a secretary could have had on his letters, it would be well to speak with caution on topics such as Pauline terminology or Pauline theology. There may be less of Paul in the Pauline corpus than we have been assuming.[2]

If one adds to this the fact that Timothy is named as co-sender of the letter, the problem becomes even more complicated.[3]

Another important implication of our investigation of the traditional materials in Colossians is that one must be very cautious about

---

[1]See Otto Roller, *Das Formular der paulinischen Briefe* (Stuttgart, 1933), p. 333 and C. F. D. Moule, *The Birth of the New Testament*, Harper Commentary Series (New York and Evanston: Harper & Row, Publishers, 1962), pp. 161-62.

[2]Bahr, "Paul and Letter Writing in the First Century," p. 447, and "Subscriptions in the Pauline Letters," pp. 27-41. See also Edward P. Sanders, "Literary Dependence in Colossians," *JBL* 85 (1966): 28-45, for a statistical comparison of Colossians with Philemon which runs counter to my argument. Sanders seeks to show that the author of Colossians depends literarily upon selected passages from the undisputed letters of Paul. He makes no mention of the problems brought about by the probable use of a secretary in many first century letters nor does he deal adequately with the fact that nearly all of the passages which he cites as literarily dependent on the Pauline letters are related to the use of traditional materials (1:15, 16; 1:20-22a; 1:26, 27; 2:12-13; and 3:5-11).

[3]Hans Dieter Betz raises these same issues with reference to the undisputed letter of Galatians. They are obviously even more appropriate for Colossians. *Galatians*, Hermeneia Series (Philadelphia: Fortress Press, 1979).

ruling out the Pauline authorship of a letter because the theological affirmations of the letter differ from those in the "undisputed" letters. This is a major flaw in Lohse's argument. He wrote:

> It is true that the thought of Col certainly exhibits Pauline features. The differences, however, that exist between Col and the theology of the major Pauline epistles must not be overlooked. *They are not at all limited to the passages that argue against the "philosophy," but also occur in passages that are free from polemic.* Consequently, the appearance of non-Pauline concepts and expressions cannot be explained simply by saying that they were coined by the specific circumstances of the controversy. Rather Pauline theology has undergone a profound change in Col, which is evident in every section of the letter and has produced new formulations in christology, ecclesiology, the concept of the apostle, eschatology, and the concept of baptism. Therefore, Paul cannot be considered to be the direct or indirect author of Col.[4]

According to our thematic analysis of Colossians (above, chapter 5), the passages that are free of polemic are precisely those which are based on traditional instruction concerning Christ and behavior (1:12-20; 2:9-15; 3:5-4:6). There are, to be sure, theological expressions in the "non-traditional" sections. But these are the sections which contain the polemical statements that reflect the historical circumstances of the controversy (2:4, 6-8, 16-23; 3:1-4). The majority of the theological affirmations, however, are located in the traditional materials and, therefore, reflect more of the style and language of the community which shaped the traditional materials than of the author.

An investigation of the use of traditional materials, therefore, shows us that a style and language analysis of the letter has little value for determining authorship and that a theological analysis must be made with great care and in full recognition of the fact that the main theological affirmations are located in the traditional sections. In the light of this, what kind of an approach will be helpful in investigating the authorship and purpose of Colossians? Since both of these matters have to do with historical considerations and since the content of the letter is made up largely of theological matters, our approach must of necessity be both historical and theological. But such an approach must be made with full awareness of the difficulties involved.

It is the historical approach that is most problematic. At first glance it would seem that the most obvious thing to do would be to try to

---

[4]Lohse, *Colossians*, pp. 180-81 (emphasis mine).

reconstruct the major tenets of the "philosophy" and then assess whether or not the theological reasoning of the writer is compatible with Paul's theology. Indeed, this has been a common approach to the problem of the authorship and purpose of the letter. However, to reconstruct the teachings of a group or movement on the basis of a polemic made against it is always hazardous even when we know who the author of the polemic was. When we are uncertain about the authorship and historical circumstances of a polemical document, the problem of reconstruction becomes extremely difficult. We run the risk of assuming a historical context, building models on the basis of individual words and phrases against the backdrop of the historical assumption, and then atomistically sorting out the phenomena of the text on the basis of those models. Fred O. Francis and Wayne Meeks were keenly aware of the danger of circular reasoning in the reconstructing of the Colossian "philosophy."[5] They were also aware of the importance of the presence of traditional materials in drawing any conclusions about it.[6] Our investigation has shown that the writer was concerned that his readers not waver from the "hope of the gospel" which they had heard and that they live in accordance with the teaching which they had received about Christ. He specifically wanted to remind them of Christ's lordship over all things, including the invisible "rulers and authorities," and of Christ's subjugation of those powers through his death. The traditional Christ-hymn celebrates these facts and the traditional baptismal and hymnic passage in 2:9-15 reaffirms that teaching and the participation of the readers in the triumph of the cross-event. What all of this means in terms of conduct is made clear in the polemical section (2:4-8; 2:16-3:4) and in the traditional paraenesis in 3:5-4:6.

---

[5]See Morna D. Hooker, "Were There False Teachers in Colossae?" in *Christ and Spirit in the New Testament*, ed. Barnabas Lindars and Stephen S. Smalley in honor of Charles Francis Digby Moule (Cambridge: University Press, 1973), pp. 315-31. She concluded that the Colossians were not endangered by actual false teachers but were pressed by the beliefs and practices of their pagan and Jewish neighbors.

[6]*Conflict at Colossae*, revised edition, ed. and trans. with an introduction and epilogue by Fred O. Francis and Wayne A. Meeks, Sources for Biblical Study 4 (Missoula: Scholars Press, 1975), pp. 209-17. Two of the ten methodological issues cited comment on the importance of observing the traditional material:

(5) Ideally, the literary form and context of a document ought to be of paramount importance in constructing an historical model. The line of argument in Colossians--its

An examination of the contents of the traditional passages in the light of the warnings in the polemical sections will enable us to establish parameters for assessing the historical situation. If it can be shown that these parameters enclose concerns akin to those which Paul faced, then Pauline authorship must not be ruled out. Moreover, if it can be shown that they comprise concerns that were of special and unique interest to Paul, Pauline authorship should be given ever more credence. Finally, if it can be shown that the traditional materials, and especially their redactions and functions within the letter, are compatible with Paul's central theological perspective, Pauline authorship should be considered likely.

With these matters in mind an appropriate way to approach the problem of the authorship and purpose of Colossians will be to examine two especially important features of the mission and message of the Apostle Paul and then to examine Colossians in the light of those features.

SPECIAL FEATURES IN THE MISSION AND MESSAGE OF PAUL

An extensive examination of the life and teachings of Paul is obviously much too large an undertaking for this study. If possible, we must narrow the investigation to those features of the Apostle's ministry and message which were of special and even unique importance to him. If the use of traditional materials in Colossians has any specific bearing on those special features, a decision as to whether or not Paul wrote the letter will be greatly aided. Fortunately there are two very specific items which stand out as of unique importance to Paul. The first has to do with the special nature of his apostleship and the second has to do with the inclusion of the Gentiles as the special feature of his gospel.

---

phrases and their inner connectedness--must be weighed carefully. The difficulty lies in the opaque allusion, the enigmatic statement, even the unexpressed presupposition. A distinct problem in Colossians and in some other documents is to know the function of traditional material (hymns, and other formulae).

(6) Careful attention must be given to establishing the common ground between writer and opponents in controversial documents such as Colossians. One cannot carry on an argument if everything is at issue. Perhaps the traditional material functions at least in part as common ground. Pp. 216, 217.

The Special Nature of Paul's Apostleship

It is well-known that Paul's apostolic status was constantly under attack and that he responded to the charges and innuendos of his opponents with a vigor nearly unmatched in the New Testament. His apostolic mission was clearly very important to him.

Acts bears witness to a tradition which asserted that one of the requirements of apostolic status was the necessity of having accompanied Jesus during his earthly ministry (Acts 1:21ff. and 10:34ff.). Such a qualification plainly excluded Paul from that unique group. No doubt his opponents used this against him. Such an argument would put him in tension with the Jerusalem apostolate. This may help to explain why Paul referred to the "Twelve" only once[7] and why he speaks of the leaders of the Jerusalem church with such reserve in Galatians.[8] The defensive way in which Paul declares his independence from Jerusalem in Galatians and the way in which he compares himself to Apostles who were "Hebrews," "Israelites," "sons of Abraham," and "servants of Christ" in 2 Corinthians 11:1-29 probably reflects his sensitivity to being compared with the Jerusalem apostles. Paul never took a stand against the Jerusalem apostolate. On the contrary, he seemed glad to receive their support and recognition (Galatians 2:7-10). The question must be asked, however, whether Paul wanted his opponents and his churches to recognize his apostleship as equal to the Jerusalem apostolate, or whether he wanted them to understand that it was in some way even more important than theirs.

The Significance of the Damascus Road Experience. Paul's experience on the road to Damascus has been interpreted in a variety of ways.[9]

---

[7]The term "Twelve" is used by Paul in 1 Cor. 15:5 in a context full of formulaic and stylistic features which characterize traditional material.

[8]The strange statement in Gal. 2:6, which at first glance seems to present a rather cavalier attitude toward the Jerusalem "pillars," probably is more of an expression of his attitude toward the argument of his opponents than an expression of his opinion of the leaders. The phrase ὁποῖοί ποτε ἦσαν should be given its full temporal meaning. "Whatsoever they were *at one time* makes no difference to me." Such a statement probably reflects Paul's sensitivity to his opponents' argument that he, unlike the Jerusalem apostles, had not been with Jesus during his earthly ministry. See Betz, *Galatians*, pp. 92-95 for a variety of interpretations of this verse.

[9]Gerhard Lohfink, *The Conversion of St. Paul: Narrative and History in Acts,* trans. and ed. by Bruce J. Malina (Chicago: Franciscan Herald, 1976), and William D.

Frequently it has been called his "conversion experience," a designation which has been rightfully criticized.[10] Paul refers to his Damascus road experience only rarely,[11] and the clearest of these is in Galatians 1:15-17. The striking contrast which he made between his former manner of life in 1:13, 14 and his call in 1:15-17 does indeed give the impression of a dramatic conversion. However, the broader context shows that Paul's purpose was not primarily to contrast his former and present situation, but to declare his independence from any human source for the gospel which he preached. Galatians 1:15-17 is not so much a description of Paul's conversion as it is a description of his call.

The call of the Apostle is depicted in ways that are reminiscent of the call of Jeremiah and the call of Israel, the servant of Yahweh, in Isaiah 49. Both of these Old Testament figures were called before they were born and both were called to minister to the Gentiles (Isaiah 49:1-6; Jeremiah 1:5). These are the same features singled out by Paul in Galatians 1:15-17. Furthermore, the Apostle pointed out that his special call to preach the gospel to the Gentiles was recognized by the Jerusalem apostolate. The Jerusalem leaders understood that Paul "had been entrusted with the gospel to the uncircumcised, just as Peter had been entrusted with the gospel to the circumcised" and that God, who had appointed Peter "for apostleship to the circumcised" had also appointed Paul "for the Gentiles" (Galatians 2:7, 8).

The significance of Paul's Damascus road experience is depicted in Acts in a way which closely corresponds to Paul's account in Galatians. It is described in Acts 9:1-19; 22:4-16; and 26:12-19. There are minor differences in the accounts but they all stress the same thing.[12] The Damascus road experience was the occasion of Paul's call to declare God's name among the Gentiles. In Acts, as in Galatians, the call is

---

Davies, *Invitation to New Testament* (Garden City: Doubleday & Co., 1966), pp. 254-65.

[10]Krister Stendahl, *Paul Among Jews and Gentiles and Other Essays* (Philadelphia: Fortress Press, 1976), pp. 7-23.

[11]Although there are numerous passages which refer to the grace of apostleship received from God, the only passages which imply the historical occasion for the reception of this gift are Gal. 1:16, 17; 1 Cor. 9:1; 15:8-10.

[12]Acts 9 differs from Acts 22 over whether the companions of Paul heard the voice of Jesus. Acts 26 differs from the other two passages in that the call to preach to the Gentiles came directly from Jesus rather than through the mediation of Ananias.

akin to the call of an Old Testament prophet.[13] The light, the voice, and the dramatic commission all bring to mind the calls of Isaiah, Jeremiah, and Enoch.[14] The main stress in each passage is the call to preach the gospel to the Gentiles (9:15; 22:15; 26:17, 18). The New Testament does not interpret Paul's experience on the Damascus road as a moral conversion or as a crisis of self understanding (in the Bultmannian sense). There is a sense in which it was a crisis of recognizing that the crucified man from Nazareth was indeed the anticipated Messiah which the primitive church declared,[15] but the primary significance of Paul's experience on the road to Damascus was that it was his call by the resurrected Lord to be His agent for the proclamation of the gospel to the Gentiles.

Conclusion. The special nature of Paul's call to be the apostle of Jesus Christ to the Gentiles is affirmed by the fact that it is regularly included in the salutations of all but four of the letters in the Pauline corpus. Even in those four (1 and 2 Thessalonians, Philippians, and Philemon) references to Paul's apostolic presence and authority play an important role. With regard to our inquiry into the Pauline authorship of Colossians, it is important to notice that it is in the letters in which Jewish ideologies and Jewish Christian pressures against Paul predominate that Paul stressed his call to be an apostle of Christ to the Gentiles (Galatians 1:16; 2:7-9; Romans 1:5, 13, 14; 11:13; 15:15-21; 16:25-27).[16] There is little doubt that Paul regarded his call by Jesus Christ to be the Apostle to the Gentiles as of special and unique importance. The Jerusalem apostolate obviously had interests in the Gentile mission, but their chief responsibility was to minister the gospel of Christ to the circumcision.[17] Paul, however, repeatedly refers

---

[13]Paul never so regarded himself, however. He is the eschatological apostle, *sui generis.*

[14]Johannes Munck, *Paul and the Salvation of Mankind,* trans. Franke Clark (Richmond: John Knox Press, 1959), pp. 24-33.

[15]Davies, *Invitation,* pp. 260-62.

[16]Paul's apostolic authority was also undermined in Corinth (probably by Jewish emissaries), 1 Cor. 9:1ff. and 2 Cor. 11-13. However, the trouble in Corinth was more related to pneumatic enthusiasm than to Jewish exclusivistic practices.

[17]Galatians 2:1-10 and 2 Cor.10:13-18 seem to indicate some kind of agreement between the Jerusalem leaders and Paul about the jurisdiction of ministry. Acts implies that a chief concern of the Jerusalem authorities was that Gentile Christians should not

to the fact that his apostleship to the Gentiles came by divine appointment. As we shall show in the next section, this understanding of the special nature of his call was rooted in eschatology.[18]

The Special Feature in Paul's Gospel

There was something about Paul's gospel that evoked a strong negative reaction from both Christian and non-Christian elements in the Jewish community. Some Jews went to extreme measures to keep him from preaching to Gentiles[19] and some Jewish Christians sought to discredit him both in Jerusalem and in the Gentile churches.[20] This Jewish opposition is much in evidence in all of the undisputed Pauline letters but is dealt with directly in Galatians and Romans. Significantly, it is in these two letters that Paul most thoroughly sets forth the contents of the gospel which he preached. Our investigation of the special feature of Paul's gospel will, therefore, be primarily based on Galatians. What was there about Paul's gospel which brought him into such severe contention with Judaism and some elements in the Jewish church? Before that question can be answered we must consider the inadequacy of the common approach to understanding the significance of Paul's gospel in his own day.

The Inadequacy of the Standard Approach to Paul. The negative heading of this section should not be taken as a lack of appreciation for

---

offend Jewish Christians with regard to certain cultic practices. Acts 15:20, 29; 21:25 ("Alexandrian" text). Paul did not trace the source of his problems to the Jerusalem leaders but to emissaries from there. The issue of Paul's own position vis-à-vis the Decree in Acts 15 is a difficult one. It is likely that he experienced tension with it. See John C. Hurd, *The Origin of 1 Corinthians* (New York: Seabury Press, 1965), pp. 246-53, for a summary of solutions to the problem. See also Marcel Simon, "The Apostolic Decree and Its Setting in the Ancient Church," *BJRL* 52 (1970): 437-60.

[18]See Munck, *Paul and the Salvation of Mankind*, pp. 36-38. Munck believed that Paul regarded himself as the eschatological prophet whose ministry to the Gentiles was ultimately aimed at the salvation of Israel and the consummation of the ages. Stendahl regarded this aspect of Munck's argument as a *tour de force* (*Paul Among Jews and Gentiles*, p. vi). I think that Stendahl is partially right but he goes too far in assuming that Paul believed that Christianity was the way of salvation for Gentiles and that the Abrahamic Covenant and Torah observance was the way for the Jews. For Paul, the Abrahamic Covenant included *both* Jews and Gentiles and the seed of Abraham through whom the Abrahamic promise would be fulfilled was Christ (Gal. 3:16, 26-29).

[19]First Thessalonians 2:15, 16; 2 Cor. 11:24; Rom. 15:31.

[20]Romans 15:31; Gal. 2:11-14; 2 Cor. 11:20-23; Phil. 3:2-7.

the standard approach to Pauline theology. In many ways the "common" approach to Paul is more relevant to the present human situation than the one that will be set forth in this part of our discussion.

For centuries the opposition between Paul and Judaism has been understood in terms of contrasting ways of salvation. Judaism, it is assumed, teaches that salvation is earned by legalistically obeying the law, whereas Paul taught that it is freely received by grace through faith in Jesus Christ. That Paul taught the latter is without question true. That Judaism taught the former is highly questionable. In any event, the standard interpretation of Paul has been set forth in terms of "faith versus works" or "grace versus law." Such is the common understanding of Paul in Protestantism and it is the reason why Protestant theology is often thought of as Pauline theology.

In his provocative article "The Apostle Paul and the Introspective Conscience of the West" Krister Stendahl sought to expose the problem of modernizing Paul. He contrasted the "robust conscience" of Paul with the introspective consciences of Augustine, Luther, and the western mind-set in general. His point was that the "introspective conscience of the West" causes one to view Paul's theology in the light of the Protestant/Catholic struggle of the Reformation period rather than in the light of the Jew/Gentile situation in Paul's own day. He indicated that when Paul speaks of the relationship between Jew and Gentile,

> We tend to read him as if his question was: On what grounds, on what terms, are we to be saved? We think that Paul spoke about justification by faith, using the Jewish-Gentile situation as an instance, as an example. But Paul was chiefly concerned about the relation between Jews and Gentiles--and in the development of this concern he used as one of his arguments the idea of justification by faith.[21]

This common way of interpreting Paul's opposition to Judaism as one dealing with salvation by grace or by merit is met with strong opposition by contemporary Jewish scholars. Rabbinic Judaism, they insist, has never taught that one can merit salvation. It has always taught that God graciously gives of Himself to His people and that out of love He freely forgives the repentant sinner. So strong is this conviction that C. G. Montefiore believed that Paul must have been

---

[21]Stendahl, *Paul Among Jews and Gentiles*, p. 3.

combating some inferior kind of Judaism that was clearly out of step with main-line Rabbinic Judaism.[22] The outward symbol of God's love and willingness to forgive, he wrote, was the Day of Atonement.

> What neither God nor man could do according to Paul, except by the incarnation of the Son, was done according to Rabbinic Judaism constantly, hour by hour, year by year. Nothing is more peculiar in the great Epistles than the almost complete omission of the twin Rabbinic ideas of repentance and forgiveness.[23]

If main-line Judaism never taught that justification was by works, then Paul was either raising the wrong issue or we have misunderstood the real issue which he was raising.

E. P. Sanders has recently attempted to show that the standard interpretation of Paul's teaching (righteousness by faith and not by works) is incorrect.[24] Such an interpretation, he asserts, is based upon secondary sources which reconstruct the primary sources of Rabbinic Judaism in a legalistic direction.[25] He investigated the Tannaitic literature, the Dead Sea Scrolls, the Apocrypha and Pseudepigrapha (all of which were written between 200 B.C.E. and 200 C.E.). He concluded that the common pattern of religion in all of these Jewish sources is that of "covenantal nomism." He declares that with the exception of *Ben Sira*,

> In all of the literature surveyed, *obedience maintains one's position in the covenant, but does not earn God's grace as such* (emphasis his). It simply keeps an individual in the group which is the recipient of God's grace.[26]

Such a conclusion would indicate that there was no major shift from the Old Testament teaching about the relationship between the cove-

---

[22]C. G. Montefiore, *Judaism and St. Paul* (London, 1914), pp. 21ff. H. J. Schoeps, *Paul: The Theology of the Apostle in the Light of Jewish Religious History*, trans. Harold Knight (Philadelphia: The Westminster Press, 1961, first published in 1959), pp. 168-218. Samuel Sandmel, *The Genius of Paul* (New York: Schocken Books, 1958), p. 59.

[23]Montefiore, *Judaism*, p. 75.

[24]Sanders, *Paul and Palestinian Judaism*.

[25]Predominent among the secondary sources are Wilhelm Bousset, *Die Religion des Judentums im neutestamentlichen zeitalter* (Berlin: Reuther & Reichard, 1903); H. Strack and P. Billerbeck, *Kommentar zum Neuen Testament aus Talmud und Midrash* (6 vols. in 7); and Ferdinand W. Weber, *System der altsynagogalen palaestinischen Theologie aus Targum, Midrasch und Talmud* (Leipzig: Doerffling & Franke, 1880).

[26]Sanders, *Paul and Palestinian Judaism*, p. 420.

nant and the law in post-biblical Judaism. Judaism did not teach that one *got in* the covenantal relationship by earning it through Torah obedience, but that one *stayed in* the covenant on that basis. This being the case, either Paul was combating a divergent form of Judaism which taught that salvation is achieved by a meritorious keeping of the law (as Montefiore and others believed) or else a "faith versus works" or a "grace versus law" interpretation of Paul is inadequate. Since the Jewish problem confronted Paul in nearly every place in which he ministered and since it came from both Christian and non-Christian Jews, it is not likely that he was dealing with a divergent form of Judaism. He dealt with a problem which he regarded to be a general one and which in some way contradicted an essential aspect of the gospel which he preached. This problem is faced most directly in his letter to the Galatian churches. It is to this letter that we now turn.

Galatians and the Truth of Paul's Gospel. The issue at stake in the letter to the Galatian churches was the truth of the gospel which Paul preached. In the startling passage which replaces the usual epistolary prayer and thanksgiving section (1:6-10), Paul rebuked the readers for turning to a different gospel and placed a double curse on those who preach a gospel different from the one which he preached. He emphatically declared that his gospel did not come from human origin but through revelation (1:11, 12) and showed a constant concern for the "truth of the gospel" (2:5, 14) and the "truth" (4:16; 5:7). It is apparent that some agitators were attempting to pervert the gospel which he preached (1:6, 7) and were insisting upon the necessity of circumcision and the "works of the law." Was the issue at stake that of salvation by works, or was there something more explicit than that which concerned Paul? An explanation of Galatians 1:11, 12 and 2:15-21 will help answer that question.[27]

Galatians 1:11, 12. Paul made it explicitly clear that his gospel was not "according to man" nor "from man" but that it came "through

---

[27]These two passages are of strategic importance in the structure of Galatians. The letter-body of Galatians falls into three sections: a "biographical" section (1:11-2:14), a "theological" section (2:15-4:13 [5:1?]), and a "paraenetic" section (5:1-6:10). The issue at stake in the "biographical" section is the source of Paul's gospel. Hence 1:11, 12 introduces that section. The issue at stake in the "theological" section is faith in Jesus Christ" over against "works of the law." Since 2:15-21 deals explicitly with that issue,

revelation of Jesus Christ." The complex issue of the seeming contradiction between these verses and 1 Corinthians 15:1-3 is important for our investigation of the special feature in Paul's gospel as well as for his use of tradition. Did he receive his gospel directly from Christ apart from human mediation as Galatians 1:11, 12 implies, or did he receive it through the regular process by which traditions were transmitted as 1 Corinthians 15:1-3 seems to indicate?[28] Erich Dinkler thought that the problem was insoluble but perhaps that is overly pessimistic.[29]

The gospel which Paul had received and transmitted to the Corinthians (1 Corinthians 15:1-3) was about the death, burial, and resurrection of Christ. Paul had no doubt heard, understood, and rejected that proclamation before his experience on the road to Damascus. Indeed, at that time he was energetically attempting to silence it. In one sense it can be said that Paul's encounter with the risen Jesus on the Damascus road verified the proclamation which he had previously rejected. However, the basic message about the death, burial, and resurrection of Christ is not the specific issue with which he dealt in Galatians.[30] It is doubtful that the agitators would have been so persuasive if they had denied the basic facts of the gospel.

There is general agreement that the phrase "through revelation of Jesus Christ" refers to the experience on the Damascus road. However, the question is often raised in commentaries whether "of Jesus Christ" is a subjective or objective genitive. The question is a difficult one, but it seems to me that the context indicates that it is an objective genitive and that the "revelation of Jesus Christ" involves a specific content which was of special importance to Paul. It is important to notice the emphatic personal pronouns in 1:11 and 1:12. Paul spoke of *his*

---

the question of whether 2:15-21 belongs to the "biographical" section or the "theological" one should probably be answered: the latter.

[28]See Jack T. Sanders, "Paul's 'Autobiographical' Statements in Galatians 1-2," *JBL* 85 (1966): 335-43; and Betz, *Galatians*, pp. 64-66, for recent discussions of this issue.

[29]Erich Dinkler, "Tradition V. Im Urchristentum," *RGG* 6 (1967): 970-74.

[30]It is true that there are references to the death of Christ in Gal. 1:4; 2:20, 21; 3:3, 13; and 6:14, but in none of these instances is the *fact* of Christ's death at issue. In each instance it is the eschatological significance of Christ's death as the means of deliverance from the evil age or world that is under discussion. In this Galatians and Colossians are much alike.

gospel.[31] As noted above, in each of the passages referring to the Damascus road experience in Acts and Galatians the single feature which stands out is Paul's call to be the Apostle to the Gentiles. As we shall point out in the next section, the "truth of the gospel" about which Paul was so concerned was that Gentiles are included in God's plan. The saving activity of God revealed in Jesus Christ is that Gentiles as well as Jews receive God's saving righteousness. Furthermore, Gentiles do not have to become Jews to receive it. This is the content of the gospel especially revealed to Paul on the road to Damascus and it is this which made it *his* gospel over against the perverted gospel of the agitators. It is also this message which brought him into conflict with both Christian and non-Christian Jews.

Galatians 2:15-21. Paul's reference to the "truth of the gospel" in 2:5, 14 and to the "truth" in 4:16 and 5:7 are in contexts which reveal what was at issue in the perversion of his gospel. In 2:5 and 5:7 the issue was circumcision. In 2:14 it was withdrawal from table fellowship with Gentiles and is called by Paul "living Jewishly ('Ιουδαϊκῶς)." Within the context of 2:15-21 Paul contrasted two things which later formed the basis for the common Protestant interpretation of Pauline theology. It is important to notice that he did not simply contrast "faith" and "works," but "faith *in Jesus Christ*" and the "works *of the law.*" An examination of these two phrases will show that something more explicit is in the mind of the apostle than to contrast believing or trusting with human effort.

(1) *The "Works of the Law."* Let us begin by examining the phrase "by the works of the law." It occurs six times in the letter.[32] The common way of interpreting the phrase can be summarized in the words of E. D. Burton: "by ἔργων νόμου Paul means deeds of obedience to formal statutes done in a legalistic spirit, and with the expectation of thereby meriting and securing divine approval and reward."[33] More recently H. D. Betz defined the phrase as referring to "meritorious works of the Torah" which are based on the "Jewish (Pharisaic) doctrine" of justification by fulfilling the ordinances of the

---

[31]Note Rom. 16:25 where the gospel is described as "my gospel."

[32]Galatians 2:16 (three times) and 3:2, 5, 10.

[33]E. D. Burton, *Galatians*, ICC (Edinburgh: T.&T. Clark, 1921), p. 120.

Torah.[34] Both of these definitions run counter to the insistence of contemporary Jewish scholars that main-line Judaism never taught that salvation was by merit and to Sanders' study of the Jewish literature written between 200 B.C.E. and 200 C.E.

Ernst Lohmeyer made a careful study of the phrase in *Probleme paulinischer Theologie*. He examined its use in the Septuagint, the Psalms of Solomon, 2 Ezra, 2 Baruch, and Paul. His conclusion was that Paul did not use the phrase to express the works which men accomplish in response to the law, but to describe a context of existence under which men live. The phrase, he said, designated "the religious system set for man" and could well be translated "nomistic service."[35]

In an article that has not received the attention it deserves, Joseph Tyson examined the phrase in Galatians in the light of Lohmeyer's analysis. On the basis of an exegesis of Galatians 2:15, 16; 3:2, 5; and 3:10-12, he concluded:

> (1) "Works of law" refers specifically to a life dedicated to nomistic service; it is not to be confused with human deeds of a possibly meritorious quality. (2) Nomistic service is primarily associated with circumcision and the food laws. (3) Paul believes that the conditions set by nomistic service had been superceded by a new set of conditions which can be denoted as faith in Jesus Christ. The death of Jesus made this possible, and it constitutes God's rejection of nomistic service. (4) Paul's understanding of this rejection involves a broadening concept of the chosen people. God's people are marked by faith and the Spirit rather than by circumcision and food laws.[36]

The "works of the law" in Galatians are those things which distinguish a Jew from a Gentile. It has to do with living Jewishly ('Ιουδαϊκῶς) and not like a Gentile (ἐθνικῶς). It is particularly illustrated in the observance of circumcision and Jewish food laws. Just as importantly, it is placed over against "faith in Jesus Christ" (2:16) and the new eschatological situation marked by the reception of the Spirit and response to the gospel (3:1-6). In other words, the "works of law" describe a mode of existence marked by Jewish exclusivism. Such a manner of life is incompatible with the new eschatological situation in

---

[34]Betz, *Galatians*, pp. 116, 117.

[35]E. Lohmeyer, *Probleme paulinischer Theologie* (Darmstadt and Stuttgart, 1954), p. 67.

[36]J. B. Tyson, " 'Works of the Law' in Galatians," *JBL* 92 (1973): 431.

Christ. Exclusivism is contrary to the gospel of Paul. Consequently, the letter ends with a declaration of the incongruity of exclusivism with the kind of life set forth in the gospel. "For neither circumcision counts for anything nor uncircumcision, but a new creation. Peace and mercy upon all who walk by this rule, upon the Israel of God" (6:15, 16).

(2) *"Faith in Jesus Christ."* The phrase which stands in direct antithesis to the "works of law" is "faith in Jesus Christ." The repeated contrast between the ideas represented by the two phrases is nearly overpowering in 2:16:

> Knowing that a man is not justified[37] by the works of the law but through faith in Jesus Christ, even we believed in Jesus Christ, in order that we might be justified by faith in Jesus Christ and not by works of the law because by works of the law shall no flesh be justified. (RSV)

The contrast is not between "works" and "faith," but between "works of law" and "faith in Jesus Christ." Just as the former phrase has specific content and meaning, so does the latter. All three uses of "faith" in Galatians 2:16 (two nouns and one verb) are modified by "Jesus Christ." The same is true in Galatians 3:22 and 26.[38] The genitive form Ἰησοῦ χριστοῦ opens up a variety of possible meanings. Some interpret the genitive as referring to the faith which Jesus himself had.[39] Such a meaning is unlikely. It more likely refers to the content of the faith as is implied in the phrase εἰς χριστὸν Ἰησοῦν ἐπιστεύσαμεν in

---

[37]The meaning of the δικ- root words in Paul is a matter too large to discuss in this study. See Manfred Brauch ("Perspectives on 'God's righteousness' in recent German discussion," in E. Sanders, *Paul and Palestinian Judaism*, pp. 523-42), and Sanders' own wise word of caution on the subject (pp. 491ff.) in which he notes that "righteousness does not have any one fixed meaning" and objects to the tendency of forcing them all into one meaning. J. A. Zeisler in *The Meaning of Righteousness in Paul* (Cambridge: University Press, 1972), seeks to distinguish between the meaning of the verb and the meaning of the noun and adjective. Some of his insights are helpful, but he approaches his task with the Protestant/Catholic problems of the Reformation period in mind rather than the Jew/Gentile problems of Paul's period. The Apostle uses the "righteousness" words almost exclusively in the context of the Jew/Gentile situation. Within that broad setting, I take the terms to refer to God's trustworthiness or covenant loyalty and to His saving activity.

[38]See also Rom. 3:22, 26 and Phil. 3:9.

[39]For this position see G. M. Taylor, "The Function of ΠΙΣΤΙΣ ΧΡΙΣΤΟΥ in Galatians," *JBL* 85 (1966): pp. 58-76; E. R. Goodenough, "Paul and the Hellenization of Christianity," *Religion in Antiquity, Essays in Memory of E. R. Goodenough*, pp. 47ff.; and G. Howard, "On the 'Faith of Christ,' " *HTR* 60 (1967): 459-65.

Galatians 2:16. Even more likely, in my opinion, it classifies faith as a "Jesus Christ" kind of faith.[40] In any event, it is not just faith or trust as an attitude that is in mind, but a faith or trust in Jesus Christ, who in Galatians 1:4 is described as the one "who gave himself for our sins in order to deliver us from the present evil age." That is to say, there is an eschatological dimension to the meaning and content of the phrase "faith in Jesus Christ."

The eschatological dimension of the phrase is made evident in at least three ways in the Galatian letter. First, it is disclosed by the contrast made between the "works of law" and the "hearing of faith (ἀκοὴ πίστεως)" in 3:1-5. The Galatians' experience of having received the Spirit was not based on living Jewishly ("the works of law") but on response to the Gospel (or the hearing of faith). The reception of the Spirit is clearly an eschatological event. The Gospel announces that God's righteousness is for Gentiles as well as Jews; therefore, Gentiles as well as Jews receive the eschatological Spirit (3:2, 5, 14).

Second, the eschatological dimension of the phrase "faith in Jesus Christ" is made known in 3:6-14, where faith is related to Abraham and the Gospel. Verse 7 asserts that "those of faith are the sons of Abraham." Is this because the men of faith had the same kind of *attitude* toward God and His promises as Abraham had?[41] Or is it because the

---

[40]See the function of the genitive case in A. T. Robertson, *A Grammar of the Greek N.T. in the Light of Historical Research*, 4th ed. (Nashville: Broadman Press, 1934), pp. 493-94.

[41]Betz implies this when he writes, "These 'men of [the] faith' are identified with the 'sons of Abraham' because they believe the same *way* (emphasis mine) as Abraham did." *Galatians*, p. 142. The statement is no doubt true, but it seems to put the emphasis in the wrong place. The passage is extremely difficult because of the way in which the O.T. texts are used and because of the variety of meanings of "law." Though Betz's interpretation seems to be supported by the argument in Gal. 3:10-13, some brief observations should be made. (1) "Those of faith who are blessed with faithful Abraham" (3:9) are contrasted with those who are of the "works of law" and are "under a curse" (3:10). As we have previously shown, the phrase "works of law" does not refer to the general idea of Torah obedience (contra Betz), but to practices related to Jewish particularism. The O.T. texts are used to support the statement that those who "live Jewishly" and hence promote Jewish exclusivism are under a curse. (2) This must be kept in mind in the interpretation of the "curse" statement in 3:10 which is based on a quotation of Deut. 27:26. The quotation differs from both the M.T. and the LXX by asserting the necessity of abiding in *all* of the things which are written in the book of the law. The "things" under discussion are Jewish things which isolate the Jew from all others. Such a manner of life is in contradiction to the gospel which Paul preached. (3) Although the emphasis in the passage seems to be upon "doing" or "working" over

content of their faith was the same as Abraham's? It would be wrong to make an either/or issue out of this since both are probably true. However, the emphasis has usually been on the former whereas the latter is clearly (if not predominantly) present in the passage. The association of Abraham with the gospel (3:8) points in this direction. As we noted above, the special feature of the gospel which Paul preached was the inclusion of the Gentiles in God's plan of salvation. Since Paul regarded himself to be uniquely called by God to be the Apostle to the Gentiles, the importance of the inclusivism motif cannot be overestimated. It was the fact that the Scripture (Genesis 12:3; 18:18) taught that all of the nations would be blessed in Abraham that enabled Paul to identify the promise to Abraham with the gospel. I do not think that Paul regarded the promise to Abraham as a kind of prototype of the gospel. It *was* the gospel because the promise to Abraham was fulfilled in Christ, the seed of Abraham (Galatians 3:16), in whom there is neither Jew nor Gentile (Galatians 3:27-29). It is for this reason that Paul can relate the blessing of Abraham to the eschatological reception of the Spirit (Galatians 3:14).[42] Faith is not just believing. It is faith in the Chirst in whom Gentiles experience the righteousness of God and the reception of the Spirit. It is faith in the eschatological Christ-event.

Third, the eschatological dimension of the phrase "faith in Jesus Christ" is revealed in the section in which Paul defined the purpose and function of the law (3:19-25). The "law" under discussion is the law given through Moses on Mt. Sinai. It had a positive function to perform,[43] but the function was temporary. It is completed now that

---

against "believing," it should be noted that the verb for "doing" is found only in the O.T. texts cited (Deut. 27:26 in verse 10 and Lev. 18:5 in verse 12), not in the application of the passage.

[42]The two most significant O.T. figures in the letters of Paul are Abraham and Adam. Both of them are inclusivistic figures which show the significance of Christ for all mankind.

[43]Some think that the statements about the law being "added because of transgressions" and "ordained by angels at the hand of a mediator" in 3:19 indicate that Paul regarded the law as evil. (For documentation of this see H. Betz, *Galatians*, fns. 64 and 66, p. 169). Such a view, it seems to me, is unlikely in view of Paul's strong denial (μὴ γένοιτο) that the law was against the promises of God (3:21a) and the implication that if the law had power to make alive, it would (3:21b). The same point is made in Rom. 7:13-25. The law is good, but it has no power to enable one to do the good.

Christ, the seed of Abraham, has come (3:19b). The eschatological setting of the passage can be seen in the repeated use of the verb ἔρχομαι in 3:19, 23, and 25. In verse 19 the subject of the verb is the "seed of Abraham." In verses 23 and 25 it is "the faith."[44] The article denotes previous reference and points back to "faith in Jesus Christ"in verse 22. "The faith" refers to the eschatological event of the coming of Jesus Christ. Before he came, the law enclosed the people of the Old Covenant as a protective fence.[45] It served as a "custodian (παιδαγω-γός, 3:24)" to watch over them and guard them from the awesome threat of idolatry. It did this by keeping them separate from the "uncleanness" of the pagan world which surrounded them through the observance of rites and ceremonies that maintained their state of ritual "cleanness." In other words, the law served as a guardian for the people of the Sinaitic Covenant who were as helpless children. They needed protection from the hostile powers and the στοιχεῖα (4:3) which so thoroughly victimized the nations. The law provided the means by which the people of the Old Covenant could be kept separate and distinct from the nations. It served an exclusivistic purpose to keep Israel separate from the nations. At one time exclusivism was maintained by the "works of law" and was necessary. But a new day has come. The law belonged to the old age. Now that Christ has come, it no longer has any function to perform. "Faith in Jesus Christ" is the believing response to the gospel announcement that the eschatological day has begun.

With the coming of the Christ who delivers us "out of the present evil age" also came the Spirit of Christ, who enables God's people to live responsibly as adults, not as children (νήπιοι) (4:1-6). The Spirit gives power to live in freedom from the στοιχεῖα of the world (4:3) and from the lusts of the flesh (5:16-26). The law which protected and isolated God's people from all others is no longer needed. Exclusivism was necessary for the preceding era, but the Spirit, who is given to both Jews and Gentiles, makes inclusivism the mark of the new eschatologi-

---

[44]An accusative of general reference or "subject accusative" construction is used in Gal. 3:22 and a genitive absolute construction is used in Gal. 3:25.

[45]It is important to note that it was not the law or the Torah which enclosed all things under sin. It was the Scripture which did that. The Scripture depicted the overpowering pressures of idolatry and concomitant immorality which constantly threatened Israel.

cal day. To require circumcision, food laws, or any other exclusively Jewish thing was, therefore, a denial of the special feature of the gospel according to Paul. "In Christ there is neither Jew nor Gentile, slave nor free, male nor female."

Conclusion

In the light of the above, our conclusion about the special and unique features in Paul's mission and message can be brief. His mission was based upon his special call to be the Apostle of Jesus Christ to the Gentiles. This mission is not only placed on a par with the mission of the Jerusalem apostolate, but in a sense it was even more important than theirs. Their ministry to the circumcision could not be completed until Paul's ministry to the Gentiles was completed.[46] Indeed, his ministry would be the catalyst which would bring about the completion of their ministry. Moreover, Paul's message was wholly bound up with his mission. He was the Apostle to the Gentiles and the gospel was the announcement that the Christ-event was for Gentiles as well as Jews. Participation in the death and resurrection of Christ meant participation in the one in whom there can be neither Jew nor Gentile. The special feature of Paul's gospel was the inclusivistic significance of the mission of Christ.

Even though we have limited our discussion to the letter to the Galatians, the inclusivistic emphasis in Paul's gospel must not be considered to be limited to that letter. The letter to the Romans sets forth an even more elaborate explanation of the theme of the inclusion of the Gentiles in the redemptive plan of God. Romans, which was no doubt written to the church at Rome, may also have been sent to the churches in Asia. Furthermore, it was written just prior to his trip to Jerusalem where he anticipated the resistance of some in the Jerusalem church to his gospel of inclusiveness. Hence, the first three chapters declare the Gentiles have as much right to experience God's saving righteousness as do the Jews. Romans 3:21-4:25 not only makes the

---

[46]Romans 11:11-32 shows that Paul regarded his ministry to the Gentiles to have implications for the future salvation of Israel. Munck, *Paul and the Salvation of Mankind*, pp. 23-25, describes Paul's call as that of the eschatological prophet whose ministry would usher in the final salvation for both Jews and Gentiles. Whether or not Paul believed that he would be involved in the events of the consummation, he surely thought that his ministry to the Gentiles was related to it.

same argument that is made in Galatians, but it uses the same terminology about the "works of law" and "faith in Jesus Christ." It also (even more thoroughly than Galatians) shows the significance of Abraham for his inclusivistic gospel. As in Galatians, so also in this section of Romans the phrases dealing with faith and works do not primarily contrast these terms as different ways of salvation, but as terms which contrast the inclusiveness of the eschatological gospel with the exclusiveness of the Old Testament covenant expressions. Chapters 5-8 declare the consequences of "being in Christ." Those consequences are freedom from the tyranny of sin and the law and the presence of the new dynamic of the Spirit. The whole section is based upon the presentation of Christ as the eschatological Adam (5:12-21). That model is plainly an inclusivistic one. Chapters 9-11 begin by turning the Jewish argument of exclusivism based on Abraham against them (9:6-13) and declaring that Christ is the way to righteousness for both Jews and Gentiles. Israel stumbled over that message, but Gentiles have responded. The paraenesis in chapters 12-14 is primarily directed toward a mutuality of love in which Gentile and Jewish Christians are urged not to discriminate against one another. In this letter Gentiles are in danger of practicing a kind of reverse exclusivism against the Jews. In Romans as well as in Galatians the gospel is the message that Gentiles as well as Jews are included in God's gracious purposes.

Before we examine Colossians in the light of the special features of Paul's message and ministry, an important item should be pointed out. The historical situation which the Apostle faced was that exclusivism was a threat to his gospel. In the earlier part of his ministry the exclusivism came from Jewish insistence that circumcision and other Jewish exclusivistic practices were necessary for salvation. In the latter part of his ministry the exclusivistic tendencies began to come from Gentiles within the church. Eventually Christianity became a Gentile religion and the issue of Jewish exclusivism lost its relevance.[47] Since the historical setting of Colossians is so widely disputed, an examina-

---

[47]The irrelevance of the issue of exclusivism versus inclusivism in Paul's Jew-Gentile situation is probably one of the main reasons for seeing Paul's references to faith and works as conflicting ways of salvation. In the light of the "introspective conscience of the West," which Stendahl's article aptly demonstrates, such an interpretation of Paul not only has had, but still does have great significance for the life of the church.

tion of the letter, in the light of this issue, may throw valuable light on the question of Pauline authorship.

COLOSSIANS AND PAUL

The preceding treatment of the special features of Paul's mission and message will pave the way for comparing the salient issues in Colossians with those special Pauline features. Our task is a difficult one and demands a cautious approach. We must seek to isolate the central theological perspective of Colossians and determine whether or not it is compatible with Paul's theological perspective. We must also seek to isolate some basic theological issues in Colossians that are of singular importance to Paul. Especially significant for our study will be to determine whether the use of traditional materials in Colossians is in clear accord with Paul's special concerns. In order to achieve these goals, we shall first consider the theological perspective of Paul and then examine three theological issues in Colossians that are of central interest to Paul.

The Theological Perspective of Colossians

An Evaluation of Lohse's Approach. It is to Lohse's credit that he saw that the question of the Pauline authorship of Colossians could not be answered on the basis of the style and language of the letter.[48] "To answer this question," he stated, "the theology of the letter must first be contrasted to that of the major Pauline letters and the mutual relation of these theologies must be thoroughly examined."[49] He is surely correct in pointing out the importance of theology in ascertaining the authorship of Colossians, but it appears that he has prejudged the conclusion by his use of the word "contrasted."

Lohse's approach to the task of investigating the theology of Colossians points out one of the major difficulties of such a task. His methodology was to pick out what he regarded to be the major theological categories in the letter (Christology, ecclesiology, eschatology, and baptism) and to contrast them with the same categories in the undisputed letters of Paul.[50] The problem with this approach is that it

---

[48]Lohse, "Excursus: The Language and Style of Colossians," *Colossians*, pp. 84-91.

[49]Ibid., p. 91.

[50]Ibid., pp. 177-83.

does not take into account the interrelatedness of the categories in the mind of the writer or of their bearing on the situation addressed in the letter. It is almost impossible for a New Testament writer to make a Christological statement without at the same time making an eschatological or soteriological one. The gospel itself is a Christological announcement in which eschatology, soteriology, and ecclesiology are necessarily related. In Pauline (and traditional) terms the gospel is that which God "promised beforehand through the prophets in the Holy scriptures, the gospel concerning his Son, who was descended from David according to the flesh and designated Son of God in power according to the Spirit of holiness by his resurrection from the dead, Jesus Christ our Lord" (Romans 1:2-4). The gospel is about Jesus Christ. It announces the fulfillment of an Old Testament hope. It has to do with the present as well as the future, with the "already" of the eschatological day as well as the "not yet" of the eschatological climax.[51] But most of all it has to do with Christ and salvation and the creation of a new people of God.

Lohse's treatment of the eschatology of Colossians tends to be restricted to the future expectation of the *Parousia*. He, consequently, says that eschatology in the letter has "receded into the background," whereas in most of the undisputed Pauline letters the soon coming of the Lord is anticipated.[52] It is quite true that many of Paul's letters draw attention to the "not yet" of the eschatological day and that Colossians focuses on the "already." However, Lohse's assertion ignores two important factors. First, it fails to observe that the "already" in Colossians is emphasized to help the readers live in a world that has "not yet" been fully delivered from the enslaving powers of the "rulers and authorities" and the "stoicheia." The Apostle, himself, is described as still enduring the "afflictions of the Messiah" (1:24) and of being in prison (4:4, 18). The paraenesis shows the tensions faced because of the "dominion of darkness." The readers clearly live in a pre-*Parousia* situation. The anticipation of that future day is surely in the writer's mind in 3:4 and the conditional statement concerning the necessity of continued response to the gospel (1:23), the purpose

---

[51]See above, chapter 2, under "The Theology of Colossians 1:12-20," for the way "eschatology" is used in this investigation, pp. 32-35..

[52]Lohse, *Colossians*, p. 180.

statement related to the apostle's proclamation of Christ (1:28b), and the reference to "hope" in 1:5, 23, and 27 all have futuristic connotations.[53]

Second, it ignores the fact that the undisputed letters of Paul also draw clear attention to the "already" of eschatology. Indeed, whenever Paul explicitly deals with the content of the gospel which he preached, the emphasis is on the "already" of the Christ-event. Practically no one disputes the Pauline authorship of Galatians, yet in that letter the emphasis is almost solely on the "already" of eschatology. There is not a single reference in Galatians to the *Parousia* or to the future resurrection. Indeed, as we shall point out later in this chapter, the letter to the Colossians has more affinities with Galatians than with any other letter in the Pauline corpus except Ephesians.

The point that I wish to make in this criticism of Lohse is that the theological perspective emphasized in any New Testament document is as much determined by the historical situation as it is by the predilections of the writer. It is both interesting and significant to observe that in the undisputed Pauline letters, the "already" eschatological aspect predominates when Jewish concerns are at stake (Galatians is the classic example) and the "not yet" aspect predominates when problems related to pneumatic enthusiasm are present (the Corinthian correspondence and Philippians are examples of this). In Romans, where Paul's gospel is explained, both the "already" and the "not yet" are present.

I have referred to Lohse, not to praise or refute him, but to point out that the theological categories of a letter must not be considered in isolation from one another. They must be viewed in terms of their relationships with other theological categories and with the historical situation of the writer and his readers in mind.

The Christological Perspective in Colossians. The central importance of the Christ-hymn and the main admonition to walk in the light of the

---

[53]See article on "ἐλπίς, ἐλπίζω" by R. Bultmann and K. Rengstorf in *TDNT* 2:517-33. See also E. Hoffman, "Hope, Expectation" in *The New International Dictionary of New Testament Theology* 2: 238-44. Lohse defines "hope" in Colossians as the content of the Gospel, *Colossians*, p. 180. See also G. Bornkamm, "Die Hoffnung im Kolosserbrief-zugleich ein Beitrag zur Frage der Echtheit des Briefes," in *Studien zum Neuen Testament und zur Patristik: Festschrift für Erich Klostermann* (Berlin, 1961), pp. 56-64.

received Christology make it clear that the primary theological category in Colossians is Christology. From what special perspective is it presented? We shall attempt to answer that question by examining the Christ-hymn and its applications (1:15-23; 2:9-15) and the passages dealing with the proclamation of the "mystery" (1:24-2:3; 3:24).

As noted above, the Christology of any New Testament document cannot be considered in isolation from other theological categories. The situation of both the readers and the writer will determine the way in which the Christology is interrelated with other theological concerns. In Colossians the situation of the writer's imprisonment and suffering and the readers' inclination to venerate or placate the "powers" through a variety of cultic and ascetic means necessitated an assessment of their situation in the light of the significance of Christ's death. The Christology of the letter was shaped by those concerns.

The Christ-Hymn and Its Applications. The hymn is introduced by a statement that we have previously identified as a traditional unit (1:12-14) which probably came from a confessional statement used in connection with a baptismal service.[54] The content of that unit is an eulogy to the Father which has both ecclesiological and soteriological meaning. The Father is described as the one "who has qualified us to share in the inheritance of the saints in light" (an ecclesiological statement) and as the one who "has delivered us from the dominion of darkness and transferred us to the kingdom of his beloved Son in whom we have redemption, the forgiveness of sins" (an eschatological-soteriological statement). The unit contains terms associated with the deliverance of Israel from Egypt and with the New Testament sacrament of baptism. Both of these have eschatological and soteriological meaning in the New Testament.[55]

The hymn, which celebrates the Son as Creator and Redeemer, probably has at least three redactions: "the church" (1:18a), "making peace through the blood of his cross" (1:20b), and "whether things upon the earth or things in the heavens" (1:20c).[56] The first one was added to give a cosmological statement an ecclesiological thrust. The hymn celebrates the Son as the Creator and Lord of all. As such he is

---

[54]See above, in chapter 2, "The Traditional Character of Colossians 1:12-14," pp. 12-19.

[55]See above, in chapter 2, "The Exodus Motif in 1:12-14," pp. 17-19.

[56]See above, in chapter 2, "Redactions in Colossians 1:15-20," pp. 32-33.

the "Head of the body." The most obvious sphere in which the Son's Lordship is now being demonstrated is in the church. Hence, the redaction contains both an ecclesiological and eschatological sense. The redaction was not intended to equate the church with the cosmos but to indicate that at the present time Christ's lordship over the cosmos is specifically demonstrated in the church.[57] The second redaction ("making peace through the blood of his cross") was added to a statement that already had soteriological meaning ("and through him to reconcile all things to himself") in order to focus attention on the cross as an eschatological event. Here, as in the Christ-hymn in 2:14, 15, the death of Christ is not seen from a juridicial or cultic perspective, but from an eschatological one. The death of Christ is the means by which Christ triumphed over the "rulers and authorities" (2:14, 15) and the way in which cosmic reconciliation is effected. The third redaction (whether things upon the earth or things in the heavens") emphasizes a feature that is already present in the hymn (the Son is Creator and Lord over all things including the heavenly powers) and relates it to the cross. Thus the redaction not only draws attention to a matter of special importance for the historical circumstances of the readers, but does it from an eschatological perspective. The readers were in danger of being tricked by the clever reasoning of the "philosophy" into venerating or placating the angels and powers through cultic and ascetic practices. They needed to be reminded that Christ was Lord over those powers and that he had subjugated them on the cross.

Since all of the redactions to the hymn place it in an eschatogical frame of reference, could it be that the author expected the whole hymn to be understood from that perspective? At first glance this seems to be an absurd question. Only the last part of the hymn celebrates the Son as the Reconciler of all things and it is only in that part of the hymn that the redactions occur. The first part celebrates the Son as the Creator of all things. Creation is associated with protology, not eschatology. It is probably true that the hymn was used in the church to celebrate Christ as both the preexistent Creator and Redeemer. Is that the only way in

---

[57]In 2:4 the reference to Christ's body as the church is also put in an eschatological perspective by relating it to the "messianic afflictions." No doubt the association of "body" with "church" in this passage is based on the redaction in 1:18a. If this is the case, the "body of Christ" motif in Colossians is an eschatological (not cosmological) one.

which it could be understood? More to the point, is that the way in which the writer of the letter intended it to be understood? Franz Zeilinger raised this question:

> Es wäre also zu fragen, ob der erst Teil des Hynnus von der Welt als Schöpfung durch den präexistenten Christus seitens des Vf verstanden wurde und verstanden sein soll, der zweite hingegen parallel dazu die Erlösung der Erstschöpfung besingt, oder ob beide Teile das gleiche Geschehen preisen, nämlich die als eschatologische Neuschöpfung aussagbare Gegebenheit der "Versöhnung" (1, 19).[58]

On the basis of the redactions related to the church in 1:18b and to the death of Christ on the cross in 1:20b, Zeilinger concluded that the author did not intend the readers to extend the hymn "back to the preexistence of Christ, but to the point of departure of the new creation, to the resurrection and exaltation as the already of 'this world'." He asserted that "this protological accentuation of eschatology makes it possible to speak of creation within the first creation which existed for the future."[59] Zeilinger's interpretation is supported by the observation that the introit to the hymn (1:12-14) indicates that the "kingdom of the beloved Son" belongs to an entirely different sphere or realm than the dominion of darkness. The kingdom then belongs to the new creation, not to the old one which was deceived and victimized by the

---

[58]Zeilinger, *Der Erstgeborene der Schöpfung*, p. 30.

[59]Ibid., p. 204; "Wie der Zusatz τῆς ἐκκλησίας V18b erweist hat der Briefautor den ihm vorliegenden Christushymnus nicht zur Darlegung einer christlichen Kosmologie verwendet, sondern als Preislied auf das Haupt des Organismus der *Kirche* verstanden. Die Aussagen des Hymnus erhalten damit eschatologish-ekklesiologisches Gewicht. Τὰ πάντα bezeichnet dann zunächst und unmittelbar die Gesamtheit der eschatologischen Schöpfung, die Himmel und Erde betrifft und umfasst, und sich innerhalb der Gegebenheiten der Erstschöpfung als *Kirche* sehen lässt. Damit hat der Verfasser die weltumspannenden Universalaussagen des Hymnus nicht eliminiert, sondern nur auf eine andere Ausgangsbasis gestellt. Es wird nicht auf den präexistenten Christus zurückgegriffen, (was im Gesamt des Briefes ohne Resonanz verbliebe), sondern auf den *eschatologischen* Ausgangspunkt der Neuschöpfung, auf die Auferstehung und Erhöhung Christi aus dem Bereich "dieser Welt." Es scheint wesenlich zu sein, dass der Verfasser mit V20b den Hymnus im Sinne der Kreuzestheologie weiterführt: Der Tod, das Sterben Christi als ein Sterben "dieses Äons" (vgl. 2 Kor 5, 21) bildet die Voraussetzung für die Existenz des mit der Auferstehung Christi kommenden neuen Äons. Innerhalb der raum-zeit-bestimmten Steinweise der Erstschöpfung ist der eschatologische Heilsäon als die Gemeinschaft der in den Todes-und Auferstehungsleib Christi Einbezogenen Wirklichkeit. Diese protologische Akzentuierung der Eschatologie ermöglicht es, von Schöpfung innerhalb der weiterhin existierenden Erstschöpfung zu sprechen."

hostile powers. It is also supported by the presence of the phrases "image of the invisible God" and "firstborn of all creation" in the opening lines of the hymn. These phrases are reminiscent of the description of Adam in the first creation. Furthermore, the statements about the old and new man in 3:9, 10 bear witness to the likelihood that the writer adhered to a tradition which presented Christ as the eschatological Adam. It is, of course, true that the first Adam was never thought of as the creator of the original creation. However, Christ, as the last Adam, is proclaimed by Paul to be the "giver of life" (1 Corinthians 15:21, 22, 45-49) and was associated with creation and reconciliation in an eschatological sense in 2 Corinthians 5:17-21.

Whether or not the author intended his readers to understand the first part of the hymn from a protological or eschatological point of view cannot be known for certain. What is certain is that the redactions in the last part of the hymn celebrate Christ from an eschatological perspective and it is the last part of the hymn that is especially and specifically applied to the readers.

The applications of the Christ-hymn are found in the verses immediately following it (1:21, 22) and in the baptismal hymn (2:9-15).[60] Both of these passages present the doctrine of Christ in an eschatological-soteriological framework. Verses 21 and 22 of chapter one are structured around contrasting adverbs. Πότε and νυνὶ δὲ contrast the old condition of existence of the readers with the present eschatological one. At one time (πότε) they lived in darkness under the hostile powers and were alienated from God. *But now* (νυνὶ δέ) in the new eschatological situation they live under the sovereignty of the Son and by virtue of his death they are reconciled to God. The baptismal hymn in 2:9-15 also presents Christ from an eschatological perspective. Verses 9 and 10 refer to 1:19 of the Christ-hymn. Verses 11-15 apply the hymn in the light of the significance of the cross (as does the redaction in 1:20b). By virtue of baptism the readers participate in the consequences of the death and resurrection of Christ (11-13). This means that they participate in Christ's triumph over the powers which he achieved on the cross (14, 15).

---

[60]See above, in chapter 2, "The Traditional Character of Colossians 2:9-15," for reasons for calling 2:9-15 a baptismal hymn, pp. 37-47.

To summarize: the Christology proclaimed in the Christ-hymn, its introduction, and applications are set forth in the frame of reference of the eschatological deliverence achieved by Christ's death and resurrection.

The Mystery Proclamation. Let us now examine the Christology of those passages which deal with the proclamation of the "mystery" (1:24-2:3; 4:2-4). In order to determine the specific aspect or perspective from which the Christology of the "mystery" is viewed, we must examine the general meaning and use of the term in the New Testament and then observe its use in the setting of Colossians.

Background of the mystery concept. Although a number of surface similarities exist between the mystery concepts in the New Testament and the cultic rites of the mystery religions and the speculations of various gnostic cosmologies and soteriologies, it is unlikely that either of these movements influenced the meaning of the term in the New Testament.[61] It is preferable to turn to the Jewish wisdom and apocalyptic literature for the backgrounds to the New Testament uses of the term.

Jewish wisdom literature was filled with the praise of wisdom. It frequently personified wisdom and declared that the righteous man was the one who listened to her and followed her precepts. She was celebrated as preexistent, associated with creation, and proclaimed as the giver of life.[62] The unrighteous man was the one who ignored or refused wisdom. Such a man was a fool and had hope only in this life. The *Wisdom of Solomon* pictures the ungodly as those who had made a covenant with death (1:15, 16) and had no hope for the future (2:1-9). Because of this, they oppress and ridicule the righteous man (2:10-20). Their dilemna was that "they did not know the secret purposes of God"

---

[61]See Zeilinger, *Der Erstgeborene der Schöpfung,* pp. 94-98; Barth, "Mystery or Secret?," *Ephesians: Introduction, Translation, and Commentary on Chapters 1-3,* pp. 123-27; and Bornkamm, "μυστήριον," *TDNT* 4:802-27.

[62]There are a number of interesting affinities between the hymn and paraenesis in Colossians with Jewish wisdom literature. As noted above (pp. 28-32), there is good reason for associating the hymn with wisdom literature. Wisdom, like the Son in the Christ-hymn, is associated with creation (Job 28:20-28; Prov. 3:19, 20; 8:22ff.; Wisd. 7:22, 26; 8:1-6; 9:1-10; Eccl. 24:3-9) and deliverance (Prov. 3:12-26; Wisd. 10:1-21 and others). In the wisdom literature the conduct that God expects from His people is related to Wisdom. In Colossians it is related to Christ.

(2:21, 22, RSV). In speaking of the origin and character of wisdom, the author wrote as though he were disclosing a mystery.

> I will hide no secrets (μυστήρια) from you But I will trace her course from the beginning of creation, And make the knowledge of her clear And I will not pass by the truth.[63]

He also described wisdom as "an initiate in the knowledge of God" (8:4). Similar motifs are found in the *Wisdom of Sirach* where wisdom is described as inscrutible (1:1-7) but accessible to those who fear the Lord (1:14-20). Comparable ideas, including preexistence, are expressed in praise of wisdom in chapter 24. Mystery motifs are also to be found in chapter 39. The one who devotes himself to the study of the Torah and seeks out wisdom will "penetrate the subtleties of parables" and "seek out the hidden meanings of proverbs and be at home with the obscurities of parables" (39:1-3). For such a one, the Lord will "direct his counsel and knowledge aright, and he will meditate on his secrets (μυστήρια 39:7)."

In the wisdom literature the secrets or mysteries are open to those who have wisdom and understanding. Such wisdom and its concomitant understanding of the mysteries was not based on esoteric experiences or cultic rites but on fearing God and desiring to know and obey His will. Wisdom and the understanding of the secrets is the gift of God to those who walk in accord with His precepts. "Mystery" in the wisdom literature is associated with the same circle of ideas (wisdom, understanding, knowledge, instruction, the disclosure of the hidden) as it is in the "mystery" passages in the New Testament.

In Jewish apocalyptic literature μυστήριον takes on an eschatological meaning. Lohse believes that the statement about the mystery in Colossians 1:26 depended upon a traditional formulation in early Christian preaching. This formulation has to do with the making known of that which was previously hidden. It is found also in 1 Corinthians 2:7ff. and the closing doxology in Romans (16:25ff.). He says:

> The concepts μυστήριον (mystery), ἀποκρύπτειν (to conceal, hide), φανε-ροῦν (to reveal, make known) have been taken into the primitive Christian language of preaching from apocalyptic tradition. The word μυστήριον

---

[63]Wisd. 6:22 (RSV).

(mystery) corresponds to the Hebrew *raz* (secret) which designates the secret of God's eschatological decree.[64]

The reasonableness of Lohse's affirmation can be seen in the apocalyptic literature. Daniel 2:28, 29 describes God as the "One who reveals mysteries (ὁ ἀποκαλύπτων μυστήρια, *LXX*)" in a context in which Daniel interprets Nebuchadnezzar's dream as referring to future events. Second Esdras likewise purports to reveal the future and includes many symbols involving mysterious numbers and strange beasts. Angelic mediators disclose hidden mysteries. In 14:5 it is said that God told Moses "many wondrous things, and showed him the secrets of the times and declared to him the end of all things." Ethiopic Enoch speaks of hidden mysteries which are kept in heaven and revealed to the seer through heavenly mediators (Ethiopic Enoch 9:6). The mysteries are about the end times when sinners would be judged and the righteous made manifest (Ethiopic Enoch 38:3; 106:19; 103:2ff.).

In both Jewish wisdom and apocalyptic literature the mysteries are related to that which was previously hidden but now can be known. In the wisdom literature the emphasis is upon understanding and knowing the instruction. In the apocalyptic literature it is upon eschatological revelation.

Mystery in the New Testament. In the Gospels μυστήριον occurs only in connection with the reason why Jesus spoke in parables (Mark 4:11; Matthew 13:11; Luke 8:10).[65] In this setting the word is used with reference to the kingdom of God (Heaven). A distinction is made between those to whom the mystery of the kingdom is given and those to whom it is not. The parables have a judgmental connotation related to the time of eschatological crisis. Jesus spoke in parables in order to conceal the mystery of the kingdom from those on the outside. On the other hand the mystery was understood by the disciples. In Mark 1:15

---

[64]Lohse, *Colossians*, p. 74.

[65]In Mark the statement ʿΥμῖν τὸ μυστήριον δέδοται τῆς βασιλείας τοῦ θεοῦ· ἐκείνοις δὲ τοῖς ἔξω ἐν παραβολαῖς τὰ πάντα γίνεται does not fit smoothly in its context. The context deals with the meaning of the parables (especially the parable of the sower). Mark 4:12, however, deals with the reason why Jesus spoke in parables. The Matthean and Lukan parallels smooth out the difficulty by introducing the statement with a question ("*Why* do you speak to them in Parables?"). They also use the plural and refer to the μυστήρια of the kingdom.

the kingdom of God is associated with the gospel of God, which in turn is associated with the presence of Jesus the Messiah. The mystery is about the incursion of the reign of God into the world in the mission of Jesus. As Bornkamm puts it, "The μυστήριον τῆς βασιλείας τοῦ θεοῦ which is revealed to the disciples is thus Jesus Himself as the Messiah."[66] The concepts of hiddenness and disclosure, understanding and knowing, and the eschatological reign of God are the primary features in the Synoptic Gospels' use of μυστήριον.

In the Pauline letters μυστήριον is used nine times from a variety of eschatological perspectives. Two of them are associated with the eschatological climax at the *Parousia*. Second Thessalonians 2:7 speaks of the "mystery of lawlessness" which is already present but which will be brought to nought by the *Parousia* of the Lord Jesus. First Corinthians 15:51 depicts the mystery as the transformation of those who are in Christ at the time of the *Parousia*. Two more of them use the word in connection with pneumatic experience and the gifts of the Spirit. "Mystery" is in the plural in both instances. In 1 Corinthians 13:2 the mysteries are understood by the pneumatic person, but in 1 Corinthians 14:2 they are spoken in "tongues" and are understood only by God. The remaining five uses are all associated with the gospel and are of special importance for our investigation of the meaning and use of the term in Colossians.

In 1 Corinthians 2:1 there is a textual problem. The "western" text has μαρτύριον and the "Egyptian" text has μυστήριον The latter is probably to be preferred.[67] Μυστήριον is used in connection with Paul's preaching in Corinth, the contents of which is summed up with the phrase "Jesus Christ and him crucified" (1 Corinthians 2:2). Μυστήριον occurs again in 1 Corinthians 2:7 where it is associated with the "wisdom of God" which was for the τέλειοι. This "wisdom in mystery"

---

[66]Gunther Bornkamm, "μυστήριον," *TDNT* 4:819.

[67]Hans Conzelmann prefers μαρτύριον and thinks that μαρτύριον "has introduced itself from v. 7." *A Commentary on the First Epistle to the Corinthians*, Hermeneia Series, trans. James W. Leitch (Philadelphia: Fortress Press, 1975), p. 53. Bornkamm thinks that it is impossible to know for certain which is the correct reading, but prefers μυστήριον and thinks that μυστήριον reflects 1:6. "μυστήριον," *TDNT* 4:819. The Editorial Committee of the United Bible Societies supports μυστήριον. Bruce Metzger, *A Textual Commentary on the Greek New Testament*, Companion volume to the United Bible Societies' Greek New Testament, 3rd ed. (London and New York, 1971), p. 545.

is not of this age. It was previously hidden and is for the "glory" of the Christian community. As in 2:1, it is also related to the death of Christ (2:8). In 1 Corinthians 4:1 Paul wants the Corinthians to regard himself, Apollos, and Cephas as "servants of Christ and stewards of the mysteries (μυστήρια) of God." Romans 16:25ff. is considered by some to be a non-Pauline doxology added to the letter. That may be true. In any event it serves as a most apt summary of the gospel which Paul preached. The "gospel," the "word of the cross," the "preaching of Jesus Christ," the "revelation of the mystery," the "mystery of God" are all interrelated in the letters of Paul. The mystery is described as that which long had been kept secret but now is disclosed to all the nations. In Romans 11, where Paul stressed his calling as the apostle to the Gentiles (v. 13ff.), the mystery is associated with the gospel (v. 28) and with the "wisdom and knowledge of God" which is made known in His inscrutable plan (vv. 33-36). The mystery was about the "hardening of Israel" (v. 25) which was associated with the inclusion of the Gentiles in God's eschatological plan (vv. 25-28).

There are twelve occurrences of μυστήριον in the so-called deutero-Pauline epistles and in the Apocalypse.[68] Six of them are in Ephesians. In some instances the use of μυστήριον in Ephesians parallels the uses in the undisputed letters of Paul. In 3:4-6 the mystery is described as the revelation of that which was formerly hidden and is linked with the gospel and the inclusion of the Gentiles in God's plan of redemption. In 6:19 it is called "the mystery of the gospel." In other instances, however, Ephesians goes beyond the undisputed letters of Paul. In 1:9, 10 the mystery involves a cosmic reconciliation or unification and is associated with eschatological language (οἰκονομίαν τοῦ πληρώματος τῶν καιρῶν). A similar idea is expressed in 3:9-11 which also includes eschatological terminology (πρόθεσιν τῶν αἰώνων). A significant feature about the mystery is that it was revealed to a venerated apostleship. Such an attitude toward the apostles is reminiscent of the postapostolic church. A similar stress on apostolic teaching seems to be present in Ephesians 5:32. Τὸ μυστήριον τοῦτο probably refers to the quotation of Genesis 2:24 in the preceding verse.[69] At first

---

[68]Excluding the references in Colossians, they are Eph. 1:9; 3:3, 4, 9: 5:32; 6:19; 1 Tim. 3:9, 16; Rev. 1:20; 10:7; 17:5, 7.

[69]It could also refer to the text that follows and function as a summary of the section on husbands and wives.

glance, the "mystery" seems to give the real or allegorical meaning of the Old Testament text.[70] Upon closer scrutiny, however, it seems more likely that it refers to the wonder of the marriage union itself. This was doubtless the meaning intended both in the Old Testament text and in the relationship between husbands and wives described in the *Haustafel*. The main stress is in the phrase ἐγὼ δὲ λέγω εἰς χριστὸν καὶ εἰς τὴν ἐκκλησίαν.[71] The emphatic pronoun indicates that this is the way the writer intended the *Haustafel* to be understood in this letter. In 1 Peter the *Haustafel* was used to aid in the understanding of eschatological suffering. In Colossians, as we have previously reasoned, it was used to curtail excessive pneumatic enthusiasm. In Ephesians it was used to proclaim the relationship between Christ and his church. The emphatic pronoun stamps the ecclesiological meaning of the *Haustafel* in Ephesians with (Pauline) apostolic authority.

In 1 Timothy 3:9, 16 μυστήριον is also used in a setting of ecclesiastical authority. Deacons are required to "hold the mystery of the faith with a clear conscience" (3:9) and the confession statement called the "mystery of our religion" immediately follows the description of the church as "the pillar and bulwark of the truth" (3:16). The "faith" and the "truth" in these passages have more to do with the content of doctrine than with eschatological proclamation.

The remaining three passages which use μυστήριον are located in the Apocalypse. They relate to the "mystery of the seven stars" (1:20), the "mystery of God" associated with the seven angels (10:7), and the "mystery of Babylon the Great, the Mother of Harlots" (17:5, 7). All of the uses interpret the meaning of symbols and foretell events in the seer's future.

To summarize: the use of μυστήριον in the Synoptic Gospels is related to the gospel of the Reign of God made present in Jesus the Messiah. In the undisputed letters of Paul the mystery is primarily related to the proclamation of the gospel and focuses attention on the significance of Christ's death, his *Parousia*, and the inclusion of the

---

[70]This view is held by Raymond E. Brown, "The Semitic Background of the New Testament Mysterion (II)," *Biblica* 40 (1959): 83-84 and Marcus Barth, *Ephesians*, Anchor Bible Series, vol. 2 (Garden City: Doubleday & Co., 1974), pp. 641-44, 729-38.

[71]For a good treatment of this see J. Sampley, "*And the Two Shall Become One Flesh*": *A Study of Traditions in Ephesians 5:21-23* (Cambridge: University Press, 1977), pp. 86-102, especially p. 96.

Gentiles in God's redemptive plan. Ephesians also connects the mystery with the proclamation of the gospel and the inclusion of the Gentiles, but it goes beyond the undisputed letters by relating the mystery to cosmic reconciliation and associating it with the ecclesiastical office (as does 1 Timothy). In the Apocalypse the word is used with reference to apocalyptic symbols which were made known and explained to the seer. With the exception of the "ecclesiastical office" statements in Ephesians and 1 Timothy, the term is always used in an eschatological-Christological frame of reference in the New Testament.

The setting of the mystery in Colossians. Four out of five of the occurrences of the term "mystery" in Colossians are located in the passage in which the writer affirms his apostolic authority and concern for his readers (1:24-2:5). There are three observations which deserve our attention.

First, the mystery which was "hidden for ages and generations" is not as closely associated with the apostolic office in Colossians as it is in Ephesians. To be sure, it is located in a context in which the (Pauline) authority to proclaim the mystery is asserted (1:25, 26),[72] but Colossians does not limit the revelation of the mystery to the "holy apostles and prophets" as Ephesians does. It rather declares that the mystery was made known to "the saints." Perhaps the phrase νῦν δὲ ἐφανερώθη τοῖς ἁγίοις αὐτοῦ could imply the ecclesiastical office. The writer of Ephesians apparently thought so and altered the statement to give that meaning. Nonetheless, ἅγιοι refers to the whole Christian community in Colossians 1:2 and probably has the same connotation in 1:26. In the following verse the ἅγιοι are described as those to whom God wished "to make known how great among the Gentiles are the riches of the glory of this "mystery" and the phrase is explicitly applied to the readers.

Second, the statements about the mystery appear in an eschatological setting. The writer declares that he rejoices in the sufferings which he endures for the sake of his readers. He describes that suffering as filling up τὰ ὑστερήματα τῶν θλίφεων τοῦ χριστοῦ. Although these words have been taken to mean that something was lacking in the

---

[72]See the emphatic pronoun in 1:25.

death of Christ on the cross,[73] such an interpretation is rendered untenable by the declarations of the triumph of the cross in 1:20 and 2:14, 15. In like maner, the interpretation of this statement as referring to a mystical union with Christ's passion has little to commend it.[74] Not only does the apostle expect to complete those sufferings in time (a feature incompatable with mysticism), but the inference that there might be some deficiency in such a mystic experience hardly seems possible. It is far more likely that the statement about suffering and filling that which is lacking in the afflictions of Christ is based upon the apocalyptic idea of the afflictions associated with the end times and the woes of the Messiah. These ideas permeate the so-called "little apocalypse" of Mark 13 and parallels. War and plague and cosmic wonders will reach a zenith of horror in the last days which immediately precede the advent of the Messiah.[75] The Messianic woes or afflictions were the signs of the impending eschatological climax.

In light of this, it is difficult to accept the theory that eschatology has "receded into the background" in Colossians or that "hope" is a "spatially determined mode of thought" which replaces a temporal longing for the future consummation.[76] Suffering in the Gospels, the Pauline letters, 1 Peter, and Hebrews is an eschatological concept which is related to living for the sake of (or in the stead of) Christ. Since the mission of Christ in waging a warfare against the powers of evil is not yet over (1 Corinthians 15:50-58), living in the stead of Christ means participation in the Messianic warfare. That means suffering. Such suffering, however, is a privilege and a joy (Philippians 1:29; 3:10; Romans 8:17-25; 1 Peter 1:5-11; 4:12-19). Just as God has set temporal limits (2 Esdras 4:36, 37; Galatians 4:4; Romans 11:25) so has He set quantitative limits on the suffering to be endured in the Messianic affliction (Mark 13:20). The apostle can rejoice not only because the

---

[73]See H. Windisch, *Paulus und Christus: Ein biblisch-religiongeschichtlicher Vergleich*, UNT 24 (Leipzig, 1934), pp. 236-50.

[74]For this interpretation see Adolf Deissmann, *Paul: A Study in Social and Religious History*, trans. William E. Wilson (New York: Harper Torchbooks, 1957, first edition published in 1957), pp. 162ff., 181ff., 202.

[75]See Strack and Billerbeck, *Kommentar zum Neuen Testament aus Talmud und Midrasch*, vol. 4, pp. 977-86, for examples of Jewish apocalyptic expectations of catastrophes.

[76]Lohse, *Colossians*, p. 180.

suffering which he endures is for the sake of Christ, but also because the more suffering he endures the less the church will have to endure. It is in such an eschatological setting as this that the "mystery of God, even Christ" (2:2) occurs in Colossians.

Third, the mystery is identified with the "word of God" (1:25, 26) which in turn is identified with the gospel. We have previously drawn attention to the cluster of words in the thematic introduction (1:1-23) which link together the gospel with the "word of truth."[77] The same cluster occurs at the beginning and ending of the thematic main argument (1:24-4:6). The gospel is equated with the "word of truth" (1:5) which proclaims a "hope" (1:5, 23). In like manner, the "mystery" is identified with the "word of God" (1:25, 26) which also declares a "hope" (1:27). The gospel was preached (κηρυχθέντος, 1:23) and the mystery proclaimed (καταγγέλλομεν, 1:28). Moreover, the gospel is not only preached, but it is taught and it involves understanding, wisdom, knowledge, and growth (1:5-7, 9, 10). The same is true of the mystery (1:27, 28; 2:2).[78] The content of the gospel is centered in Christ. So also is the mystery (1:27, 28; 2:2, 3). The gospel is not for a select few but for "all the world" (1:6). Christ, "the mystery of God" (2:2) is proclaimed for "every man" (1:28). In Romans 15:15-19 Paul described himself as the divinely appointed "minister of Christ to the Gentiles" and declared that he had "fully preached the gospel of Christ (πεπληρωκέναι τὸ εὐαγγέλιον τοῦ Χριστοῦ)" all the way from Jerusalem to Illyricum. In Colossians 1:25, 26 Paul is described as the divinely appointed minister of the church to "make the word of God fully known, the mystery hidden for ages and generations (πληρῶσαι τὸν λόγον τοῦ θεοῦ, τὸ μυστήριον τὸ ἀποκεκρυμμένον ἀπὸ τῶν αἰώνων καὶ ἀπὸ τῶν γενεῶν)." As the apostle to the Gentiles, Paul had the territorial responsibility of proclaiming the gospel to the Gentiles in every place. The proclamation of the "word of God" means the same as

---

[77]See above, in chapter 5, "The Introduction (1:1-23)," p. 167.

[78]It is interesting to observe that 1 Cor. 2:1ff. also connects the gospel with the wisdom of God, growth, and maturity. The Gospel is both proclaimed and taught. It has a clear bearing upon the deportment of the hearer and learner. The Corinthians' lack of understanding of the significance of the gospel resulted in excessively enthusiastic and libertine behavior. The Colossians' lack of understanding led to the almost opposite effects. It did not lead to disorder (2:5) but it did lead to an ascetic and legalistic mode of expression (at least in the context of worship if not also in daily life).

the proclamation of the gospel. In Colossians, as in the Pauline passages mentioned above, the proclamation of the mystery means the proclamation of the significance of the gospel.

The Content of the Mystery. The identification of the proclamation of the gospel with the proclamation of the mystery is made more clear by the fact that the basic content or subject matter of each is the same. In Colossians 2:2, a text with a bewildering variety of readings,[79] the content of the mystery is set forth in one word: "Christ." More specifically, the contents are summarized in the phrase: "Christ in you, the hope of glory (ὅ ἐστιν Χριστὸς ἐν ὑμῖν, ἡ ἐλπὶς τῆς δόξης, 1:27)." The brevity of the clause raises the question of meaning. Does the ἐν mean "in" or "among"? Does it refer to the mystical indwelling of Christ in the individual,[80] the indwelling of Christ in the church,[81] or the presence of Christ among his people?[82]

The interpretation of the clause as referring to the mystical indwelling of Christ in the individual can be ruled out on at least two grounds: (1) the apocalyptic and eschatological setting of the term "mystery" makes it incompatible with the mystic union conceptions related to the mystery religions or gnosticism and (2) the context is related to the apostle's divine appointment to minister the word of God to the Gentiles. ᾽Εν τοῖς ἔθνεσιν and ἐν ὑμῖν doubtless refers to the Colossians who were Gentiles. This is not to say that the concept of the indwelling Christ is not compatible with the Pauline teaching. Second Corinthians 13:5, Romans 8:10, and Ephesians 3:17 all speak of Christ ἐν ὑμῖν or ἐν ταῖς καρδίαις ὑμῶν. Second Corinthians 13:5 may mean "among you," but the other two clearly refer to the indwelling Christ.

---

[79]The U.B.S. Greek text gives the reading χριστοῦ strong support (a "B" rating) "(a) because of strong external testimony (p[46], B Hilary Pelagius Ps-Jerome) and (b) because it alone provides an adequate explanation of the other readings as various scribal attempts to ameliorate the syntactical ambiguity of τοῦ θεοῦ, χριστοῦ. Metzger, *Textual Commentary on the New Testament.* p. 622.

[80]For this position see Martin Dibelius and Heinrich Greeven, *An die Kolosser, Epheser, an Philemon,* Begründet von Hans Lietzmann in Verbindung mit Fachgenossen, Herausgegeben von Günther Bornkamm (Tübingen: J. C. B. Mohr [Paul Siebeck], 1953), pp. 24-25; M. Wagenführer, *Die Bedeutung Christi für Welt und Kirche: Studien zum Kolosser- und Epheserbrief* (Leipzig, 1941), p. 96.

[81]Bornkamm, "Die Haresie des Kolosserbriefes," in *Conflict at Colossae*, p. 820.

[82]Lohse, *Colossians*, p. 76, and Martin, *Colossians and Philemon*, p. 72.

However, it must be noted that the indwelling Christ is always associated with the eschatological Spirit and, therefore, has eschatological, not mystical, meaning.

The issue as to whether Christ indwells the individual and/or the community is a complicated one. In Romans 8, where being-in-Christ means practically the same as being-in-the Spirit, both Christ and the Spirit indwell people (verses 9, 10). An interesting intermingling of Christ and Spirit and of the singular and plural of the second person pronoun occurs in this passage. In verse 9a the Spirit dwells in you (plural) and in verse 10 Christ is in you (plural). In 9b Christ and Spirit are again very closely associated and the possession of "the Spirit of Christ" is applied to the individual (εἰ δέ τις πνεῦμα Χριστοῦ οὐκ ἔχει, οὗτος οὐκ ἔστιν αὐτοῦ). In verse 10 a community sense is implied by the use of the plural pronoun and the singular "body" (εἰ δέ Χριστὸς ἐν ὑμῖν, τὸ μὲν σῶμα νεκρόν). However, in verse 11b the plural is used with the plural pronoun (σώματα) connoting a reference to individual persons. The corporate or community sense of "body" is also present in Romans 6:12. There also the use of the plural pronoun and the singular σῶμα occurs (ἐν τῷ θνητῷ ὑμῶν σώματι). In Romans 12:1 the individual person is implied again (τὰ σώματα ὑμῶν), but in 12:4 the corporate or community meaning is clearly stressed (οἱ πολλοὶ ἕν σῶμά ἐσμεν ἐν Χριστῷ). It seems safe to say that in Pauline theology the Spirit and Christ indwells both individuals and communities. It seems quite clear that in Colossians 1:27 the ἐν ὑμῖν refers to the community. The mystery might be Christ in you or Christ among you, but the "you" refers to the community (not the individual) and it is specifically related to Gentiles. Christ "in" or "among" the Gentiles is announced to be "the hope of glory." Both the present and the future are bound together in the proclamation of the mystery. Christ *is* in you and he is the *hope* of glory. Hope is related to the mystery in 1:27 and to the gospel in 1:5 and 23. First Corinthians 2:1-8 also clusters together the concepts of gospel, wisdom, mystery, and glory. There, as in Colossians, these words are placed in an eschatological frame of reference. There, as in Colossians, the cross stands over against the "rulers of this age" who are coming to nought. There, as in Colossians, the wisdom of God in the mystery is for the glory of those who understand the significance of the cross.

To summarize: Colossians places the mystery in an eschatological setting and associates it with the proclamation of the gospel. Its central message is about Christ and the specific content of the mystery is concerned with the presence of Christ in or among the Gentiles. He is the Gentiles' hope of glory. In Christ, the eschatological Adam, "there cannot be Greek and Jew, circumcised and uncircumcised, barbarian, Scythian, slave, free man, but Christ is all, and in all" (Colossians 3:11).[83]

Summary. We began this section on the theological perspective of Colossians by drawing attention to the fact that no theological category can be considered properly without observing its relationship to other theological categories. The core of all of the New Testament theologies is related to the proclamation and interpretation of the Christ-event. Ecclesiology, soteriology, pneumatology, eschatology, the meaning of the sacraments, and every other classification of theological inquiry are all centered on the mission and message of Jesus Christ, the Lord. This means that the gospel lies at the center of all New Testament theology. The gospel was both proclaimed and taught. The way in which this was done was determined not only by the special situation and concern of the writer, but also by the circumstances of those to whom he wrote.

The writer of Colossians, as we have noted time and again, desired his readers to walk in the light of the instruction which they had received about Christ. They were in danger of being tricked by a system of teaching which the writer considered to be under the aegis of the hostile world rulers. This "philosophy" was contrary to the new situation brought about by the "kingdom" of God's "Beloved Son." The readers were especially in need of understanding the significance of the cross-event as the triumph of Christ over the hostile powers. Such an understanding had very real implications for their manner of life in worship and in their relationships with one another and with society in general. The concern was therefore a Christological one which was

---

[83]In using Col. 3:11 to throw light on the implication of the relationship of the mystery to the Gentiles, I am going contrary to Lohse who says that Col. 3:11 "was adopted from the tradition" and that the "distinctions between Greeks and Jews is of no concern to Colossians." *Colossians*, p. 143, fn. 70. Whether or not it belongs to the baptismal paraenesis (I think it does), it affirms the inclusiveness that is characteristic of the new eschatological situation. This inclusiveness is the focal point of the mystery disclosed in Colossians as well as the focal point of the gospel set forth in Galatians (3:8, 16, 27-29).

deeply related to the new eschatological situation. Consequently, the Christology of Colossians was set forth in an eschatological perspective which focused on the significance of the death of Christ. The readers' participation in the triumph of Christ's death was connected with baptism. For this reason a large portion of the letter is made up of Christological and paraenetic traditions associated with baptism.

The Christology of Colossians is primarily set forth in the Christ-hymn and its applications (1:15-23; 2:9-15) and in the sections of the letter dealing with the "mystery" (1:24-2:5; 4:2-4). The eschatological dimension of the hymn is introduced by the eulogy to the Father (1:12-14), a traditional unit used as an introit to the hymn. It contrasts the dominion of darkness and the "kingdom of the Beloved Son." The protological-cosmological hymn is put in an eschatological perspective by the redactions concerning the church (1:18b), the significance of the cross (1:20b), and by the eschatological application of the hymn to the readers by the use of the temporal adverbs πότε and νυνί in 1:21, 22. The eschatological "now" of the readers' situation is related to the death of Christ (1:22) and the eschatological "not yet" is related to the Hope of the gospel (1:23).

The Christ-hymn is further applied to the readers in 2:9-15. This is done in 2:9 and 10 by a reference back to the πλήρωμα statement in 1:19 and to the κεφαλή, ἀρχαί, and ἐξουσίαι concepts in 1:16, 18. The eschatological "fullness" or completeness is totally centered in Christ, who is the head of all rule and authority. His sovereign Lordship was made present in the triumph of the cross (1:20; 2:14, 15). Participation in the consequences of that victory comes about by being "in him" (2:10) by virtue of sharing in his death and resurrection through baptism (2:11-13). The Christ-hymn and its application, therefore, is of central importance in the letter because it points out the eschatological significance of Christ's death and resurrection as a victory over the "rulers and authorities."

The eschatological perspective of the Christology of Colossians is also evident in the "mystery" passages (1:24-2:5; 4:2-4). In Colossians the term μυστήριον is used in a way very similar to its use in the Synoptic Gospels, 1 Corinthians, and Romans. In those documents the mystery is associated with the proclamation of the gospel, the significance of the death and resurrection of Christ, and the inclusion of the Gentiles in God's redemptive plan. In the Gospels the word is used only in connection with the parables of the kingdom of God, which kingdom has become present in the mission, death, and resurrection of Jesus, the Christ. In 1 Corinthians the gospel is called the "word of the cross" and is centered in the proclamation of "Jesus Christ and him crucified." In chapter two the mystery is called the "mystery of God" and "wisdom of God in mystery." It is not of "this age" and involves the eschatological significance of the death of Christ which brings to nought the "rulers of this age." The mystery about the *Parousia* (1 Corinthians 15:50ff.) proclaims the ultimate defeat of death and is connected with the resurrection of Christ (1 Corinthians 15:20-23). In Romans the mystery is associated with the "hardening" of Israel "until the full number of the Gentiles come in" (11:25) and is equated with the gospel which is to be made known "to all the nations" (16:25, 26). All three of these eschatological concerns (proclamation of gospel, significance of the death of Christ, and the inclusion of the Gentiles) are also present in the "mystery" passages in Colossians. The mystery passages are associated with knowledge, wisdom, and understanding. The writer was concerned that his readers be filled with knowledge, wisdom, and understanding about the significance of the cross-event, which brought about the subjugation of the "rulers and authorities." The mystery is called the "word of God" (1:25) which is identified with the gospel (1:5, 23). The special significance of the mystery/gospel for the Colossians was that it declared the inclusion of the Gentiles in the "hope of glory" (1:27).

The Colossians needed to be reminded of what they had been taught in the gospel of Christ. Christ is the eschatological ruler of all by virtue of his triumph on the cross. The "all" included the heavenly powers. The readers needed to remember that in the eschatological "now" (1:22) they participated in the triumph of Christ through baptism (2:9-15). The gospel was the gospel of hope (1:23) and the Pauline apostolic ministry was that of proclaiming that hope to the Gentiles.

In short, the theological perspective in Colossian is an eschatological one. It is centered in the significance of the death of Christ, which authenticated and established his sovereignty over the "rulers and authorities" and the *stoicheia* of this world. The triumph of the cross has implications for the life and worship of the church, which includes Gentiles as well as Jews. These implications relate both to the "now" of the times of the "messianic affliction" and to the future "hope of glory."

Is such a perspective compatible with the hypothesis of the Pauline authorship of Colossians? In the next section we shall attempt to show that an affirmative answer to that question is probable by examining three theological issues which are of central importance in both Colossians and Galatians.

INCLUSIVISM, THE STOICHEIA, AND THE DEATH OF CHRIST IN COLOSSIANS AND GALATIANS

Inclusivism

As noted above, Paul's special call to be the apostle to the Gentiles was closely linked to the emphasis in his message on the inclusion of Jews and Gentiles in God's purpose of redemption. Galatians was written to oppose the threat of Jewish exclusivism which ran counter to Paul's gospel of inclusivism. Our task is to determine whether or not Colossians also shows a concern for inclusiveness.

The difficulty of reconstructing the historical situation of the letter to the Colossians is well-known. As helpful as various reconstructions have been, we are still faced with the dilemma that they frequently raise questions which cannot be adequately answered from the contents of the letter. Hypotheses about the history of religions background of the opposed "philosophy" range from Jewish to Gnostic to syncretistic Jewish Gnosticism. The theory that the opposed teaching was influenced by Jewish legalistic concerns faces the problem that there is not a single reference to νόμος or Torah obedience in the letter. The hypothesis that the "philosophy" was based upon the dualistic teachings of gnostic self-denial encounters the twofold dilemma that the paraenetic sections are directed against libertinism (the vice and virtue catalogues) and excessive pneumatic enthusiasm (the *Haustafel*) and that the primary concerns of the letter are cosmological and eschatological, not anthropological. The theory that the opposed teaching was based upon a combination of both Jewish and gnostic ideas is probably the correct one, but it does not really solve the problems just mentioned. If anything, it doubles them.[84]

---

[84]This is not written to devalue the significant contributions of the history of religions approach to the background of the Colossian "philosophy." It is rather an acknowledgment of the complicated difficulties faced by such an approach. For

Whatever the historical background of the opposed teaching may have been, there are a number of indications that the writer was clearly concerned about the issue of inclusivism. Every chapter contains several statements which point to this. In chapter one (verse 4) he gives thanks for the readers' faith in Jesus Christ[85] and for their love for "*all* the saints.*" He celebrates the fact that the Gospel, which bears fruit in all the world, has also borne fruit among the readers (1:6, 23). The important Christ-hymn, which has cosmological and eschatological meaning, is specifically applied to the Gentile readers (1:12, 21, 22). Of special importance is the fact that the mystery proclamation declares the presence of Christ among the Gentiles (1:27)[86] was preached and taught to every (πάντα) man (1:28); and is associated with Paul's apostolic ministry to the Gentiles (1:23, 29). In chapter two concern is expressed for other Christians in the Lycus valley that their hearts might be knit together in love and that they might have full assurance of the inclusivistic mystery (2:1, 2). In the "baptismal hymn" (2:9-15), the readers' participation in the victory of the cross over the evil powers is celebrated.[87] The polemic in 2:16-23 is directed against practices

---

example, there are a number of key words or phrases which are obviously central to the writer's response to the teachings of the "philosophy." One must ask whether words like πλήρωμα, μυστήριον, γνῶσις, and σοφία are borrowed from the system of teaching being refuted or are terms which belong to the writer's own theological vocabulary. Πλήρωμα, for instance, is in the Christ-hymn (1:19). If the hymn is a corrected one which previously reflected the teachings of the "philosophy," πλήρωμα may be a key word in the opponent's teaching. If, on the other hand, the hymn came from an "approved" source in the primitive Christian community, πλήρωμα would be a term belonging to the accepted tradition of the church. In addition, many reconstructions are based on Col. 2:18 and 2:23. These verses are notoriously difficult to interpret. As is evident from the vigorous debates over the meaning of these passages, lexical, syntactical, and historical problems abound in them. See F. O. Francis, "Humiliation and Angelic Worship in Colossians 2:18," *ST* 16 (1963): 109-34.

[85]See above, in this chapter, "(2) 'Faith in Jesus Christ'," for the eschatological and inclusivistic meaning of the phrase "faith in Jesus Christ, pp. 190-94."

[86]See above, in this chapter, "The Mystery Proclamation, pp. 203-14."

[87]See above, fn. 58. The meaning of χειρόγραφον and δόγμασιν in 2:14 also have a bearing on the issue of whether the opposed teaching in Colossians included elements of Jewish exclusivism. The χειρόγραφον may refer to a legal certificate of indebtedness signed by men (Lohse, *Colossians*, p. 108) or to an indictment of human guilt presented in the heavenly court by hostile angels or spirits (O. A. Blanchette, "Does the Cheirographon of Colossians 2:14 Represent Christ Himself?," *CBQ* 23 [1961]: 306-12; A. J. Bandstra, *The Law and the Elements of the World: An Exegetical Study in Aspects of Paul's Teaching* [Kampen: J. H. Kok, 1964], pp. 158-60; Martin, "Reconciliation and

which are akin to the exclusivistic Jewish conventions condemned in Galatians but it includes a criticism of visionary and ascetic elements which seem to indicate that the situation in Colossae was not identical with the one in the Galatian churches. Nevertheless, some form of noninclusion was apparently a feature of the "philosophy."

In chapter three a statement very much like the one in Galatians 3:28 occurs: "Here there cannot be Greek and Jew, circumcised and uncircumcised, barbarian, Sythian, slave, free man, but Christ is all, and in all" (3:11).[88] In addition, the virtue catalogue focuses attention on mutual forebearance, forgiveness, love, and the reminder that the church is called "in one body" (3:12-15). All of these have a clear bearing on the inclusiveness that marks the church in the new age.

In chapter four a request is made that the imprisoned Paul might carry out his apostolic obligation to preach the inclusivistic "mystery of Christ" to still others (4:2-4) and a clear concern is shown for "outsiders" (4:5, 6). As we have noted before, it is probably significant that the list of final greetings in 4:10-17 is headed by salutations from the only three Jewish Christian leaders among Paul's fellow-workers (4:10, 11). No doubt the readers knew these men, who were powerful evidence of the conviction that the former importance of circumcision under the Old Testament Torah had given way to the new eschatological situation in which "neither circumcision nor uncircumcision is anything" (Galatians 6:15). Finally, if the preferred textual reading of

---

Forgiveness in the Letter to the Colossians," pp. 120-21). The δόγματα may refer to the commandments and ordinances of the O.T. law, Eph. 2:15 (Lohse, *Colossians*, p. 109), or to the ascetic way of life and the worship of angels demanded by the "philosophy" (Martin, "Reconciliation and Forgiveness," p. 121). If χειρόγραφον refers to a legal certificate of indebtedness stating an agreement to keep the exclusivistic demands of the O.T. law and δόγμασιν refers to the statements of those demands, then some form of Jewish exclusivism was a treat to the Colossians. If not, some other (gnostic?) form of exclusivism was at issue.

[88]Compare 1 Cor. 12:13. It is not known whether Col. 3:11 is an application of Gal. 3:28 (Martin, *Colossians*, p. 108) or a reference to a traditional baptismal confession. The two theories are not mutually exclusive. The catalogues probably were associated with baptismal instruction (see above pp. 65-73) and Col. 3:11 is located in the middle of the catalogues. Lohse believes that the verse "corresponds to tradition" and that the "distinction between Greeks and Jews is of no concern to Colossians" (*Colossians*, p. 143, fn. 70). However, the strategically located references to the Jewish leaders (see below) makes this unlikely. In any event, the context of Col. 3:11 depicts the condition of the "new man" in which there are no exclusivistic distinctions.

4:15 is correct (Νύμφαν καὶ τὴν κατ' οἶκον αὐτῆς ἐκκλησίαν),[89] the salutation to a leading woman in the Christian communities of the Lycus valley would have clear implications for the importance of inclusiveness in the message of Colossians.

We may not know the precise teachings of the "philosophy" opposed in Colossians, but it seems clear that a Jewish element was present, if not predominant. The many references in every chapter to matters which have a bearing on the inclusivistic nature of the Gospel point to the threat of exclusivism in the contrary teaching.

The Stoicheia

Of the seven occurrences of στοιχεῖα in the New Testament, four appear in the Pauline corpus (Galatians 4:3, 9 and Colossians 2:8, 20). Three of the four uses in the Pauline letters are modified by τοῦ κόσμου. Fundamentally, the word refers to a member of a series or to the basic elements out of which everything is formed.[90] The letters of the alphabet are a good example of the former and the ancient's belief that the world is made of earth, fire, water, and air illustrates the latter.[91] The *Wisdom of Solomon* speaks of the στοιχεῖα as active forces which are related to times, seasons, and the cycle of years.[92] The word is used in a derogatory manner to refer to rudimentary teachings in Hebrews 5:12 and is used in connection with the dissolution of the world by fire on the Day of the Lord in 2 Peter 3:10, 12.[93]

A matter of dispute in Colossians and Galatians is whether στοιχεῖα should be understood in a personal or impersonal way. At the impersonal side of the spectrum is the view of the Church Fathers and Reformers who tended to associate the στοιχεῖα with the Law of

---

[89]See B. Metzger, *Textual Commentary on the Greek New Testament*, on Col. 4:15, p. 627.

[90]For an extensive survey of the literature on the meaning of στοιχεῖα see G. Delling, "στοιχέω, συστοιχέω, στοιχεῖον," *TDNT* 7:670.

[91]E. Lohse (*Colossians*, p. 97) cites a passage in Diogenes Laertius in which Zeno lists the above mentioned elements as the basic components of the universe. A similar meaning is found in 4 Macc. 12:13; Wis. 19:18-21; Philo, *Rer, div. her.* 134.

[92]Wisdom 7:17-19.

[93]It may refer to the basic materials out of which the world is made or, since the words οὐρανοί, στοιχεῖα, and γῆ are mentioned in a series in v. 10, it may refer to the heavenly bodies.

Moses.[94] This view was also held by DeWette, Meyer, Weiss, Ewald, Ellicott, Lightfoot, Knox, Grant, Moule, and Delling.[95] In a similar vein, others think that στοιχεῖα refers not only to the teachings of the Mosaic law but also to the basic religious principles shared by both Jews and Gentiles.[96] A mediating position between the personal and impersonal meanings of στοιχεῖα is held by A. J. Bandstra. He sees a close relationship between δύναμις and στοιχεῖα.[97] The στοιχεῖα are not personal agents as such, but are "forces of order" or "component forces" in the structure of the universe.[98] He identifies these components in Pauline theology as the law and the flesh which enslave men.[99] An increasing number of scholars belong on the personal side of the spectrum of views and regard the στοιχεῖα as hostile powers or spirit-forces.[100]

---

[94]Tertullian understood the term both as the material elements of the world and as the rudimentary knowledge of the Law (*Adv. Marc.* V.iv.1, xix.7). Jerome associated the term with the Law of Moses and the declarations of the prophets (Com. on Gal. 4:2, 8, 9). Luther identified it with the Mosaic Law (Com. on Gal. 4) and Calvin maintained that the word referred to the O.T. laws in Galatians and rudimentary lessons used for the instruction of children in Colossians (On Galatians: *Corpus Reformatorum* 78:233ff.; on Colossians: *Corpus Reformatorum* 80:103ff.

[95]W. DeWette, *Kurze Erklärung der Brief an die Kolosser, an Philemon, und die Epheser und Philipper* (Leipzig: Weidemann, 1847), p. 44; H. A. W. Meyer, *Critical and Exegetical Handbook to the Epistle to the Galatians*, 2nd ed., trans. G. H. Venables from the 5th German edition (Edinburgh: T.&T. Clark, 1884), pp. 219, 220; B. Weiss, *Biblical Theology of the New Testament*, trans. David Eaton from the 3rd German edition (Edinburgh: T.&T. Clark 1882), 1:358, 372, 377; P. Ewald, *Die Briefe des Paulus an die Epheser, Kolosser, und Philemon*, 2nd ed. (Leipzig: A Deichert, 1910), pp. 167-68; C. J. Ellicott, *St. Paul's Epistle to the Galatians*, 4th ed. (London: Longmans Green, 1867), p. 75; J. B. Lightfoot, *St. Paul's Epistles to the Colossians and to Philemon*, 3rd ed. (London: Macmillan, 1904), pp. 178-79; W. L. Knox, *St. Paul and the Church of the Gentiles* (Cambridge: University Press, 1939), pp. 108-109, 140, 141; R. M. Grant, "Like Children," *HTR* 39 (1946): 72; C. F. D. Moule, *The Epistle of Paul the Apostle to the Colossians and to Philemon* (Cambridge: University Press, 1957), p. 92; G. Delling, "στοιχέω, συστοιχέω, στοιχεῖον," *TDNT* 7:684-85.

[96]For example, A. W. Cramer, *Stoicheia Tou Kosmou*, p. 45.

[97]A. J. Bandstra, *The Law and the Elements of the World*, pp. 39, 40.

[98]Ibid., p. 48.

[99]Ibid., p. 60.

[100]F. F. Bruce, *Commentary on the Epistle to the Colossians* (Grand Rapids: Eerdmans, 1959), pp. 165ff., 231-32; R. Bultmann, *Theology of the New Testament*, trans. K. Grobel (New York: Scribner's Sons, 1951), 1:173; E. Lohse, *Colossians*, pp. 96-98; G. H. C. MacGregor, "Principalities and Powers: The Cosmic Background of

At first glance the στοιχεῖα τοῦ κόσμου in Colossians 2:8 and 20 seems to refer to the impersonal teaching of the "philosophy." The "philosophy and empty deceit" which threatens the readers is described as κατὰ τὴν παράδοσιν τῶν ἀνθρύπων and κατὰ τὰ στοιχεῖα τοῦ κόσμου. The prepositional phrases seem to have a synonomous relationship and describe the opposed teaching as human and wordly. A similar idea seems to be expressed in Colossians 2:20. There dying from the στοιχεῖα τοῦ κόσμου is related to living in the world (ζῶντες ἐν κόσμῳ) and subjecting one's self to ordinances (δογματίζεσθε). A closer look, however, shows that the phrase probably has personal meaning in both verses and refers to the spirit-powers. As Percy points out, in 2:8 the writer places the στοιχεῖα in direct antithesis to Christ.[101] Thus the translation of στοιχεῖα as the "elemental spirits" is in accord with the syntactical structure of verse 8 as well as in harmony with the following passage which proclaims Christ's sovereignty over the "rulers and authorities" (2:10) and his triumph over them on the cross (2:15). This meaning also makes clearer sense of Colossians 2:20.

In Galatians 4:3, 9 στοιχεῖα also at first glance seems to refer to the impersonal teachings of the law. In Galatians 3:23-25 the law is pictured as a wall which enclosed the people who lived under the Torah and as a pedagogue who looked after children. In 4:1-3 the pedagogue concept of the law is applied by asserting that a person is under "guardians and trustees" and the στοιχεῖα when he is a minor. The στοιχεῖα appear to refer to the law of Moses. Similarly, in 4:9, the Galatians are asked why they want to turn back again to the "weak and beggarly" στοιχεῖα. Since the agitators were pressuring them to submit to circumcision and other practices demanded in the Torah, it seems that the στοιχεῖα must refer to the teachings of the law of Moses. However, as in Colossians, so also in Galatians one must look more

---

Paul's Thought," *NTS* 1 (1954): 21ff.; Martin, *Colossians*, pp. 10-14; C. Masson, *L'Epître de Saint Paul aux Colossiens*, in Commentaire du Nouveau Testament 10 (Neuchâtel and Paris: 1950), p. 121; Percy, *Die Probleme der Kolosser- und Epheserbriefe*, p. 167; Reicke, "The Law and the World According to Paul," *JBL* 70 (1951): 261-63; H. Schlier, *Principalities and Powers in the New Testament* (New York: Herder and Herder, 1961); E. Schweizer, "Die'Elemente der Welt.' Gal. 4. 3, 9; Kol. 2, 8.20," *Verborum Veritas*, Festschrift für G. Stahlin (Wuppertal: Brockhaus, 1970), pp. 245-59; C. Toussant, *L'Epître de S. Paul aux Colossiens* (Paris: Emile Nourray, 1922), p. 139.

[101] E. Percy, *Die Probleme der Kolosser- und Epheserbriefe*, p. 167.

closely at the context and the general teaching of the letter. The eschatological dimension of Paul's thought in Galatians must be kept in mind.[102] He described the pre-Christian condition as one of slavery (4:1-7). The new situation in Christ is one of freedom (1:4; 2:4; 4:22-31; 5:1, 13). The στοιχεῖα in 4:3 as well as the "guardians and trustees" are treated as slave-holders. Furthermore, the στοιχεῖα in 4:9 are associated with "the beings that by nature are no gods" and which at one time enslaved the Galatians (4:8). They are treated like the hostile agents, which in the Jewish apocalyptic scheme of the two ages belonged to this "present evil age" or to a world order that was in antithesis to the "new creation" (Galatians 6:15) brought about by Christ.

In both Colossians and Galatians, the στοιχεῖα τοῦ κόσμου do not appear to be the basic teachings of the Jewish or Gentile religions, but hostile agents who use those teachings to keep the world under bondage. Both those who venerate the gods of paganism and those who rely on the works of the law are victims of the στοιχεῖα.

The Death of Christ

The central theological focus of Colossians is upon Christology and the focal point of its Christology is the significance of the death of Christ. The death of Christ is also a matter of singular importance in Galatians. In Colossians the redactions in the Christ-hymn (1:15-20) and its applications (1:21-23 and 2:9-15) draw attention to the significance of the cross. If the phrase τὰ ὁρατὰ καὶ ἀόρατα, εἴτε θρόνοι εἴτε κυριότητες εἴτε ἀρχαι εἴτε ἐξουσίαι is a redactional comment by the author of the letter, it shows his special concern for the relationship of the readers to the heavenly powers.[103] If the phrase is not redactional, then the hymn itself stresses Christ's lordship over the heavenly "rulers and authorities." The addition of τῆς ἐκκλησίας in 1:18b shows that the headship of Christ over the powers should especially be known and experienced in the church. By far the most significant redaction in the hymn is the participial phrase in 1:20bc in which it is asserted that the

---

[102]See above, in this chapter, "(1) The 'Works of the Law'," for the eschatological significance of the phrases "works of law" and "faith in Jesus Christ."

[103]Martin notes that these words disturb the symmetry of the passage. "Reconciliation and Forgiveness in the Letter to the Colossians," p. 111.

means by which universal reconciliation takes place is through the cross (εἰρηνοποιήσας διὰ τοῦ αἵματος τοῦ σταυροῦ αὐτοῦ, [δι' αὐτοῦ] εἴτε τὰ ἐπὶ τῆς γῆς εἴτε τὰ ἐν τοῖς οὐρανοῖς). Thus, the death of Christ has both cosmological (1:20) and ecclesiological significance. Christ, through the "blood of the cross" (1:20b) and the "body of his flesh" (1:22) had reconciled the cosmos as well as the readers to God.

In 2:9-15 the death of Christ is again related to the "rulers and authorities" as well as the readers. It is clear that the Christ-hymn is in mind because of the references to the πλήρωμα (2:9 and 1:19), the σώματος τῆς σαρκός (2:11 and 1:22), and the ἀρχαί and ἐξουσίαι (2:10, 15 and 1:16). The one in whom the divine fullness dwells bodily and in whom the readers are made full is also the head of all rule and authority. It seems likely that the choice of the word σωματικῶς in 2:9 is an allusion to σῶμα in 1:18, which by means of the probable redaction in 1:18b and its use in 2:4, has ecclesiological meaning. Thus the divine fullness which dwells in Christ is also resident in the church. Consequently, the church participates in the sovereignty of Christ over the heavenly powers. It shares in that sovereignty through participation in Christ's death through baptism. The passage comes to a climax in the victory-song of 2:14, 15[104] in which the cross is celebrated as the means by which Christ triumphed over the heavenly powers.

The importance of the death of Christ and the church's participation in its subjugating effect on the heavenly powers is further made clear by repeated references to it in the polemical and paraenetic sections of the letter (2:20; 3:1, 3, 5, 9,[105] 10, 12).

Now let us turn to the significance of the death of Christ in Galatians. The following seven passages contain references to the death of Christ:

> Who gave himself for our sins to deliver us from the present evil age, according to the will of our God and Father. (1:4)

> I have been crucified with Christ; it is no longer I who live, but Christ who lives in me; and the life I now live in the flesh I live by faith in the Son of God, who loved me and gave himself for me. (2:20)

---

[104]The investigation of the traditional hymnic character of these verses is found above, in chapter 2, "Colossians 2:14-15, pp. 44-47."

[105]For the significance of ἀπέκδυσις and ἀπεκδύμαι in 2:11, 14 and 3:9 see Martin, "Reconciliation and Forgiveness," pp. 121-23.

O foolish Galatians! Who has bewitched you, before whose eyes Jesus Christ was publicly portrayed as crucified? (3:1)

Christ redeemed us from the curse of the law, having become a curse for us--for it is written, "cursed be every one who hangs on a tree." (3:13)

But if I, brethren, still preach circumcision, why am I still persecuted? In that case the stumbling block of the cross has been removed. (5:11)

And those who belong to Christ Jesus have crucified the flesh with its passions and desires. (5:24)

But far be it from me to glory except in the cross of our Lord Jesus Christ, by which the world has been crucified to me, and I to the world. (6:14)

At some length in a previous section of this chapter we drew attention to the eschatological perspective from which the Christology of Colossians is viewed.[106] It is significant to note that there is an eschatological dimension in every reference to the death of Christ in Galatians. A thorough examination of each passage would be ideal, but we shall limit our discussion to the strategically important passages located in the salutation and conclusion of the letter (1:4 and 6:14) and briefly comment on the others in the light of them.

In Galatians 1:4 Jesus Christ is described with a participial phrase and a purpose clause. The participial phrase (τοῦ δόντος ἑαυτὸν ὑπὲρ τῶν ἁμαρτιῶν ἡμῶν) possesses a formulaic character and probably represents a primitive Jewish-Christian understanding of the death of Christ as an expiatory sacrifice.[107] The purpose clause, however, represents the way in which Paul wanted the Galatians to understand the significance of Christ's death. It is clearly an eschatological declaration. Christ died "in order to deliver us from the present evil age" (ὅπως ἐξέληται ἡμᾶς ἐκ τοῦ αἰῶνος τοῦ ἐνεστῶτος πονηροῦ). The evil age is marked by bondage to the "elemental spirits of the universe" (4:3) and by false gods (4:8).[108] The death of Christ liberates from those evil powers.

---

[106]See above, "The Christological Perspective in Colossians," pp. 198-202.

[107]For the formulaic character of Gal. 1:4 and other passages see W. Popkes, *Christus Traditus: Eine Untersuchung zum Begriff der Dahingabe im Neuen Testament*; W. Kramer, *Christ, Lord, Son of God*, trans. Brian Hardy, Studies in Biblical Theology (London: SCM, 1966), pp. 115ff.; H. Betz, *Galatians*, pp. 41, 42.

[108]The purpose clause in Gal. 1:4 expresses a concept similar to the one in Col. 1:13, though the latter celebrates the activity of the Father rather than the Son.

Galatians 6:14-16 functions as the letter's theological climax. It concludes a passage in which Paul exposes the motives of the circumcisers and contrasts himself with them. They boasted in getting Gentiles to submit to circumcision. Paul boasted in nothing except "the cross of our Lord Jesus Christ, through which[109] the world is crucified to me, and I to the world." There are three crucifixions presented in the text: Christ's, the world's, and Paul's. The latter two are involved in the former. How could the death of Christ bring about the crucifixion of the world to Paul and Paul to the world? This question brings the eschatological significance of the death of Christ to the fore. Whatever the world (κόσμος) is, it is set in an abjuratory light and is contrasted with the "new creation" in which there is neither circumcision nor uncircumcision (6:15). The agitators who boast in getting the Galatians to submit to circumcision, therefore, belong to the world and have no part in the "new creation." Paul Minear aptly describes the "world" in 6:14 as follows:

> This reality was as ordered as the system of traditions, customs and laws that had become enshrined in the Torah. This mode of ordering social behavior had persisted over many centuries and through many cultural changes. Kosmos was as cohesive as the ethnic group that accepted the sovereignty of Jahweh, as pervasive as the distinction between Jew and Gentile, as elemental as the observance of sacred geographies and calendars, as universal as the desire for internal and external securities, as deeply rooted as divisions between sexes and classes. Wherever people accepted the importance of such divisions, there could be discerned the presence of this kosmos. It existed at the point where the στοιχεῖα claimed sovereignty and that sovereignty was accepted. This kosmos was grounded in primordial religious traditions, structured by perennial religious needs, articulated in elaborate liturgies and fealties.[110]

To summarize, it was the cross that brought an end to the enslaving powers of the world over Paul and set him free to live in the new

---

[109] Δι' οὗ in 6:14 can refer either to Christ or to the cross. The latter is to be preferred. However, Betz's comment is appropriate: "Whether δι' οὗ refers to the cross of Christ, or to the person of Christ is of no consequence, since for Paul 'Christ' is always the crucified redeemer Christ." (*Galatians*, p. 318).

[110] P. S. Minear, "The Crucified World: The Enigma of Galatians 6:14," *Theologia Crucis-Signum Crucis*, Festschrift für Erich Dinkler zum 70. Geburtstag, Herausgegeben von Carl Andresen und Günter Klein (Tübingen: J. C. B. Mohr [Paul Siebeck], 1979), pp. 402, 403.

creation. Both Galatians 1:4 and 6:14 set forth the death of Christ as the means by which the enslaving powers of the στοιχεῖα, the evil age, and the world are brought to an end.

All of the other references to the death of Christ in Galatians can be understood in the light of the eschatological deliverance from the present evil age dominated by the στοιχεῖα and false gods. In 2:20 Paul uses baptismal terminology to declare that he had died to the law which belonged to the pre-Christian age (2:19, 21) by participating in the crucifixion of Christ. Galatians 5:24 contains a similar statement about involvement in the consequences of Christ's death. It is located in the center of the catalogue of virtues described as the fruit of the Spirit. Belonging to Christ and thus having experienced the crucifixion of the flesh is intimately associated with living in the Spirit. In 3:1 and 3:13 the death of Christ is also related to the Spirit. Galatians 3:1 introduces rhetorical questions which indicate that the Galatians did not receive the Spirit by the "works of law" but by response to the gospel. Galatians 3:13, which is based upon a complicated use of Deuteronomy 21:23 (which was probably used in connection with the sacrifice of Isaac motif),[111] declares that Christ redeemed us from the curse of the law in order that Gentiles might receive the blessing of Abraham and the eschatological Spirit (3:14). The reference to the cross in 5:11 is extremely difficult to interpret because of our ignorance of the precise historical situation that would compel Paul to make such a statement. We are also uncertain about whether the concluding statement in 11b is a conclusion to the question in 11a or the conclusion to the entire pericope (5:1-12). In either case circumcision stands in opposition to the scandal of the cross which brought about the defeat of the στοιχεῖα and the religious practices belonging to the evil age.

It can be seen from this discussion about the death of Christ in Colossians and Galatians that it has the same significance in both letters. The cross is the means by which Christ brought about the ultimate defeat of the powers belonging to the evil age and it is an event in which those who belong to Christ share by means of their participation in the death of Christ through baptism.

---

[111]See M. Wilcox, " 'Upon the Tree'—Deut. 21:22-23 in the New Testament," *JBL* 96 (1977): 85-99.

SUMMARY AND CONCLUSION

At the beginning of this chapter we noted that the large amount of traditional material in Colossians makes a lexical and stylistic analysis of the letter of little value for establishing its authorship. We also noted that any judgments about authorship made on the basis of the theological affirmations must be made with great care. Most of the theological assertions are located in the passages which we have identified as traditional and, therefore, reflect the mode of expression, not so much of the author, but of the backgrounds from which they came. Furthermore, caution must be exercised in isolating theological categories in the letter without recognizing their interrelationships in the mind of the writer and in the light of the historical situation. Care must also be taken in making judgments about the historical situation of Colossians on the basis of a history of religions analysis of the opposed teaching. One cannot be certain whether significant words and concepts come from the opposed teaching, the traditions used, or the writer's own theological vocabulary. Also, strategic texts such as 2:18 and 2:23 are too fraught with lexical and syntactical difficulties to produce a clear picture of the "philosophy."

The approach which we have taken in this chapter is that of comparing matters of special theological importance to Paul with the major theological concerns in Colossians. Specific attention was given to the significance of the redactions in the traditional materials. The integrating motif of Pauline theology is the eschatological gospel. Paul was convinced that with the coming of Jesus Christ a new creation had begun, at least proleptically. He had been uniquely called by Christ to be the Apostle to the Gentiles. The focal point of the Gospel which he had been called to preach was the inclusion of both Jews and Gentiles in the redemptive purpose of God. Any attempt by Jewish Christians to force Jewish exclusivistic practices upon Gentile Christians was regarded by Paul as a reversion to the pre-Christian situation of enslavement under the law of Moses and the wordly powers. An attempt by Gentile Christians to force Jewish Christians to abandon circumcision would have been equally offensive to Paul. In the new situation neither circumcision nor uncircumcision means anything.

In our investigation of Colossians and Paul, we drew attention to the special significance of the death of Christ as a triumph over the στοιχεῖα τοῦ κόσμου and the "rulers and authorities" in Colossians and of the special importance to the Gentiles of the proclamation of the "mystery of Christ." The fact that in Christ there can be neither Jew nor Gentile and that the cross was the means by which Christ triumphed over the world and its enslaving powers are presented in practically identical ways in Colossians and Galatians. In both letters the issue of exclusivistic religious practices threatens to place the readers under the influence of the στοιχεῖα from which the death of Christ had freed them. On these grounds it seems justifiable to believe that the author of Colossians was Paul the Apostle and that he wrote to the churches of the Lycus valley to warn them about a teaching which advocated practices which would put them in a pre-Christian situation and which contradicted the teaching which they had received about Christ in the Gospel and in baptismal instruction.

Bibliography of Major Works Cited

Texts and Translations

Aland, K., M. Black, B. Metzger, and A. Wikgren, eds. *The Greek New Testament.* 1st ed. Stuttgart: Württemberg Bible Society, 1966.

Brownlee, William H. *The Dead Sea Manual of Discipline.* Bulletin of the American Schools for Oriental Research. Supplementary Studies 10-12. New Haven, 1951.

Charles, R. H. *The Apocrypha and Pseudepigrapha of the Old Testament.* 2 vols. London: Oxford University Press, 1913.

———. The Testaments of the Twelve Patriarchs. London: S.P.C.K., 1917.

Cohn, L., and P. Wendland, eds. *Philonis Alexandri. Opera quae supersunt.* Vol. 4. Berlin: Topelmann, 1962-1963.

Dupont-Sommer, A. *The Essene Writings from Qumran.* Translated by G. Vermes. Oxford and Cleveland: World Publishing Company, 1962.

Goodspeed, Edgar J. *The Apostolic Fathers, An American Translation.* New York: Harper and Brothers, 1950.

Herford, R. Travers. *Pirk Aboth—The Ethics of the Talmud: Sayings of the Fathers.* New York: Schocken Books, 1962.

Lightfoot, J. B. *The Apostolic Fathers.* Edited and completed by J. R. Harmer. London: Macmillan, 1907.

Metzger, Bruce M., ed. "The Apocrypha of the Old Testament." *The Oxford Annotated Bible with the Apocrypha (Revised Standard Version).* 2d. ed. New York: Oxford University Press, 1973.

Rahlfs, Alfred, ed. *Septuaginta.* 2 vols. Stuttgart: Privilegierte Württembergische Bibelanstalt, 1952; first published in 1935.

Richardson, Cyril C. *Early Christian Fathers*. Newly translated and edited by C. C. Richardson in collaboration with E. R. Fairweather, E. R. Hardy, and M.H. Shepherd. Library of Christian Classics. Vol. 1. Philadelphia: Westminster Press, 1953.

Schaff, Philip. *Teaching of the Twelve Apostles: the Didache and Kindred Documents*. Bryennios edition. Edinburgh: T. & T. Clark, 1885.

Reference Works

Blass, Friedrich, Albert Debrunner, and Robert Funk. *A Greek Grammar of the New Testament and Other Early Christian Literature*. Translated by Robert Funk. Chicago: University of Chicago Press, 1961.

Dana, H. E., and Julius R. Mantey. *A Manual Grammar of the Greek New Testament*. New York: Macmillan Company, 1927.

The Interpreter's Dictionary of the Bible. George Arthur Buttrick, general editor. 4 vols. New York and Nashville: Abingdon, 1962.

The Jewish Encyclopedia: A Descriptive Record of the History, Religion, Literature, and Customs of the Jewish People from the Earliest Times to the Present Day. Prepared under the direction of Cyrus Adler (and others). Edited by Isidore Singer. 12 vols. New York and London: Funk and Wagnalls, Co., 1901-1906.

The New International Dictionary of New Testament Theology. Edited by Colin Brown. Translated with additions and revisions from *Theologisches Begriffslexikons zum Neuen Testament*. 3 vols. Grand Rapids: Zondervan, 1975. Originally published in German, 1967, 1969, 1971.

Robertson, A. T. *A Grammar of the Greek New Testament in the Light of Historical Research*. 4th ed. Nashville: Broadman Press, 1934.

Strack, H. L., and P. Billerbeck. *Kommentar zum Neuen Testament aus Talmud und Midrasch*. München: C. H. Becksche Verlagbuchhandlung, 1922-1961.

Theological Dictionary of the New Testament. Edited by Gerhard Kittel and Gerhard Friedrich. Translated and edited by Geoffrey W. Bromiley. 9 vols. Grand Rapids: Eerdmans, 1964.

Commentaries

Barth, Marcus. *Ephesians*. 2 vols. Anchor Bible Series, numbers 34, 34a. Garden City: Doubleday and Company, Inc., 1974.

Beare, Francis Wright. *The First Epistle of Peter*. Oxford: B. Blackwell, 1947.

Betz, Hans Dieter. *Galatians*. Hermeneia Series. Philadelphia: Fortress Press, 1979.

Bruce, F. F. (with E. K. Simpson). *Commentary on the Epistles to the Ephesians and Colossians*. New International Commentary. Grand Rapids: Eerdmans, 1959.

Burton, Ernest. *A Critical and Exegetical Commentary on the Epistle to the Galatians*. The International Critical Commentary. Edinburgh: T. & T. Clark, 1921.

Conzlemann, Hans. *A Commentary on the First Epistle to the Corinthians*. Translated by James W. Leitch. Philadelphia: Fortress Press, 1975.

DeWette, W. *Kurze Erklärung der Brief an die Kolosser, an Philemon, und die Epheser und Philipper.* Leipzig: Weidemann, 1847.

Dibelius, Martin, and Heinrich Greeven. *An die Kolosser, Epheser, und Philemon. Handbuch zum Neuen Testament.* Edited by Hans Leitzmann and Günther Bornkamm. Tübingen: J. C. B. Mohr (Paul Siebeck), 1953.

Ellicott, C. J. *St. Paul's Epistle to the Galatians.* 4th ed. London: Longmans Green, 1867.

Ewald, P. *Die Briefe des Paulus an die Epheser, Kolosser, und Philemon.* 2nd ed. Leipzig: A. Deichert, 1910.

Houlden, James Leslie. *Paul's Letters from Prison: Colossians, Philemon, and Ephesians.* Harmondsworth: Penguin, 1970.

Lietzmann, Hans. *An die Römer. Handbuch zum Neuen Testament.* Edited by Hans Leitzmann and Günther Bornkamm. Tübingen: J.C.B. Mohr (Paul Siebeck), 1933.

Lightfoot, J. B. *St. Paul's Epistles to the Colossians and to Philemon.* 3rd ed. London: Macmillan, 1904.

_____. *The Epistle of St. Paul to the Galatians.* Grand Rapids: Zondervan Publishing House, n.d.

Lohmeyer, Ernst. *Die Briefe an die Philipper, an die Kolosser und an Philemon. Kritisch-exegetischer Kommentar über das Neue Testament, begründet von Heinrich August Wilhelm Meyer.* Göttingen: Vandenhoeck and Ruprecht, 1953.

Lohse, Eduard. *A Commentary on the Epistles to the Colossians and to Philemon.* Translated by William R. Poehlmann and Robert J. Karris. Hermeneia Series. Philadelphia: Fortress Press, 1971.

Martin, Ralph P. *Colossians and Philemon.* New Century Bible. Greenwood SC: Attic Press, Inc., 1974.

Masson, Charles. *L'epître de Saint Paul aux Colossiens. Commentaire du Nouveau Testament 10.* Neuchatel and Paris: Delachaux et Niestle, 1950.

Meyer, H. A. W. *Critical and Exegetical Handbook to the Epistle to the Galatians.* Translated by G. H. Venables from the fifth German edition. 2nd ed. Edinburgh: T. & T. Clark, 1884.

Moule, C. F. D. *The Epistle of Paul the Apostle to the Colossians and to Philemon.* Cambridge: Cambridge University Press, 1957.

Scott, Ernest, F. *The Epistles of Paul to the Colossians, to Philemon, and to the Ephesians.* The Moffat New Testament Commentary. New York: Harper & Row, n.d.

Selwyn, E. G. *The First Epistle of St. Peter.* 2nd ed. London: Macmillan, 1961.

Toussant, C. *L'epître de S. Paul aux Colossiens.* Paris: Emile Nourray, 1921.

Books

Audet, Jean-Paul. *La Didachè: Instructions des Apôtres.* Etudes Biblique. Paris: Gabalda, 1958.

Bandstra, A. J. *The Law and the Elements of the World.* Kampen: J. H. Kok, 1964.

Barnard, L. W. *Studies in the Apostolic Fathers and Their Background.* New York: Schoken Books, 1966.

Beardslee, William A. *Literary Criticism of the New Testament.* New Testament Series. Philadelphia: Fortress Press, 1970.

Beasley-Murray, George R. *Baptism in the New Testament.* Grand Rapids: Eerdmans, 1974. Originally published in 1962.

Bousset, Wilhelm. *Die Religion des Judentums im neutestamentlichen Zeitalter.* Zweite Auflage. Berlin: Reuther and Reicard, 1906.

Bultmann, Rudolph. *Theology of the New Testament.* Translated by Kendrick Grobel. 2 vols. New York: Charles Scribner's Sons, 1951, 1955.

Bryennios, Philotheé. Διδαχὴ τῶν Δώδεκα ἀποστόλων. Constantinople, 1883.

Carrington, Phillip. *The Primitive Christian Catechism.* Cambridge: Cambridge University Press, 1940.

Crouch, John E. *The Origin and Intention of the Colossian Haustafel,* Forschungen zur Religion und Literatur des Alten und Neuen Testaments. Göttingen: Vandenhoek and Ruprecht, 1972.

Daube, David. *The New Testament and Rabbinic Judaism.* Jordan Lectures 1952. University of London: Athlone Press, 1956.

Davies, W. D. *Paul and Rabbinic Judaism: Some Rabbinic Elements in Pauline Theology.* London: S.P.C.K., 1962.

————. *Invitation to the New Testament: A Guide to Its Main Witnesses.* Garden City: Doubleday & Company, Inc., 1966.

Deichgräber, Richard. *Gotteshymnus und Christushymnus in der frühen Christenheit: Untersuchungen zu Form, Sprache, und Stil der frühchristlichen Hymnen.* Studien zur Umwelt des Neuen Testaments 5. Göttingen: Vandenhoeck and Ruprecht, 1967.

Deissmann, Adolf. *Paul: A Study in Social and Religious History.* Translated by William E. Wilson. New York: Harper Torchbooks, 1957. First edition published in 1912.

————. *Bible Studies.* Translated by A. Grieve. Edinburgh: T .& T. Clark, 1901.

Dibelius, Martin. *A Fresh Approach to New Testament and Early Christian Literature.* New York: Charles Scribner's Sons, 1976.

Dinkler, Erich. *Signum Crucis: Aufsätze zum Neuen Testament und zur christlichen Archäologie.* Tübingen: J.C.B. Mohr (Paul Siebeck), 1951.

Dodd, Charles H. *The Gospel and Law: The Relation of Faith and Ethics in Christianity.* New York: Columbia University Press, 1951.

Doty, William G. *Contemporary New Testament Interpretation.* Englewood Cliffs: Prentice-Hall, 1972.

————. *Letters in Primitive Christianity.* New Testament Series. Philadelphia: Fortress Press, 1973.

Dunn, James D. G. *Christology in the Making.* Philadelphia: Westminster Press, 1980.

Feine, Paul, Johannes Behm, and Werner George Kummel. *Introduction to the New Testament.* Translated by A. J. Mattill, Jr. 14th rev. ed. Nashville: Abingdon, 1966. Revised edition translated by Howard Clark Kee. Nashville: Abingdon, 1975.

Feuillet, Andre. *Lè Christ sagesse de Dieu d'après les èptres pauliniennes.* Etudes Biblique. Paris, 1966.

Francis, Fred. O., and Wayne A. Meeks, eds. *Conflict at Colossae.* Society for Biblical Literature. Sources for Biblical Study 4. Missoula: Scholars Press, 1973.

Funk, Robert W. *Language, Hermeneutics, and Word of God.* New York: Harper and Row, 1966.

Furnish, Victor Paul. *Theology and Ethics in Paul.* Nashville and New York: Abingdon Press, 1968.

Gabathuler, Hans-Jakob. *Jesus Christus, Haupt der Kirche-Haupt der Welt: Der Christhymnus Colosser 1:15-20 in der theologischen Forschung der letzen 130 Jahre.* Abhandlungen zur Theologie des Alten und Neuen Testaments 45. Zürich: Zwingli Verlag, 1965.

Gavin, Frank Stanton Burns. *Jewish Antecedents of the Christian Sacraments.* New York: Ktav Publishing House, 1969; reprint of the 1928 edition.

Gegermann, Harold. *Die Vorstellung vom Schöpfungsmittler im hellenistischen Judentum und Urchristentum.* Texte und Untersuchungen zur Geschichte der altchristlichen Literatur. Berlin: Topelmann, 1961.

Gerhardsson, Birger. *Memory and Manuscript: Oral Tradition and Transmission in Early Christianity.* Lund-Copenhagen: Munksgaard, 1964.

Gibbs, John G. *Creation and Redemption: A Study in Pauline Theology.* Leiden: E. J. Brill, 1971. Based on the author's thesis, Princeton, 1968.

Giet, Stanislaus. *L'Enigme de la Didachè.* Paris: Ophrys, 1970.

Goodspeed, Edgar J. *The Key to Ephesians.* Chicago: University of Chicago Press, 1956.

Harnack, Adolph. *Die Lehre der Zwölf Apostel.* Leipzig, 1884.

Hunter, Archibald M. *Paul and His Predecessors.* Philadelphia: Westminster Press, 1961.

Hurd, John C., Jr. *The Origin of I Corinthians.* London: S.P.C.K.; New York: Seabury Press, 1965.

Jervell, Jacob. *Imago Dei: Gen 1,26f im Spätjudentum und in den paulinischen Briefen.* Forschungen zur Religion und Literatur des Alten und Neuen Testament 58. Edited by Hans Lietzmann and Günther Bornkamm. Göttingen: Vandenhoeck and Ruprecht, 1960.

Kamlah, Erhard. *Die Form der katalogischen Paränese im Neuen Testament.* Wissenschaftliche Monographien zum Alten und Neuen Testament 7. Tübingen: J.C.B. Mohr, 1964.

Käsemann, Ernst. *Essays on New Testament Themes.* Studies in Biblical Theology 41. London: SCM Press Ltd., 1964.

Kehl, Nikolaus. *Der Christhymnus im Kolosserbrief: Eine motivgeschichtliche Untersuchung zu Kol 1, 12-20.* Stuttgarter Biblische Monographien 1. Stuttgart: Verlag Katholisches Bibelwerk, 1967.

Klein, Rabbi G. *Der älteste Christliche Katechismus und die Jüdische Propoganda-Literatur.* Berlin: George Reimer, 1909.

Knox, Wilfred L. *St. Paul and the Church of the Gentiles.* Cambridge: Cambridge University Press, 1939.

Kramer, Werner. *Christ, Lord, Son of God.* Translated by Brian Hardy. Studies in Biblical Theology 50. Naperville IL: Alec R. Allenson, 1966.

Kroll, J. *Die christliche Hymnodik bis zu Klemens von Alexandreia. Verzeichnis der Vorlesungen an der Akademie zu Braunsberg im Sommer 1921.* Königsberg, 1921; reprinted Darmstadt: Wissenschartliche Buchgesellschaft, 1968.

Lohfink, Gerhard. *The Conversion of St. Paul: Narrative and History in Acts.* Translated and edited by Bruce J. Malina. Chicago: Franciscan Herald Press, 1976.

Martin, Ralph P. *Carmen Christi: Phil ii. 5-11 in Recent Interpretation and in the Setting of Early Christian Worship.* London: Cambridge University Press, 1967.

Metzger, Bruce M. *A Textual Commentary on the Greek New Testament.* Companion volume to the United Bible Societies' Greek New Testament, 3rd ed. London and New York, 1971.

Montefiore, C. G. *Judaism and St. Paul: Two Essays.* London: Arno Press, 1914.

Mowinckel, Sigmund. *La Decalogue.* Paris, 1927.

Muilenburg, J. *The Literary Relations of the Epistle of Barnabas and the Teaching of the Twelve Apostles.* Marburg, 1929.

Munck, Johannes. *Paul and the Salvation of Mankind.* Translated by Frank Clarke from *Paulus und die Heilsgeschichte* (Copenhagen, 1954). Richmond: John Knox Press, 1959.

Neufeld, Vernon H. *The Earliest Christian Confessions.* Edited by Bruce M. Metzger. New Testament Tools and Studies. Grand Rapids: Eerdmans, 1963.

Norden, Eduard. *Agnostos Theos, Untersuchungen zur Formengeschichte religiöser Rede.* Leipzig, 1913; reprinted Darmstadt: Wissenschaftliche Buchgesellschaft, 1956.

O'Brien, Peter Thomas. *Introductory Thanksgiving in the Letters of Paul.* Supplements to Novum Testamentum. Vol. 49. Leiden: E. J. Brill, 1977.

Percy, Ernst. *Die Probleme der Kolosser-und Epheserbriefe.* Acta reg. Societatis Humaniorum Litterarum Lundensis 39. Lund: C.W.K. Gleerup, 1946.

Popkes, Wiard. *Christus Traditus. Eine Untersuchung zum Begriff der Dahingabe im Neuen Testament.* Stuttgart and Zürich: Zwingli, 1967.

Rad, G. von. *Old Testament Theology.* Translated by D.M. Stalker. Vol. 1. New York: Harper and Row, 1962.

Riesenfeld, H. *The Gospel Tradition and Its Beginnings: A Study in the Limits of Formgeschichte.* London: Mowbray, 1957.

Robinson, John A. T. *The Body.* Studies in Biblical Theology 5. London: SCM Press, 1963; first published in 1952.

Sampley, J. Paul. *'And the Two Shall Become One Flesh': A Study of Traditions in Ephesians 5:21-33.* Cambridge: Cambridge University Press, 1971.

Sanders, E. P. *Paul and Palestinian Judaism: A Comparison of Patterns of Religion.* Philadelphia: Fortress Press, 1977.

Sanders, Jack T. *The New Testament Christological Hymns: Their Historical Religious Background.* Cambridge: Cambridge: University Press, 1971.

————. *Ethics in the New Testament: Change and Development.* Philadelphia: Fortress Press, 1975.

Sandmel, Samuel. *The Genius of Paul.* New York: Schocken Books, 1958.

Schlier, H. *Principalities and Powers in the New Testament.* New York: Herder and Herder, 1961.

Schille, Gottfried. *Frühchristliche Hymnen.* Berlin: Evangelische Verlagsanstalt, 1962.

Schmithals, Walter. *Gnosticism in Corinth.* Translated by John E. Steely. New York and Nashville: Abingdon, 1971.

Schoeps, H. J. *Paul: The Theology of the Apostle in the Light of Jewish Religious History.* Translated by Harold Knight. Philadelphia: Westminster Press, 1961. Originally appeared as *Paulus: Die Theologie des Apostels im Lichte der jüdischen Religiongeschichte.* Tübingen: J. C. B. Mohr, 1959.

Schubert, Paul. *Form and Function of the Pauline Thanksgivings.* Beinefte zur Zeitschrift für die neutestamentliche Wissenschaft 20. Berlin: Topelmann, 1939.

Schwartz, Eduard. *Ethik der Griechen.* Stuttgart: Teubner, 1951.

Schweitzer, Albert. *The Mysticism of Paul the Apostle.* With a preface by F. C. Burkitt. London: Adam and Charles Black, 1956. First printed in 1931.

Stamm, J. T. (with M. E. Andrew). *The Ten Commandments in Recent Research.* Studies in Biblical Theology, 2d series, 2. Naperville IL: Alec R. Allenson, Inc.,1967

Stendahl, Krister. *Paul Among Jews and Gentiles and Other Essays.* Philadelphia: Fortress Press, 1976.

Vögtle, Anton. *Die Tugend-und Lasterkataloge: exegetische, religions-und formgeschichtlich Untersucht.* Munster: Aschendorff, 1936.

Wagenführer, Max Adolph. *Die Bedeutung Christi für Welt und Kirche: Studien zum Kolosser-und Epheserbrief.* Leipzig, 1941.

Wegenast, Klaus. *Das Verständnis der Tradition bei Paulus.* Wissenschaftliche Monographien zum Alten und Neuen Testament 8. Neukirchen: Kreis Moers, Neukirchener Verlag, 1962.

Weidinger, Karl. *Die Haustafeln: Ein Stück urchristlicher Paränese.* Untersuchungen zum Neuen Testament 14. Leipzig: Englemann, 1928.

Weiss, Bernhard. *Biblical Theology of the New Testament.* Translated by David Eaton from the 3rd German edition. Edinburgh: T. & T. Clark, 1882.

Wengst, K. *Christologische Formeln und Lieder des Urchristentums.* Studien zum Neuen Testament 8d 7. Gütersloh: Gütersloher Verlaghaus (Gerd Mohr), 1972.

White, John L. *The Form and Function of the Body of the Greek Letter: A Study of the Letter-Body in the Non-literary Papyri and in Paul the Apostle.* Society of Biblical Literature Dissertation Series. 2nd ed. cor. Missoula: Scholars Press, 1972.

Wibbing, Siegfried. *Die Tugend-und Lasterkataloge im Neuen Testament und ihre Traditionsgeschichte unter besonderer Berücksichtigung der Qumran-Texte.* Beihefte zur Zeitschrift für die neutestamentliche Wissenschaft 25. Berlin: Topelmann, 1959.

Windisch, H. *Paulus und Christus: Ein biblischreligiongeschichtlicher Vergleich.* Untersuchungen zum Neuen Testament 24. Leipzig: Englemann, 1934.

Wundt, Max. *Geschichte der griechischen Ethik.* Vol. 2. Leipzig: Englemann, 1911.

Zeilinger, Franz. *Der Erstgeborene der Schöpfung: Untersuchungen Formalstruktur und Theologie des Kolosserbriefes.* Wien: Verlag Herder, 1974.

Zeisler, J. A. *The Meaning of Righteousness in Paul.* Society for New Testament Studies Monograph Series 20. Cambridge: Cambridge University Press, 1972.

Articles

Alt, Albrecht. "The Origins of Israelite Law." *Essays on Old Testament History and Religion.* Translated by R. A. Wilson, pp. 81-132. Oxford, 1966.

Audet, Jean-Paul. "Les affinities littérarires et doctrinales du 'Manuel de discipline.' " *Revue Biblique* 59 (1952): 219-38; 60 (1953): 41-82.

Bammel, Ernst. "Versuch zu Kol 1:15-20." *Zeitschrift für die Wissenschaft und die Kunde der älteren Kirche* 52 (1961): 88-95.

Bahr, Gordon J. "Paul and Letter Writing in the First Century." *The Catholic Biblical Quarterly* 28 (1966): 465-77.

_____. "The Subscriptions in the Pauline Letters." *Journal of Biblical Literature* 87 (1968): 27-41.

Bornkamm, Günther. "Zum Verständnis des Christus-Hymnus Phil. 2,6-11." *Studien zu Antike und Urchristentum, Gesammelte Aufsätze.* Vol. 2. Beiträge zur Evangelischen Theologie 28. Munich, 1959.

_____. "Die Häresie des Kolosserbriefes." *Theologische Literaturzeitung* 73 (1948): 11-20. Also in *Conflict at Colossae,* edited and translated by Fred O. Francis and Wayne A. Meeks. Society of Biblical Literature. Sources for Biblical Study 4. Missoula: Scholars Press, 1973.

_____. "Die Hoffnung im Kolosserbriefe-zugleich ein Beitrag zur Frage der Echtheit des Briefes." *Studien zum Neuen Testament und zur Patristik: Festschrift für Erich Klostermann,* p. 56-64. Berlin, 1961.

Bradley, David G. "The *Topos* as a Form in the Pauline Paraenesis." *Journal of Biblical Literature* 72 (1953): 238-46.

Brown, Raymond. "The Semitic Background of the New Testament *mysterion* (II)." *Biblica* 40 (1959): 70-87.

Burney, C. F. "Christ as the APXH of Creation. (Prov. viii 22, Col. i 15-18, Rev. iii 14.)" *The Journal of Theological Studies* 27 (1926): 160-77.

Connolly, R. "New Fragments of the Didache." *The Journal of Theological Studies* 24 (1923): 151-53.

_____. "The Didache in Relation to the Epistle of Barnabas." *The Journal of Theological Studies* 32 (1932): 237-53.

Craddock, Fred B. "All Things in Him: A Critical Note on Col. 1:15-20." *New Testament Studies* 12 (1966): 78-80.

Daube, David. "Appended Note: Participle and Imperative in I Peter," in Edward G. Selwyn, *The First Epistle of St. Peter*, pp. 467-88. London: Macmillan Press, 1974; first edition 1946.

Davies, William D. "Reflections on Traditions: The Aboth Revisited." *Christian History and Interpretations: Studies presented to John Knox*. Edited by William R. Farmer, C. F. D. Moule, and R. R. Niebuhr. Cambridge: Cambridge University Press, 1967.

Dibelius, Martin. "The Isis Initiation in Apuleuis and Related Initiatory Rites." *Conflict at Colossae*. Edited and translated by Fred O. Francis and Wayne A. Meeks, pp. 61-121. Society of Biblical Literature. Sources for Biblical Study 4. Missoula: Scholars Press, 1973. Originally published in *Botschaft und Geschichte*. Edited by Günther Bornkamm with Heinz Kraft. Vol. 2. Tübingen: J. C. B. Mohr (Paul Siebeck), 1956.

Dinkler, Erich. "Tradition V. Im Urchristentum." *Die Religion in Geschichte und Gegenwart* 6 (1967): 970-74.

Doty, William G. "The Classification of Epistolary Literature." *The Catholic Biblical Quarterly* 31 (1969): 183-99.

_____. "Identifying Eschatological Language." *Continuum* 7 (1970): 546-61.

Easton, Burton Scott. "The New Testament Ethical Lists." *Journal of Biblical Literature* 51 (1932): 1-12.

Ellingsworth, P. "Colossians 1:15-20 and Its Context." *Expository Times* 73 (1962): 252-53.

Ellis, Earl E. "Dating the New Testament." *New Testament Studies* 26 (1980): 487-502.

Feuillet, André. "L'hymne christologique de l'epître aux Philippiens (II, 6-11)." *Revue Biblique* 62 (1955).

Francis, Fred O. "The Form and Function of the Opening and Closing Paragraphs of James and I John." *Zeitschrift für die neutestamentliche Wissenschaft und die älteren Kirche* 61 (1970): 110-26.

Funk, Robert W. "The Apostolic *Parousia:* Form and Significance." *Christian History and Interpretation: Studies presented to John Knox*. Edited by William R. Farmer, C. F. D. Moule, and R. R. Niebuhr, pp. 249-69. Cambridge: Cambridge University Press, 1967.

Gager, John G. "Functional Diversity in Paul's Use of End-time Language." *Journal of Biblical Literature* 89 (1970): 325-37.

Goodenough, Edwin R. "Paul and the Hellenization of Christianity." *Religions in Antiquity: Essays in Memory of E. R. Goodenough*. Edited by Jacob Neusner, pp. 23-68. Studies in the History of Religion 14. Leiden: Brill, 1968.

Goppelt, Leonhard. "Jesus und die Haustafel-Tradition." *Orientierung an Jesus: zur Theologie der Synoptiker*, für Josef Schmid, herausgegeben von Paul Hoffmann in Zusammenarbeit mit Norbert Brox und Wilhelm Pesch, pp. 93-106. Frieburg, Basel, Wein: Herder, 1973.

————. "Die Herrschaft Christi und die Welt nach dem Neuen Testament." *Lutherische Rundschau* 17 (1967): 21-50.

Grant, Robert M. "Like Children." *Harvard Theological Review* 39 (1946).

Greenwood, David. "Rhetorical Criticism and Formgeschichte: Some Methodological Considerations." *Journal of Biblical Literature* 89 (1970): 418-26.

Hinson, E. G. "The Christian Household in Colossians 3:18-4:1." *Review and Expositor* 70 (1973): 495-507.

Hooker, Morna D. "Were There False Teachers in Colossae?" *Christ and Spirit in the New Testament.* Edited by Barnabas Lindars and Stephen S. Smalley. p. 315-31 Cambridge: Cambridge University Press, 1973.

Van der Horst, P. W. "Observations on a Pauline Expression." *New Testament Studies* 19 (1973): 181-87.

Howard, G. "On the 'Faith of Christ.'" *Harvard Theological Review* 60 (1967): 459-65.

Jewett, Robert. "Conflicting Movements in the Early Church as Reflected in Philippians." *Novum Testamentum: An International Quarterly for New Testament and Related Studies* 12 (1970): 362-90.

————. "The Form and Function of the Homiletic Benediction." *Anglican Theological Review* 51 (1969): 18-34.

————. "The Epistolary Thanksgiving and the Integrity of Philippians." *Novum Testamentum: An International Quarterly for New Testament and Related Studies* 12 (1970): 40-53.

Käsemann, Ernst. "Primitive Christian Baptism Liturgy." *Essays on New Testament Themes.* Studies in Biblical Theology 41. pp. 154-59 London: SCM Press, 1964.

Kelly, J. N. D. Book review: "La Didaché: instructions des Apôtres by Jean-Paul Audet." *Journal of Theological Studies* 12 (1961): 329-33.

Knox, John. "Philemon and the Authenticity of Colossians." *Journal of Religion* 18 (1938): 144-60.

Lillie, W. "The Pauline House-tables." *Expository Times* 86 (1975): 179-83.

Lohmeyer, Ernst. "Probleme paulinischer Theologie, I Briefliche Grussüberschriften." *Zeitschrift für die neutestamentliche Wissenschaft und die Kunde der älteren Kirche* 26 (1927): 158-73. Reprinted as *Probleme paulinischer Theologie.* Darmstadt and Stuttgart, 1954.

Lohse, Eduard. "Pauline Theology in the Letter to the Colossians." *New Testament Studies* 15 (1969): 211-20.

Macgregor, G. H. C. "Principalities and Powers: The Cosmic Background of Paul's Thought." *New Testament Studies* 1 (1954): 17-28.

Martin, Ralph P. "Reconciliation and Forgiveness in the Letter to the Colossians." *Reconciliation and Hope,* Leon Morris Festschrift. Edited by R. J. Banks, pp. 104-24. Grand Rapids: Eerdmans, 1974.

————. "An Early Christian Hymn." *Evangelical Quarterly* 36 (1964): 95-205.

Maurer, G. "Die Begründung der Herrschaft Christi über die Machte nach Kolosser 1:15-20." *Wort und Dienst, Neue Folge* 5 (1955): 79-93.

McEleney, Neil J. "The Vice Lists of the Pastoral Epistles." *The Catholic Biblical Quarterly* 36 (1974): 203-19.

Mendenhall, George. "Covenant Forms in Israelite Tradition." *The Biblical Archaeologist* 17 (1954): 50-76.

Minear, Paul S. "The Crucified World: The Enigma of Galatians 6,14." *Theologia Crucis-Signum Crucis.* Festschrift für Erich Dinkler zum 70. Geburtstag, edited by Carl Andresen and Günter Klein, pp. 395-407. Tübingen: J. C. B. Mohr (Paul Sie beck), 1979.

Moule, C. F. D. " 'The New Life' in Colossians." *Review and Expositor* 70 (1973): 481-93.

Mullins, Terrence Y. "Disclosure: A Literary Form in the New Testament." *Novum Testamentum: An International Quarterly for New Testament and Related Studies* 7 (1964): 44-50.

————. "Greeting as a New Testament Form." *Journal of Biblical Literature* 87 (1968): 418-26.

————. "Formulas in the New Testament Epistles." *Journal of Biblical Literature* 91 (1972): 380-90.

————. "Visit Talk in New Testament Letters." *The Catholic Biblical Quarterly* 35 (1973): 350-58.

Munro, Winsome. "Col iii. 18-iv. 1 and Eph. v. 21-vi. 9: Evidences of a Late Literary Stratum?" *New Testament Studies* 18 (1972): 434-37.

O'Brien, Peter Thomas. "Thanksgiving and the Gospel in Paul." *New Testament Studies* 21 (1974): 144-55.

Polhill, J. B. "The Relationship Between Ephesians and Colossians." *Review and Expositor* 70 (1973): 439-50.

Rad, G. von. "The Form Critical Problem of the Hexateuch." *The Problem of the Hexateuch and Other Essays.* Translated by E. W. Dicher, pp. 1-78. Edinburgh and London, 1966.

Reicke, Bo. "The Law and the World According to Paul." *Journal of Biblical Literature* 70 (1951): 259-76.

Rengstorf, Karl Heinrich. "Die neutestamentlichen Mahnung an die Frau, sich dem Manne unterzuordnen." *Verbum Dei manet in aeternum.* Festschrift für Otto Schmitz. Edited by Werner Forester, pp. 131-45. Witten, 1953.

Robinson, James M. "A Formal Analysis of Col. 1:15-20." *Journal of Biblical Literature* 76 (1957): 270-87.

————. "Die Hodajot-Folmel in Gebet und Hymnus des Frühchristentums."

Apophoreta. Festschrift für Ernst Haenchen, pp. 194-235. Berlin: Verlag Alfred Topelmann, 1964.

242 The Use of Traditional Materials in Colossians

Robinson, J. Armitage. "The Problem of the *Didache.*" *Journal of Theological Studies* 13 (1912): 339-56.

———. "The Epistle of Barnabas and the Didache." Published posthumously by R. Connolly in *The Journal of Theological Studies* 35 (1934): 113-46; 225-48.

Salom, A. P. "The Imperatival Use of the Participle in the New Testament." *Australian Biblical Review* 11 (1963): 41ff.

Sanders, Jack T. "The Transition from Opening Epistolary Thanksgiving to Body in the Letters of the Pauline Corpus." *Journal of Biblical Literature* 81 (1962): 348-62.

Schrage, W. "Zur Ethik der neutestamentlichen Haustafeln." *New Testament Studies* 21 (1974): 1-22.

Schubert, Paul. "Form and Function of the Pauline Letters." *The Journal of Religion* 19 (1939):365-77.

Schweizer, Eduard. "The Church as the Missionary Body of Christ." *New Testament Studies* 8 (1961): 1-11.

———. "Christ in the Letter to the Colossians." *Review and Expositor* 70 (1973): 429-514.

———. "Die 'Elements der Weld' Gal. 4.3,9; Kol. 2.8,20." *Verborum Veritas*, Festschrift für Gustav Stählin zum 70. Geburtstag. Edited by O. Böcher and K. Haacker, pp. 245-49. Wuppertal, 1970.

———. "Die Weltlichkeit des Neuen Testaments: Die Haustafeln." *Beiträge zur alttestamentlichen Theologie*, Festschrift für Walther Zimmerli zum 70. Geburtstag, hrsg. H. Donner, R. Hanhart, R. Smend, pp. 397-413. Göttingen: Vandenhoeck & Ruprecht, 1977.

———. "Die Kirche als Leib Christi in den paulinischen Antilegomena." *Theologische Literaturzeitung* 86 (1961): 241-56.

———. "Traditional Ethical Patterns in the Pauline and Post-Pauline Letters and Their Development (lists of vices and house-tables)." *Text and Interpretation: Studies in the New Testament presented to Matthew Black*. Edited by Ernest Best and R. Mcl. Wilson, pp. 195-209. Cambridge: Cambridge University Press, 1979.

Simon, Marcel. "The Apostolic Degree and Its Setting in the Ancient Church." *Bulletin of the John Rylands Library* 52 (1970): 437-60.

Smith, Morton. "A Comparison of Early Christian and Rabbinic Tradition." *Journal of Biblical Literature* 82 (1963): 169-76.

Spivey, Robert A. "Structuralism and Biblical Studies: The Uninvited Guest." *Interpretation* 28 (1974): 15-45.

Stirewalt, M. L. "Paul's Evaluation of Letter Writing." *Search the Scriptures*, Festschrift for R. T. Stamm. Edited by J. M. Myers et. al., pp.179-96. 1969.

Taylor, Greer M. "The Function of PISTIS CHRISTOU in Galatians." *Journal of Biblical Literature* 85 (1966): 58-76.

Tyson, Joseph B. " 'Works of Law' in Galatians." *Journal of Biblical Literature* 92 (1973): 423-31.

Vawter, Bruce. "The Colossian Hymn and the Principle of Redaction." *Catholic Biblical Quarterly* 33 (1971): 62-81.

Vokes, F. E. "The Didache—Still Debated." *Church Quarterly* 3 (1970): 57-62.

Warfield, Benjamin. "Text, Sources, and Content of the 'Two Ways' of the First Section of the Didache." *Biblica Sacra* 43 (1886): 100-61.

Wendland, H. D. "Zur sozialethischen Bedeutung der neutestamentlichen Haustafeln." *Die Leibhaftigkeit des Wrotes (Festgabe* A. Korberie), pp. 34-46. Hamburg, 1959. Reprinted in *Botschaft an die soziale Welt,* pp. 104-14. Hamburg, 1959.

White, John L. "Introductory Formulae in the Body of the Pauline Letter." *Journal of Biblical Literature* 90 (1971): 91-97.

Wilcox, Max. " 'Upon the Tree'—Deut. 21:22-23 in the New Testament." *Journal of Biblical Literature* 96 (1977): 85-99.

Wilder, Amos N. "The Rhetoric of Ancient and Modern Apocalyptic." *Interpretation* 25 (1971): 437-53.

Author Index

Text Index

**EARLY CHRISTIAN
WRITINGS**

THE USE OF TRADITIONAL MATERIALS IN COLOSSIANS

Designed by Haywood Ellls

Composition by Omni Composition Services, Macon, Georgia
  typefaces—11/13 Times (text), Mediaeval Roman (display)
  the text was "read" by a Hendrix Typereader OCR Scanner and formatted on an
  Addressograph/Multigraph Comp/Set 5404, then paginated on an A/M Comp/
  Set 4510.

Production specifications:
  text paper—60 pound Warren's Olde Style
  endpapers—Process Materials Corporation Multicolor Antique, Bombay
  cover (on .088 boards)—Holliston Crown Linen 13460, stamped with Kurz-
  Hastings Colorit 931
  jacket—100 pound enamel, printed by offset lithography and varnished

Printing (offset lithography) by Omnipress of Macon, Inc., Macon, Georgia
Binding by John H. Dekker and Sons, Inc., Grand Rapids, Michigan